# "Yellow Woman"

## Women Writers
### Texts and Contexts

SERIES EDITORS

THOMAS L. ERSKINE
*Salisbury State University*

CONNIE L. RICHARDS
*Salisbury State University*

SERIES BOARD

MARTHA BANTA
*University of California at Los Angeles*

BARBARA CHRISTIAN
*University of California at Berkeley*

PAUL LAUTER
*Trinity College*

VOLUMES IN THE SERIES

# "Yellow Woman"

□ LESLIE MARMON SILKO ■

*Edited and with an introduction by*
MELODY GRAULICH

Rutgers University Press
New Brunswick, New Jersey

Melody Graulich would like to thank the Dean of Liberal Arts at the University of New Hampshire, Stuart Palmer, for the generous support of a Summer Faculty Fellowship to complete this project.

**Library of Congress Cataloging-in-Publication Data**

Silko, Leslie, 1948–
    Yellow woman / Leslie Marmon Silko ; edited and with an
introduction by Melody Graulich.
        p.     cm. — (Women writers : Text and contexts)
    Includes bibliographical references.
    ISBN 0-8135-2004-5 (hardback) — ISBN 0-8135-2005-3 (pbk.)
    1. Indians of North America—Women—Fiction.  I. Graulich, Melody,
1951–    . II. Title.  III. Series: Women writers (New Brunswick,
N.J.). Texts and contexts.
PS3569.I44Y4     1993
813'.54—dc20                                      93-20141
                                                            CIP

British Cataloging-in-Publication information available.

*For Brock, who lured me up the mountain*

# ❑ Contents ■

# Contents

# ❑ Introduction

# Introduction

*Remember the Stories*

> You don't have anything
> If you don't have the stories.
> —LESLIE SILKO, *Ceremony*
>
> Everywhere he looked, he saw a world
> made of stories, the long ago, time immemorial
> stories, as old Grandma called them. It was a world
> alive, always changing and moving . . .
> —LESLIE SILKO, *Ceremony*
>
> I know Aunt Susie and Aunt Alice would tell me stories
> they had told me before but with changes in details
> or descriptions. The story was the important thing
> and little changes here and there were really part
> of the story. There were even stories about the
> different versions of the stories and how they
> imagined these differing versions came to be.
> —LESLIE SILKO, *Storyteller*

## Storytelling

"Within one story there are many other stories coming together," Leslie Silko has said of the cultural traditions of her tribe, the Laguna Pueblo Indians.[1] To borrow an image from another culture, "Yellow Woman" is a chinese box: story within story within story. The Yellow Woman stories the narrator has heard construct her sense of herself and her actions. In turn, she makes them her own. When she decides at the story's end that she will tell her family a story about how "some Navajo

---

The title is adapted from advice given to Tayo, the central character in *Ceremony:* "Next time just remember the story."

3

had kidnaped" her, she claims the cultural inheritance the story explores: she becomes a storyteller, passing on the stories, in her own voice. As the stories have shaped her, so will she shape them; they must evolve to respond to her particular experience and point of view. The story "Yellow Woman," yet another telling of her abduction by a mountain spirit, constructed from many Yellow Woman stories, becomes only the most recent telling in an ongoing tradition.

My opening paragraph self-consciously repeats the word "story," used in its various forms twelve times in"Yellow Woman," because it is the most important and recurring word in Leslie Silko's work. Although "Yellow Woman" was originally published separately, Silko later placed the story in a book some call a collection, some an autobiography, *Storyteller,* which contains numerous other retellings of Yellow Woman stories, in varied voices and tones, some mythic, some comic.[2] In a poem called "Storytelling," for instance, the Yellow Woman story is embellished with "a red '56 Ford," "wine bottles and / size 42 panties," and the husband confronts his returning wife with the comment:

> "You better have a damn good story . . .
> about where you been for the past
> ten months and how you explain these
> twin baby boys."

Apparently her story was not good enough for after he heard it he left "and moved back in with his mother." "Storytelling" begins with the lines, "You should understand / the way it was / back then, / because it is the same / even now." Silko asks her readers to look at the interrelationships among her Yellow Woman stories, to understand the past's influence on the present and the present's connection to the past, to read backward and forward simultaneously, a point Bernard A. Hirsch explores more fully in an essay included in this volume.

*Storyteller* is composed of Silko's retellings of the stories she heard as a child; in its dedication, she pays tribute to the oral tradition, "to the storytellers as far back as memory goes and to the telling which continues and through which they all live and we with them." In the opening poem she es-

4

tablishes herself as one of many storytellers in the book and accepts responsibility for passing on her Aunt Susie's stories.

> What she is leaving with us—
> the stories and remembered accounts—
> is primarily what she was able to tell
> and what we are able to remember.
>
> As with any generation
> the oral tradition depends upon each person
> listening and remembering a portion
> and it is together—
> all of us remembering what we have heard together—
> that creates the whole story
> the long story of the people.
>
> I remember only a small part.
> But this is what I remember.
>
> (6–7)

Storytelling establishes one's place within tribal culture and history. "At Laguna," Silko says, it is "a way of interacting . . . a whole way of seeing yourself, the people around you, your life, the place of your life in the bigger context, not just in terms of nature and location but in terms of what has gone on before, what's happened to other people. It's a whole way of being."[3] Becoming part of the stories and passing them on is also central to Silko's sense of herself as an evolving, individual "being." While the stories "make [the Pueblo] a community," they also define individual identity.

> [T]hat's how you know you belong, if the stories incorporate you into them. There have to be stories. It's stories that make this a community. People tell those stories about you and your family or about others and they begin to create your identity. In a sense, you are told who you are, or you know who are you by the stories that are told about you.[4]

And you claim who you are by the stories you accept as your own, the particular stories you tell and retell.

In the past twenty-five years, termed the "Native American Renaissance" by Kenneth Lincoln, many American Indian writers have retold the traditional stories of powerful mythological women: Corn Woman, Changing Woman, Serpent Woman. Thought Woman, who with her sisters created all life by thinking it into being and who is embodied in spider grandmother, has been especially important to feminist writers because she offers an empowering model for female creativity. Silko too retells Thought-Woman stories to direct her own creative power as a storyteller and to link the mythological past to the present, as in the opening poem to her novel *Ceremony.*

> Ts'its'tsi'nako, Thought-Woman,
> is sitting in her room
> and whatever she thinks about
> appears. . . .
>
> Thought-Woman, the spider,
> named things and
> as she named them
> they appeared.
>
> She is sitting in her room
> thinking of a story now
> I'm telling you the story
> she is thinking.

Like spider grandmother, Silko weaves a web of stories, "narratives within narratives within narratives."[5] By connecting herself to Thought-Woman, even speaking for her, Silko asserts confidence in her public role as an artist, yet in her work, as in Paula Gunn Allen's poem "Grandmother," Thought-Woman, "having created," tends "to disappear."[6] Yellow Woman, however, is a continuing presence in Silko's first two books, *Ceremony* and *Storyteller*, written when she was still a very young woman, in her mid-twenties.[7] Young and often rebellious, Yellow Woman searches for a different kind of creative spirit, sexuality and passion, discovered in the mountains beyond the Pueblo. Yellow Woman's story is the one Silko clearly claims

6

as her own. As she has said, "We need certain tellers to look after certain myths. The ones I'm looking after have always been around."[8]

The essays in this collection compare Silko's many retellings of Yellow Woman stories from a variety of angles, looking at crucial themes like storytelling, cultural inheritances, memory, continuity, identity, interconnectedness, ritual, tradition, symbolic and literal mothers. The links between Silko's stories and her narrator's are unmistakable, suggesting that they are in many ways explorations into what one critic has called "the preserve of wilderness within."[9]

## Growing Up Laguna

Born in 1948 in Albuquerque, Leslie Silko defined the major biographical influences on her writing in a very brief autobiographical note in the 1974 collection, *The Man to Send Rain Clouds,* where "Yellow Woman" was first published: "I grew up at Laguna Pueblo. I am of mixed-breed ancestry, but what I know is Laguna. This place I am from is everything I am as a writer and human being."[10]

Silko's work suggests that growing up at Laguna Pueblo shaped her view of the world, her "self," and her art; her early work focuses on growing up as an Indian and as a mixed-breed, on young people who come to understand the "I" in relation to their cultural practices and to the land, a significant theme in American Indian literature.

Perhaps Silko has repeatedly emphasized the ever-changing nature of cultural inheritances and stories and the inclusiveness of Indian culture because she grew up in a family that practiced and celebrated the traditional ways of Pueblo life but also borrowed freely from Anglo and Mexican cultures, a family that valued learning. Indeed, *Storyteller* begins with a striking image which implies cultural interminglings: a description of a Hopi basket filled with family photographs taken by Silko's grandfather and father. Later Silko describes both the oral stories she heard from Grandma A'mooh *and* the little book without a cover her grandmother loved to read from, *Brownie the Bear.*

Silko's great-grandmother Marie Anaya married Robert Marmon, a Civil War veteran from Ohio who with his brother settled in New Mexico and influenced Pueblo politics; in *Storyteller* Silko recounts that when he left Laguna "white people who knew / sometimes called him 'Squaw Man'" and retells a family story about how he stood up to a hotel manager in Albuquerque who said his "Indian" sons were not welcome. Many family members were schooled away from the Pueblo; both Marie Anaya and Aunt Susie attended the Carlisle Indian School, and Susie went on to Dickinson College. One of three sisters who were encouraged to read widely, to write, and to try anything, Silko was taken from a poor Indian school at the Pueblo and sent to a private day school in Albuquerque, a hundred mile round trip. She later attended the University of New Mexico, where she married and had a son and began to write in earnest, publishing her first story in 1969. While she was attending law school, after the birth of her second son, Silko was awarded a National Endowment for the Arts Discovery Grant in 1971. She quit law school and, like many writers, supported herself by teaching, first at Navajo Community College in Tsaile, and later at the University of Arizona and the University of New Mexico. She spent two influential years in Ketchikan, Alaska, while finishing *Ceremony,* published in 1977. A MacArthur Foundation fellowship in 1981 allowed her to quit teaching and devote herself to her massive novel, *The Almanac of the Dead,* published in 1991. Twice divorced, Silko now lives on a ranch in the foothills outside of Tucson with a friend and a variety of animals, perhaps following the advice of her photographer father who felt "most at home in the canyons and sandrock" and saw "regular jobs" as "a confinement":

> As I got older
> he said I should become a writer
> because writers worked their own hours
> and they can live anywhere and do their own work.
>> "You could even live
>> up here in these hills if you wanted."
>
> (160–161)

Like her descriptions of storytelling and the oral tradition, Silko's comments about growing up in the Laguna Pueblo illuminate some of the themes of "Yellow Woman." In the interview with Kim Barnes included in this volume, Silko praises simultaneously her pueblo's fluid gender boundaries and its "matriarchal" culture, both of which she sees as encouraging her development. Growing up in a close community of powerful, creative, and hard-working women like Aunt Susie and Grandma A'mooh helped her "remember"—another word she often repeats—helped her find her voice as a storyteller, part of the ongoing tradition. Yet she also suggests that women, and particularly mothers, can use their power to "thwart you or frighten you." Although she discusses close relationships with aunts and grandmothers, fathers and uncles, Silko presents her mother as a mysterious absence in *Storyteller* and her other works, perhaps satirized in an elliptical reference to the narrator's mother in "Yellow Woman"—"my mother was telling my grandmother how to fix the Jell-O"—or in the defensive voice of the narrator's mother in "Storytelling":

> "No! That gossip isn't true.
> She didn't elope
> She was *kidnapped* by
> that Mexican
> at Seama feast.
> You know
> my daughter
> isn't
> *that* kind of girl."
> (95–96)[11]

Silko denies Barnes's suggestion that Pueblo women run to the wilderness to escape "from a kind of social and sexual domination [by men]," but she may find Yellow Woman stories appealing because their young and rebellious heroines seek their (hetero)sexuality in the defiance of a different kind of domination, perhaps to escape from matriarchal control or to evade turning into their mothers.[12]

In another interview not included in this volume, Silko suggests that as a mixed breed, she grew up simultaneously within pueblo culture and "on the fringes." She talks of how her family lived on the outskirts of town near the river, the setting where the "Yellow Woman" narrator meets her ka'tsina spirit.[13] Water imagery is central to all of Silko's work, and she portrays the river as a "special place where all sorts of things could go on" that couldn't happen in town, a place where young people experiment with behavior on the fringes of acceptability. "There are willows and tamarack," she says, "and there are always stories. You just hear them." Perhaps the stories helped her find what she calls new "possibilities" in the river:

> The river was a place to meet boyfriends and lovers and so forth. I used to wander around down there and try to imagine walking around the bend and just happening to stumble upon some beautiful man. Later on I realized that these kinds of things that I was doing when I was fifteen are exactly the kinds of things out of which stories like the Yellow Woman story [came]. I finally put the two together: the adolescent longings and the old stories.[14]

Silko's "finally" suggests that this moment of "putting together" her individual longings, her emerging desire, and the "old stories" was a kind of epiphany, a leap forward in both personal and artistic development. Both the story "Yellow Woman" and the collection which contains it explore the process of putting together the search for self and the old stories.

### Cultural Context

Silko presents her ability to put together as a cultural inheritance: "Within one story there are many other stories together again. There is always, *always,* this dynamic of bringing things together, of interrelating things."[15] She borrows imagery from spider grandmother to suggest the importance of such interrelationships: "the structure of Pueblo expression resembles something like a spider's web—with many little threads radiating from a center, criss-crossing each other."[16] Criss-crossings are at the center of Silko's art.

As I have already suggested, the Yellow Woman stories of the oral tradition criss-cross in "Yellow Woman." There are numerous versions, some recorded by anthropologists like Franz Boas, some still alive in the oral tradition, as Silko demonstrates.[17] Several of the essays included in this volume summarize versions of the story. As Allen points out, Yellow Woman stories are about all sorts of activities, but the stories Silko retells concern a young woman, married and often a mother, who wanders beyond the pueblo and has a sexual encounter with a spirit-man, a ka'tsina spirit from the mountains. Sometimes she is abducted by him; sometimes she seeks him out. Sometimes she is killed, by either her abductor or her husband. Often she returns to her tribe with new spiritual offerings, the result of her encounter.

In her influential *The Sacred Hoop: Recovering the Feminine in American Indian Traditions,* Paula Gunn Allen explores the Yellow Woman stories, using Yellow Woman's tribal name, Kochinnenako.* Because Allen also grew up at Laguna Pueblo, she can best assess the story's significance and widespread appeal. In "Kochinnenako in Academe," the essay included in this volume, she calls the stories "always female-centered, always told from Yellow Woman's point of view," implying that the story belongs to the young woman, focuses on her needs, her perspective, and her changes. Although often somewhat "alienated" from her people, "Kochinnenako is a role model," whose stories do not necessarily imply

> that difference is punishable; on the contrary, it is often her very difference that makes her special adventures possible, and these adventures often have happy outcomes for Kochinnenako and for her people. This is significant among a people who value conformity and propriety. . . . It suggests that the behavior of women, at least at certain times or under

---

*Silko herself spells it "Kochininako," a spelling also used by other contributors to this volume.

certain circumstances, must be improper or nonconformist for the greater good of the whole.

As Allen's comment implies, Kochinnenako is a liberating figure, especially for young women attempting to understand individual longings and desires in a cultural context. She combines the mundane and the sacred and has an enduring presence, as Allen argues in *Spider Woman's Granddaughters*.

> Yellow Woman, like the tradition she lives in, goes on and on. She lives in New Mexico (or that's what they call it at present), around Laguna and other Keresan pueblos as well. She is a Spirit, a Mother, a blessed ear of corn, an archetype, a person, a daughter of a main clan, an agent of change and of obscure events, a wanton, an outcast, a girl who runs off with Navajos, or Zunis or even Mexicans. She is also mother of the little war twins, consort of the sun, granddaughter of the one who plays with stars, somehow (obscurely?) related to Grandmother Spider . . .[18]

In another essay from this volume, "Earthy Relations: Carnal Knowledge," Patricia Clark Smith extends Allen's analysis of Kochinnenako's "nonconformity" by explicitly addressing the exploration of sexual transgressions: "These stories somehow concern an inevitable human need to go forth and experience wilderness—and the sexual wilderness that it encompasses." Through her encounters with spirit-men from the mountains, Yellow Woman claims a daring, creative sexuality: "The preserve of wilderness within her—her energy, curiosity, sexuality—is not forcibly repressed, as if it were shameful and unnatural, but brought into contact with the outer wilderness."

Exploring this theme in the work of Silko, Luci Tapahonso, and Joy Harjo, Smith suggests that the search for "wilderness" is widespread in contemporary Indian writers, a point Paula Gunn Allen echoes in her essay, "This Wilderness in My Blood: Spiritual Foundations of the Poetry of Five American Indian Women," also included in *The Sacred Hoop*. In her own fiction, Allen, like Silko, explores a narrator's confusions about

Yellow Woman's identity, as can be seen in "Whirlwind Man Steals Yellow Woman," an excerpt from Allen's novel, *The Woman Who Owned the Shadows,* included in this volume.

As her connections to Allen and other writers demonstrate, Silko writes within and in response to the evolving traditions of contemporary Indian writers. A key passage in *Ceremony,* for instance, comments on the recurring story about the Indian male who becomes a defiant victim at the story's end—the plot of one of the earliest Indian novels, D'Arcy McNickle's *The Surrounded* and echoed in works by N. Scott Momaday, James Welch, and others. A mysterious woman associated with yellow and blue and with the land, Ts'eh, helps the main character Tayo escape the "end of the story" one of his fellow Indians, influenced by white culture, has planned for him: the story of the crazed veteran "'fighting to your death alone in these hills.'" Ts'eh is *Ceremony's* Yellow Woman, and she possesses a healing sexuality; through a sexual relationship with her, Tayo "remembers" his relationship to the land and to the old stories and realizes that everything is interconnected. Tayo is healed through recognizing what many of Silko's yellow women know: that through the stories he can understand himself and his place in his culture. The end of *Ceremony,* where Tayo becomes a tribal storyteller and passes on Ts'eh's lessons, is a much fuller treatment of the cultural reintegration only hinted at in the ending of Momaday's influential *House Made of Dawn,* published in 1968, which many believe began the Native American Renaissance.

Silko's interest in storytelling as central to the creation of community and self is shared by many contemporary Indian writers, Paula Gunn Allen, Simon Ortiz, Louise Erdrich, and especially Scott Momaday, who says:

> Storytelling is imaginative and creative in nature. It is an act by which man strives to realize his capacity for wonder, meaning, and delight. It is also a process in which man invests and preserves himself. . . . Man tells stories in order to understand his experience, whatever it may be. . . . Only when he is embodied in an idea, and the idea is realized in language, can man take possession of himself.[19]

This passage from his essay, "Man Made of Words," published in 1970, has become a classic articulation of the interrelationship between language and self in contemporary American Indian literature. In acknowledging and acting out her sexual desires, encouraged by the stories she has heard about other women who walked outside the confines of the pueblo, the "Yellow Woman" narrator finds wonder, meaning, and delight. Telling her story, she takes possession of a self with fluid boundaries.

### Yellow Woman

Ambiguous and unsettling, the story "Yellow Woman" focuses on the narrator's efforts to figure out who she really is. Walking away from her everyday identity as daughter, wife, and mother, she takes possession of transgressive feelings and desires by recognizing them in the stories she has heard, by blurring the boundaries between herself and Yellow Woman: "This is the way it happens in the stories, I was thinking, with no thought beyond the moment she meets the ka'tsina spirit and they go." And, in turn, the narrator attempts to imagine Yellow Woman's feelings in order to understand her own confusions. In the midst of her second sexual encounter with the mysterious man she met by the river, she wonders "if Yellow Woman had known who she was—if she knew that she would become part of the stories." This moment brings together the story's four major themes, sexual desire, the natural landscape, the search for self, and the nature of storytelling. Although one can argue that by the end of the story the narrator finds some answers to her questions about Yellow Woman and about herself, Silko characteristically leaves those answers ambiguous. To complement the diverse approaches to "Yellow Woman" in the essays included in this volume, I offer a close reading of the story, looking at the important elements of any short story: its motifs, settings, plot, character development, themes, point of view, and style.

Throughout "Yellow Woman" Silko uses recurring naturalistic image patterns to explore the narrator's desires and changes, to show her opening herself to a richer sensuality. The story begins with images of transgression. The narrator has crossed the river, the boundary between the sandrock mesas of the pueblo and the mountains. The opening line, "My thigh clung to his with dampness," evokes an intimacy connected to the river's flow. The narrator twice comments on seeing the moon, an image of female sexuality, reflected in the river. As it contains the reflection of the moon, the river embodies sexual desire, its current running through "the narrow fast channel [that] bubbled and washed green ragged moss and fern leaves."

As the river imagery evokes the female body, so do images of flowers, and the narrator sees the moon blossom into "moonflowers" later in the story. Thinking about why she followed Silva into the mountains, she presents her act as instinctive, a natural need to express her sexuality: "I did not decide to go. I just went. Moonflowers blossom in the sand hills before dawn, just as I followed him." The narrator first made love with Silva "before dawn" and this passage suggests that act opened her to a yellow light, a new awareness. Silko brings this imagery to fruition later in the story when after a fuller expression of her sexual desires, the narrator sees flowers alongside the trail she is following:

> Only the waxy cactus flowers bloomed in the bright sun, and I saw every color that a cactus blossom can be; the white ones and the red ones were still buds, but the purple and the yellow were blossoms, open full and the most beautiful of all.

In her cactus flowers, Silko describes "every color" of the human races, subtly suggesting the university of the Yellow Woman stories. By coming to understand and accept her desires through her connection to Yellow Woman, and acting upon them, the narrator becomes the yellow blossom, an image of her awakening.

This awakening takes place as the narrator moves further and further from the pueblo. Beside the river, she cannot "look beyond the pale red mesas to the pueblo." "[P]ulled . . . close" by Silva, she follows him north into the mountains, which also embrace her: "the dark lava hills . . . all around." By using encircling imagery that recalls the female body, Silko

15

suggests that embracing heterosexual desire leads a woman to self-discovery, to embrace herself and her connection to Yellow Woman. As the mountains encircle her, so does Silva's stone house, "made with black lava rock and red mud." The house's traditional "window facing east" connects it, perhaps opens it, to Yellow Woman; as Silko has said, "Yellow in the Pueblo culture is an important color..., connected with the East, and corn, and corn pollen, and dawn, and Yellow Woman.[20] Like the house, certainly a female image with its interior space and its warmth, the narrator learns to open herself to the dawn; she discovers her own sexual spaces, literal and metaphorical, in her experiences beside the river and in the mountains.

In the mountains encircling Silva's house, where they are "too far away" to see the pueblo but can recognize its "boundaries," the narrator can see for miles. She is able to open herself to the world, now embraced by the wind. "I was standing in the sky with nothing around me but the wind that came down from the blue mountain peak behind me." She has reached this viewpoint by taking a "narrow trail through the black rim rock," and her pleasure in the wind leads her to wonder who else "walks on the pine needles in those blue mountains." Her vision unites the separate self, standing alone in the sky, with others who walked the same "trail through the pine trees," perhaps other yellow women. Trails, roads, and paths criss-cross throughout the rest of Silko's story, turning the landscape into spider woman's web. Images of her ongoing search, for self and for connection, they present her with choices and map a final, if ambiguous, resolution.

The narrator twice walks on the mountain trail in the pines at moments when she recognizes how she is changing. The first time she "remembered yesterday," the day she and Silva first made love, "and the day before"; thinking about the difference between these two days, between the self "before" and the self emerging, leads her to go outside in search of the wind, a wonderful symbol of her passion and turmoil. The second time she walks when she realizes that she has become Yellow Woman and regrets her grandpa's death because only he could connect her experience to the cultural tradition, only he would understand, through the traditional Yellow Woman stories, that "'She'll come home—they usually do.'"

When the narrator sees "something ancient and dark" in Silva's eyes and the story turns violent, she may recall thinking he could "hurt" or "destroy" her. Perhaps she remembers that some yellow women die, and she had better claim Grandpa's version as her own. She takes off when Silva tells her to go back up the mountain but when she reaches a place "where the trail forked," she chooses to head down the mountain to a "safer" place. Turning Silva's horse loose, she wonders "if it would go back to its corral under the pines on the mountain." Her instincts lead her back to her own corral, the pueblo. Trails of self-exploration and change are domesticated into a "paved road," with its suggestions of the conformity of communal life, which she knows will lead her back to her ordinary domestic life; the road recalls "the highways and pick-up trucks" she initially believes Yellow Woman never saw. But she rejects the pavement and chooses a compromise: she follows instead the well worn "path up from the river into the village," arriving at sunset at the house filled with her grandmother, her mother, her husband, her baby, and the ghost of her grandfather, where she is defined by her relationships and roles.

The narrator has discovered a self that defies the confines of everyday domestic life, an awakened spiritual self, free, open, passionate, reflected in the natural world, a self whose desires are apparently not satisfied in her relationship with her husband Al. These desires still require expression at the story's end, as is suggested by her hope that she will once more find Silva by the river. Yet the narrator, like most yellow women, has chosen to return to the pueblo, her settled life there apparently satisfying other needs and desires. Like the story's trails, her needs criss-cross, intersect. We have only for a moment to think of another woman who discovered such a self— Nathaniel Hawthorne's Hester Prynne—to realize the value of Yellow Woman stories. Providing the narrator with a model for breaking the rules, they also allow her to integrate herself back into pueblo life because her cultural traditions implicitly accept female sexual longings and transgressions, and because she, like her creator, can discover herself within a tradition and contribute to "the telling which continues."

By the story's end, the narrator has become a storyteller. She has passed on pieces of her grandfather's stories and told of her own experience on the mountain in the form of a Yellow Woman story. As Allen's comments about Kochinnenako imply, Silko's decision to tell the story from the narrator's point of view is traditional, but her use of first person narration and the story's much praised ambiguity nevertheless brilliantly reinforce her themes. Like traditional yellow women, the narrator is unnamed. By choosing not to reveal her name in the story she tells us, she claims the role of Yellow Woman.

Yet naming, identity, and storytelling are complicated matters, as one of the narrator's speculations about Yellow Woman reveals: "Maybe she'd had another name that her husband and relatives called her so that only the ka'tsina from the north and the storytellers would know her as Yellow Woman." The lyrical, intimate story the narrator tells the reader is quite different from the offhand story about being kidnapped by a Navajo she intends to tell her family, a story she does not believe is true, though she thinks her grandfather would have recognized it as a Yellow Woman story. While the story she tells the reader seems much "truer" to her interior experience, the projected story may be what really happened, for the narrator has often wondered if Silva might be a Navajo. Silko thus suggests that different stories reflect different interpretations of the same experience, even when told from the same point of view. The many Yellow Woman stories in *Storyteller* reinforce this point.

Silko's ambiguity about what actually happened to her narrator raises the question of whether both stories, or parts of both stories, are fantasies, perhaps inspired by the traditional Yellow Woman stories the narrator heard. The narrator's comment at the story's end—that because she "believes" it, Silva will return for her—implies that perhaps she has "believed" him into being. In the autobiographical comment I quoted earlier, Silko herself fantasized about meeting a man by the river, as Yellow Woman had. In such a reading, the link between the traditional stories and the particular experiences of the narrator suggests that the Yellow Woman stories speak to a fundamental female need to express desire, whether women act out such urges or not; Silko suggests that such desire is an essential part of life when Silva defines the narrator's desire as "breathing so hard." From Yellow Woman, the narrator receives encouragement to look more deeply into herself, to explore desires beyond the confines of the pueblo boundaries and of everyday life. As the teller of a Yellow Woman story, Silko also receives encouragement to transgress propriety and write explicit sexual scenes. Some critics find the story unnerving, seeing the narrator's encounters with Silva as blurring into rape, but read as a fantasy, the story elliptically explores the desire to give up sexual control, to be overpowered by sexual urges. As feminist psychologists have suggested, so-called "rape fantasies" are safe: the fantasizer imagines a man with the sexual power to "overcome" her inhibitions, but finally, as storyteller, retains control over what happens. As Silko's use of her first-person narrator makes clear, the Yellow Woman stories offer women control over their sexual fantasies, ways to express unsanctioned desires.

Finally Silko's ambiguous treatment of the narrator's identity leaves us with questions about the nature of storytelling; about whether Yellow Woman really was a woman just like her, her ordinary life overlooked as she was mythologized; about how much the stories have shaped the narrator's interpretations of her desires and her experience; about how to understand the stories she tells. We are presented with two names, one ordinary, never revealed, one mythological, often repeated; with two stories, one prosaic and commonplace, one lyrical and mysterious; with a woman whose family makes jello and a woman who follows the spirit. "Yellow Woman" asks us to put them all together, to recognize the interrelationships, the criss-crossing strands of the web, of everyday life and the oral tradition, of self and culture.

## The Critical Response

Two of Silko's stories, "Yellow Woman" and "Lullaby," are among the most often reprinted stories in American Indian literature.[21] First appearing in *The Man to Send Rain Clouds* (1974), "Yellow Woman" received immediate attention and praise and has been reprinted in a number of other collections including Martha Foley's *Two Hundred Years of Great American Short Stories* (1975).

Although critics have written extensively on *Ceremony* and *Storyteller,* no essays have focused solely on "Yellow Woman." In the introduction to *The Man to Send Rain Clouds,* Kenneth Rosen identifies qualities in Silko's work all later critics have pursued—her rich style and her exploration of the intersection between the cultural tradition and the individual voice:

> Using Indian lore and history as a kind of counterpoint to her special music, she writes with a depth and intensity which, to my mind, set her work apart and mark her as a talent from whom we can expect new, important work.

In an early influential essay, "Ritual and Renewal: Keres Traditions in the Short Fiction of Leslie Silko" (1978), excerpted in this volume, A. LaVonne Ruoff examines tribal stories and traditions and concludes that "Silko emphasizes the need to return to the rituals and oral traditions of the past in order to rediscover the basis for one's cultural identity." Other critics have followed Ruoff's lead in discussing "Yellow Woman." In an introductory pamphlet on Silko published in 1980, Per Seyersted suggests that "Yellow Woman" is about cultural loss. He argues that the narrator "is the only one in the pueblo to credit and love her dead grandfather's stories about Yellow Woman" and that the story "seems to say that white influence has made most Pueblos forget the old myths."[22] In *Spider Woman's Granddaughters* (1989), Paula Gunn Allen also describes a gap between traditional and contemporary life in the story, but she focuses on the narrator's "confusion" and isolation from her culture.

> Silko's use of the Yellow Woman stories, for example, leans more toward isolation of the protagonist from her people than toward connectedness—though even here her connection to herself is of necessity through the stories by way of her family.[23]

20

Perhaps because Silko tells many Yellow Woman stories and insists upon connecting individual stories with cultural traditions, the critics included in this volume all offer larger contexts in which to read the story, many treating it as a piece of a whole, *Storyteller*. An interview with Silko conducted by Kim Barnes follows the story, providing general biographical background, information about Pueblo life, and some discussion of writers who influenced Silko and her attitudes about writing and art. Ruoff's pioneering piece begins the essay section because it also presents useful background information about Laguna Pueblo history and rituals influenced by many cultures. The essay also offers an introduction to Silko's use of material from the oral tradition; the second part has been excerpted to focus specifically on "Yellow Woman."

The next two essays by Paula Gunn Allen and Patricia Clark Smith provide overviews of the ways Indian women interpret, retell, and revise traditional stories. Although Allen's "Kochinnenako in Academe" does not directly discuss "Yellow Woman," it provides both a "Feminist-Tribal Interpretation" of the traditional stories and their relationships to contemporary women's lives and a context in which to read Silko's story. Because Allen's retellings of Yellow Woman stories provide a useful counterpoint to Silko's, "Kochinnenako in Academe" is followed by "Whirlwind Man Steals Yellow Woman," a short section from Allen's novel, *The Woman Who Owned the Shadows*. In "Earthy Relations, Carnal Knowledge: Southwestern American Indian Women Writers and Landscape," Smith identifies a recurring pattern in American Indian women's literature: the use of "spirit-figures" to understand female sexuality and to explore the "preserve of wilderness" within women embodied in women's connections with the land.

The essays by Ruoff, Allen, and Smith help readers to see "Yellow Woman" in relation to tribal oral storytelling traditions and to American Indian women's traditions. The next four essays all focus more narrowly on *Storyteller*. Bernard A. Hirsch's "'The Telling Which Continues': Oral Tradition and the Written Word" introduces readers to the design of *Storyteller*, physically describing the unusual text and examining the interrelationships between Silko's poems, fiction, and autobiography, and her placement of photographs. Hirsch extends his discussion of the text's formal properties into an analysis of how it shapes reader response: "The reader learns by accretion." In looking at how "successive narrative episodes cast long shadows both forward and back, lending different complementary shades of meaning to those preceding them," he focuses particularly on the various retellings of Yellow Woman stories.

Arnold Krupat's "The Dialogic of Silko's *Storyteller*" also helps readers to understand *Storyteller*'s overarching structures, but it focuses primarily on speech, language, and theories of meaning. Krupat reads the text as a "Native American autobiography in the dialogic mode," a "strongly polyphonic text." Krupat's essay first appeared in *Narrative Chance: Postmodern Discourse on Native American Indian Literatures,* edited by Gerald Vizenor, a collection of essays which use critical theory to understand the "narrative discourse" of Indian writers. Krupat borrows the "heteroglossic, polyvocal" view of human language developed by the Russian theorist Mikhail Bakhtin to explore how Silko's text envisions individual identity—and voice—in the context of a "dialogue" of voices all committed to seeing "Pueblo ways as a reference point."

The final two essays center most narrowly on individual themes in *Storyteller* and in the Yellow Woman retellings. As the title suggests, Linda Danielson's "The Storytellers in *Storyteller*," concentrates on storytelling, using the "traditional" approach to Silko—an exploration of her use of cultural materials—to elaborate on the collection's recurring metaphors. Presenting Grandmother Spider as an important influence on Silko's methods of storytelling and use of metaphor, she examines the collection's "spiderweb structure" and its exploration of the "values underlying traditional verbal art," discussing, as Silko has, the relation of storytelling to local gossip as well as to the old stories. She also implicitly connects storytelling, which she calls a "survival strategy," to healing, a major theme of *Ceremony*. In "The Web of Meaning: Naming the Absent Mother in *Storyteller*," Patricia Jones, like earlier critics, reads *Storyteller* as an autobiography, an "album," in which Silko defines herself through her relationships to "people, places and stories that were important to her." Like Hirsch and Krupat, Jones uses contemporary critical theories

22

such as reader response, exploring what readers bring to a text and how a text implicitly shapes it readers. She also borrows from deconstruction, which often focuses on a key "gap" in the text, to explore the absent mother. And she uses feminist theory, which often suggests that a woman's identity is shaped by her connections to and separations from her mother, to examine the mother/daughter relationship explored elliptically throughout *Storyteller*.

Together these essays demonstrate that all readers must indeed "remember the story." The telling continues. Storytelling keeps the past alive; through it we also create ourselves, always in relation to memory, tradition, and ritual.

## ☐ Notes ∎

1. Leslie Silko, "Language and Literature from a Pueblo Indian Perspective," *English Literature: Opening Up the Canon,* ed. Leslie A. Fiedler and Houston A. Baker, Jr. (Baltimore: The Johns Hopkins University Press, 1981): 64.

2. *Storyteller* (New York: Seaver Books, 1981) is a collection of stories, lyrical and narrative poems, autobiographical anecdotes, and photographs of Silko's family and of the New Mexico landscape, many taken by her father. As the essays in this volume reveal, there has been considerable critical attention to the volume's structure, organizing principles, and genre, as well as to the blurred line between various forms of storytelling.

3. Kim Barnes, "Leslie Marmon Silko Interview," reprinted in this volume.

4. Larry Evers and Denny Carr, "A Conversation with Leslie Marmon Silko," *Sun Tracks* 3:1 (Fall, 1976): 29–30.

5. Laura Coltelli, "Leslie Marmon Silko," *Winged Words: American Indian Writers Speak* (Lincoln: University of Nebraska Press, 1990), 141.

6. "Grandmother" appears in a number of collections. See, for instance, *That's What She Said: Contemporary Poetry and Fiction by Native American Women,* ed. Rayna Green (Bloomington: Indiana University Press, 1984), 15.

7. Although it is based on fragmentary Mayan almanacs, Silko's most recent novel, *The Almanac of the Dead* (1991), is very

different from her first two books. An angry exposé of the effects of imperialism in the western hemisphere, nearly eight hundred pages long, it contains dozens of characters, loosely interconnected in a vast, sprawling plot which defies summary. Despite its anger, the novel's tone is oddly detached and distanced, and its style has little of the sensuous lyricism of Silko's early work or its rich treatment of tradition.

8. Dexter Fisher, "Stories and Their Tellers: A Conversation with Leslie Marmon Silko," *The Third Woman: Minority Women Writers of the United States* (Boston: Houghton Mifflin, 1980), 23.

9. Patricia Clark Smith with Paula Gunn Allen, "Earthy Relations, Carnal Knowledge," reprinted in this volume.

10. Kenneth Rosen, ed., *The Man to Send Rain Clouds: Contemporary Stories by American Indians* (New York: Viking Press, 1974), 176.

11. Since questions about marriage and fidelity pervade traditional Yellow Woman stories, it is interesting to note that Silko's parents were separated at about the time she was writing "Yellow Woman" and conceiving *Storyteller*, perhaps influencing her portrayal both of mothers and of marital relations.

12. Although they treat the mother/daughter relationship more elliptically, the Yellow Woman stories resemble the ancient Demeter/Persephone myths of Greek culture, where Persephone leaves her mother, sometimes willingly, sometimes not, to establish a relationship with a man.

13. Ka'tsinas are mythical spirits who embody the land, particularly the wilderness; they commonly live in the mountains, where they often gamble and upset the nature of things. They are sometimes helpful, sometimes dangerous.

14. Evers and Carr, "A Conversation with Leslie Marmon Silko," 29.

15. Silko, "Language and Literature from a Pueblo Indian Perspective," 64.

16. "Language and Literature," 54.

17. For examples of stories from the oral tradition, see Boas, *Keresean Texts.* 2 vols. Publications of the American Ethnological Society 8 (New York: G. E. Stechert and Company, 1928).

18. Paul Gunn Allen, *Spider Woman's Granddaughters* (Boston: Beacon Press, 1989), 182.

19. N. Scott Momaday, "Man Made of Words," *The Remem-*

*bered Earth,* ed. Gerry Hobson (Albuquerque: University of New Mexico Press, 1979), 168.

20. Coltelli, "Leslie Marmon Silko," 141.

21. It is interesting to note that "Lullaby," a far less ambiguous and more overtly political story about an aging Indian woman whose children have been taken from her, has more frequently been chosen by the editors of general textbook anthologies like *Norton* and *Heath,* than the more mysterious and explicitly sexual story about a young woman who breaks the rules, "Yellow Woman." "Yellow Woman," with its rich mythological context, has been more often reprinted in collections of American Indian literature.

22. Per Seyersted, *Leslie Marmon Silko* (Boise: Boise State University Western Writers Series, 1980), 19, 20.

23. Allen, *Spider Woman's Granddaughters,* 19.

# ❑ Chronology ▪

| | |
|---|---|
| 1948 | Born in Albuquerque, New Mexico. Grows up at Laguna Pueblo, fifty miles west of Albuquerque, in a close, extended family. |
| 1953–1964 | Attends Laguna Day School, where she is not allowed to use the Laguna language, and then after fourth grade, Manzano Day School in Albuquerque, a small private school. |
| 1964–1969 | Attends the University of New Mexico, marries, has her first son, and publishes her first story, "Tony's Story." Graduates with a B.A. in English. |
| 1969 | Publishes "The Man to Send Rain Clouds." |
| 1969–1971 | Hoping to file land claims suits as her father had, attends law school at the University of New Mexico; her second son is born. |
| 1971 | Receives a National Endowment of the Arts Discovery grant and decides to quit law school. |
| 1974 | Publishes seven stories in *The Man to Send Rain Clouds,* and a collection of poetry, *Laguna Woman.* |
| 1974–1976 | Teaches at Navajo Community College at Tsaile, Arizona. |
| 1976–1978 | In Ketchikan, Alaska writing *Ceremony,* published in 1977. |
| 1978 | Moves to Tucson and begins teaching at the University of Arizona. |
| 1981 | Publishes *Storyteller* |
| 1981 | Receives a MacArthur Foundation fellowship, which enables her to give up teaching and devote herself to *The Almanac of the Dead.* |
| 1991 | Publishes *The Almanac of the Dead* |

# ❏ Yellow Woman

# ☐ Yellow Woman

My thigh clung to his with dampness, and I watched the sun rising up through the tamaracks and willows. The small brown water birds came to the river and hopped across the mud, leaving brown scratches in the alkali-white crust. They bathed in the river silently. I could hear the water, almost at our feet where the narrow fast channel bubbled and washed green ragged moss and fern leaves. I looked at him beside me, rolled in the red blanket on the white river sand. I cleaned the sand out of the cracks between my toes, squinting because the sun was above the willow trees. I looked at him for the last time, sleeping on the white river sand.

I felt hungry and followed the river south the way we had come the afternoon before, following our footprints that were already blurred by lizard tracks and bug trails. The horses were still lying down, and the black one whinnied when he saw me but he did not get up—maybe it was because the corral was made out of thick cedar branches and the horses had not yet felt the sun like I had. I tried to look beyond the pale red mesas to the pueblo. I knew it was there, even if I could not see it, on the sandrock hill above the river, the same river that moved past me now and had reflected the moon last night.

From *Storyteller* (New York: Seaver Books, 1981), 54–62.

The horse felt warm underneath me. He shook his head and pawed the sand. The bay whinnied and leaned against the gate trying to follow, and I remembered him asleep in the red blanket beside the river. I slid off the horse and tied him close to the other horse, I walked north with the river again, and the white sand broke loose in footprints over footprints.

"Wake up."

He moved in the blanked and turned his face to me with his eyes still closed. I knelt down to touch him.

"I'm leaving."

He smiled now, eyes still closed. "You are coming with me, remember?" He sat up now with his bare dark chest and belly in the sun.

"Where?"

"To my place."

"And will I come back?"

He pulled his pants on. I walked away from him, feeling him behind me and smelling the willows.

"Yellow Woman," he said.

I turned to face him. "Who are you?" I asked.

He laughed and knelt on the low, sandy bank, washing his face in the river. "Last night you guessed my name, and you knew why I had come."

I stared past him at the shallow moving water and tried to remember the night, but I could only see the moon in the water and remember his warmth around me.

"But I only said that you were him and that I was Yellow Woman—I'm not really her—I have my own name and I come from the pueblo on the other side of the mesa. Your name is Silva and you are a stranger I met by the river yesterday afternoon."

He laughed softly. "What happened yesterday has

nothing to do with what you will do today, Yellow
Woman."

"I know—that's what I'm saying—the old stories
about the ka'tsina spirit and Yellow Woman can't
mean us."

My old grandpa liked to tell those stories best.
There is one about Badger and Coyote who went hunting and were gone all day, and when the sun was going
down they found a house. There was a girl living there
alone, and she had light hair and eyes and she told
them that they could sleep with her. Coyote wanted to
be with her all night so he sent Badger into a prairie-
dog hole, telling him he thought he saw something in
it. As soon as Badger crawled in, Coyote blocked up
the entrance with rocks and hurried back to Yellow
Woman.

"Come here," he said gently.

He touched my neck and I moved close to him to
feel his breathing and to hear his heart. I was wondering if Yellow Woman had known who she was—if she
knew that she would become part of the stories. Maybe
she'd had another name that her husband and relatives
called her so that only the ka'tsina from the north and
the storytellers would know her as Yellow Woman. But
I didn't go on; I felt him all around me, pushing me
down into the white river sand.

Yellow Woman went away with the spirit from
the north and lived with him and his relatives. She was
gone for a long time, but then one day she came back
and she brought twin boys.

"Do you know the story?"

"What story?" He smiled and pulled me close to
him as he said this. I was afraid lying there on the red

blanket. All I could know was the way he felt, warm, damp, his body beside me. This is the way it happens in the stories, I was thinking, with no thought beyond the moment she meets the ka'tsina spirit and they go.

"I don't have to go. What they tell in stories was real only then, back in time immemorial, like they say."

He stood up and pointed at my clothes tangled in the blanket. "Let's go," he said.

I walked beside him, breathing hard because he walked fast, his hand around my wrist. I had stopped trying to pull away from him, because his hand felt cool and the sun was high, drying the river bed into alkali. I will see someone, eventually I will see someone, and then I will be certain that he is only a man—some man from nearby—and I will be sure that I am not Yellow Woman. Because she is from out of time past and I live now and I've been to school and there are highways and pickup trucks that Yellow Woman never saw.

It was an easy ride north on horseback. I watched the change from the cottonwood trees along the river to the junipers that brushed past us in the foothills, and finally there were only piñons, and when I looked up at the rim of the mountain plateau I could see pine trees growing on the edge. Once I stopped to look down, but the pale sandstone had disappeared and the river was gone and the dark lava hills were all around. He touched my hand, not speaking, but always singing softly a mountain song and looking into my eyes.

I felt hungry and wondered what they were doing at home now—my mother, my grandmother, my husband, and the baby. Cooking breakfast, saying "Where did she go?—maybe kidnapped." And Al going to the tribal police with the details: "She went walking along the river."

The house was made with black lava rock and red mud. It was high above the spreading miles of arroyos and long mesas. I smelled a mountain smell of pitch and buck brush. I stood there beside the black horse, looking down on the small, dim country we had passed, and I shivered.

"Yellow Woman, come inside where it's warm."

He lit a fire in the stove. It was an old stove with a round belly and an enamel coffeepot on top. There was only the stove, some faded Navajo blankets, and a bedroll and cardboard box. The floor was made of smooth adobe plaster, and there was one small window facing east. He pointed at the box.

"There's some potatoes and the frying pan." He sat on the floor with his arms around his knees pulling them close to his chest and he watched me fry the potatoes. I didn't mind him watching me because he was always watching me—he had been watching me since I came upon him sitting on the river bank trimming leaves from a willow twig with his knife. We ate from the pan and he wiped the grease from his fingers on his Levi's.

"Have you brought women here before?" He smiled and kept chewing, so I said, "Do you always use the same tricks?"

"What tricks?" He looked at me like he didn't understand.

"The story about being a ka'tsina from the mountains. The story about Yellow Woman."

Silva was silent; his face was calm.

"I don't believe it. Those stories couldn't happen now," I said.

35

He shook his head and said softly, "But someday they will talk about us, and they will say, 'Those two lived long ago when things like that happened.'"

He stood up and went out. I ate the rest of the potatoes and thought about things—about the noise the stove was making and the sound of the mountain wind outside. I remembered yesterday and the day before, and then I went outside.

I walked past the corral to the edge where the narrow trail cut through the black rim rock. I was standing in the sky with nothing around me but the wind that came down from the blue mountain peak behind me. I could see faint mountain images in the distance miles across the vast spread of mesas and valleys and plains. I wondered who was over there to feel the mountain wind on those sheer blue edges—who walks on the pine needles in those blue mountains.

"Can you see the pueblo?" Silva was standing behind me.

I shook my head. "We're too far away."

"From here I can see the world." He stepped out on the edge. "The Navajo reservation begins over there." He pointed to the east. "The Pueblo boundaries are over here." He looked below us to the south, where the narrow trail seemed to come from. "The Texans have their ranches over there, starting with that valley, the Concho Valley. The Mexicans run some cattle over there too."

"Do you ever work for them?"

"I steal from them," Silva answered. The sun was dropping behind us and the shadows were filling the land below. I turned away from the edge that dropped forever into the valleys below.

"I'm cold," I said, "I'm going inside." I started

wondering about this man who could speak the Pueblo language so well but who lived on a mountain and rustled cattle. I decided that this man Silva must be Navajo, because Pueblo men didn't do things like that.

"You must be a Navajo."

Silva shook his head gently. "Little Yellow Woman," he said, "you never give up, do you? I have told you who I am. The Navajo people know me, too." He knelt down and unrolled the bedroll and spread the extra blankets out on a piece of canvas. The sun was down, and the only light in the house came from outside—the dim orange light from sundown.

I stood there and waited for him to crawl under the blankets.

"What are you waiting for?" he said, and I lay down beside him. He undressed me slowly like the night before beside the river—kissing my face gently and running his hands up and down my belly and legs. He took off my pants and then he laughed.

"Why are you laughing?"

"You are breathing so hard."

I pulled away from him and turned my back to him.

He pulled me around and pinned me down with his arms and chest. "You don't understand, do you, little Yellow Woman? You will do what I want."

And again he was all around me with his skin slippery against mine, and I was afraid because I understood that his strength could hurt me. I lay underneath him and I knew that he could destroy me. But later, while he slept beside me, I touched his face and I had a feeling—the kind of feeling for him that overcame me that morning along the river. I kissed him on the forehead and he reached out for me.

When I woke up in the morning he was gone. It gave me a strange feeling because for a long time I sat there on the blankets and looked around the little house for some object of his—some proof that he had been there or maybe that he was coming back. Only the blankets and the cardboard box remained. The .30-30 that had been leaning in the corner was gone, and so was the knife I had used the night before. He was gone, and I had my chance to go now. But first I had to eat, because I knew it would be a long walk home.

I found some dried apricots in the cardboard box, and I sat down on a rock at the edge of the plateau rim. There was no wind and the sun warmed me. I was surrounded by silence. I drowsed with apricots in my mouth, and I didn't believe that there were highways or railroads or cattle to steal.

When I woke up, I stared down at my feet in the black mountain dirt. Little black ants were swarming over the pine needles around my foot. They must have smelled the apricots. I thought about my family far below me. They would be wondering about me, because this had never happened to me before. The tribal police would file a report. But if old Grandpa weren't dead he would tell them what happened—he would laugh and say, "Stolen by a ka'tsina, a mountain spirit. She'll come home—they usually do." There are enough of them to handle things. My mother and grandmother will raise the baby like they raised me. Al will find someone else, and they will go on like before, except that there will be a story about the day I disappeared while I was walking along the river. Silva had come for me; he said he had. I did not decide to go. I just went. Moonflowers blossom in the sand hills before dawn, just as I followed him.

That's what I was thinking as I wandered along the trail through the pine trees.

It was noon when I got back. When I saw the stone house I remembered that I had meant to go home. But that didn't seem important any more, maybe because there were little blue flowers growing in the meadow behind the stone house and the gray squirrels were playing in the pines next to the house. The horses were standing in the corral, and there was a beef carcass hanging on the shady side of a big pine in front of the house. Flies buzzed around the clotted blood that hung from the carcass. Silva was washing his hands in a bucket full of water. He must have heard me coming because he spoke to me without turning to face me.

"I've been waiting for you."

"I went walking in the big pine trees."

I looked into the bucket full of bloody water with brown-and-white animal hairs floating in it. Silva stood there letting his hand drip, examining me intently.

"Are you coming with me?"

"Where?" I asked him.

"To sell the meat in Marquez."

"If you're sure it's O.K."

"I wouldn't ask you if it wasn't," he answered.

He sloshed the water around in the bucket before he dumped it out and set the bucket upside down near the door. I followed him to the corral and watched him saddle the horses. Even beside the horses he looked tall, and I asked him again if he wasn't Navajo. He didn't say anything; he just shook his head and kept cinching up the saddle.

"But Navajos are tall."

"Get on the horse," he said, "and let's go."

The last thing he did before we started down the steep trail was to grab the .30-30 from the corner. He slid the rifle into the scabbard that hung from his saddle.

"Do they ever try to catch you?" I asked.

"They don't know who I am."

"Then why did you bring the rifle?"

"Because we are going to Marquez where the Mexicans live."

The trail leveled out on a narrow ridge that was steep on both sides like an animal spine. On one side I could see where the trail went around the rocky gray hills and disappeared into the southeast where the pale sandrock mesas stood in the distance near my home. On the other side was a trial that went west, and as I looked far into the distance I thought I saw the little town. But Silva said no, that I was looking in the wrong place, that I just thought I saw houses. After that I quit looking off into the distance; it was hot and the wildflowers were closing up their deep-yellow petals. Only the waxy cactus flowers bloomed in the bright sun, and I saw every color that a cactus blossom can be; the white ones and the red ones were still buds, but the purple and the yellow were blossoms, open full and the most beautiful of all.

Silva saw him before I did. The white man was riding a big gray horse, coming up the trail towards us. He was traveling fast and the gray horse's feet sent rocks rolling off the trail into the dry tumbleweeds. Silva motioned for me to stop and we watched the white man. He didn't see us right away, but finally his horse whinnied at our horses and he stopped. He looked at us briefly before he lapped the gray horse across the three hundred yards that separated us. He stopped his horse in front of Silva, and his young fat face was shadowed by the brim of his hat. He didn't look mad, but his small, pale eyes moved from the blood-soaked gunny sacks hanging from my saddle to Silva's face and then back to my face.

"Where did you get the fresh meat?" the white man asked.

"I've been hunting," Silva said, and when he shifted his weight in the saddle the leather creaked.

"The hell you have, Indian. You've been rustling cattle. We've been looking for the thief for a long time."

The rancher was fat, and sweat began to soak through his white cowboy shirt and the wet cloth stuck to the thick rolls of belly fat. He almost seemed to be panting from the exertion of talking, and he smelled rancid, maybe because Silva scared him.

Silva turned to me and smiled, "Go back up the mountain, Yellow Woman."

The white man got angry when he heard Silva speak in a language he couldn't understand. "Don't try anything, Indian. Just keep riding to Marquez. We'll call the state police from there."

The rancher must have been unarmed because he was very frightened and if he had a gun he would have pulled it out then. I turned my horse around and the rancher yelled, "Stop!" I looked at Silva for an instant and there was something ancient and dark—something I could feel in my stomach—in his eyes, and when I glanced at his hand I saw his finger on the trigger of the .30-30 that was still in the saddle scabbard. I slapped my horse across the flank and the sacks of raw meat swung against my knees as the horse leaped up the trail. It was hard to keep my balance, and once I thought I felt the saddle slipping backward; it was because of this that I could not look back.

I didn't stop until I reached the ridge where the trail forked. The horse was breathing deep gasps and there was a dark film of sweat on its neck. I looked down in the direction I had come from, but I couldn't see the place. I waited. The wind came up and pushed warm air past me. I looked up at the sky, pale blue and full of thin clouds and fading vapor trails left by jets.

I think four shots were fired—I remember hearing four hollow explosions that reminded me of deer hunting. There could have been more shots after that, but I couldn't have heard them because my horse was running again and the loose rocks were making too much noise as they scattered around his feet.

Horses have a hard time running downhill, but I went that way instead of uphill to the mountain because I thought it was safer. I felt better with the horse running southeast past the round gray hills that were covered with cedar trees and black lava rock. When I got to the plain in the distance I could see the dark green patches of tamaracks that grew along the river; and beyond the river I could see the beginning of the pale sandrock mesas. I stopped the horse and looked back to see if anyone was coming; then I got off the horse and turned the horse around, wondering if it would go back to its corral under the pines on the mountain. It looked back at me for a moment and then plucked a mouthful of green tumbleweeds before it trotted back up the trail with its ears pointed forward, carrying its head daintily to one side to avoid stepping on the dragging reins. When the horse disappeared over the last hill, the gunny sacks full of meat were still swinging and bouncing.

I walked toward the river on a wood-hauler's road that I knew would eventually lead to a paved road. I was thinking about waiting beside the road for someone to drive by, but by the time I got to the pavement I had decided it wasn't very far to walk if I followed the river back the way Silva and I had come.

The river water tasted good, and I sat in the shade under a cluster of silvery willows. I thought about Silva, and I felt sad at leaving him; still, there was something strange about him, and I tried to figure it out all the way back home.

I came back to the place on the river bank where he had been sitting the first time I saw him. The green willow leaves that he had trimmed from the branch were still lying there, wilted in the sand. I saw the leaves and I wanted to go back to him—to kiss him and to touch him—but the mountains were too far away now. And I told myself, because I believe it, he will come back sometime and be waiting again by the river.

I followed the path up from the river into the village. The sun was getting low, and I could smell supper cooking when I got to the screen door of my house. I could hear the voices inside—my mother was telling my grandmother how to fix the Jell-O and my husband, Al, was playing with the baby. I decided to tell them that some Navajo had kidnaped me, but I was sorry that old Grandpa wasn't alive to hear my story because it was the Yellow Woman stories he liked to tell best.

# ❑ Background
## to the Story

# A Leslie Marmon Silko Interview

KB: The first question I want to ask you is, who do you consider to be your audience? Who are you writing for?

LS: I've never thought too much about an audience per se. When I first started writing, I wasn't sure that anyone would want to read or listen to the work that I did. I didn't think about it at first. In a way, it's good not to think about an audience. If you start thinking about the audience, it can inhibit what you do. When I was younger, there was concern about what will Grandma think, or what will Mama say or something like this, and that in a sense is being concerned about audience and can really inhibit a writer. Initially, I guess I assumed that I wouldn't have to worry about an audience because there would not be an audience. I didn't think about it, and I didn't even worry too much about what Mama would think or what Grandma would think or what Uncle So-and-So would think or what the people would think because at first I didn't think that I would ever have to worry that they would see what I had written. Now, I'm working on this new novel which is long and complex to the point of being foolhardy. Who knows, a polite way would be to call it an ambitious project. But I'm so caught up in trying to see if I can make it happen. It's sort of a personal challenge, and again I'm not thinking about an audience. I've been quoted in other interviews as saying that I want this novel to be a novel that, when you shop at a Safeway store, it will be in the little wire racks at the check-out station and that I don't want to write something that the MLA

From *The Journal of Ethnic Studies* 13 (Winter 1986): 83–105.

[Modern Language Association] will want. I want something that will horrify the people at the MLA. Mostly, I'm teasing, but in another way I'm not. I'm sad to see that so little serious fiction gets out into the world. I was amazed that Umberto Eco's *The Name of the Rose* and Mark Helprin's book *Winter's Tale* made it to the wire racks at the check-out stands in the United States. So I'm probably only part-way serious when I say that I don't think about an audience.

KB: So you didn't write a book like *Storyteller* for a particularly white or Indian audience.

LS: I don't think about Indian and white. What I wanted to do was clarify the interrelationship between the stories I had heard and my sense of storytelling and language that had been given to me by the old folks, the people back home. I gave examples of what I heard as best I could remember, and how I developed these elements into prose, into fiction and into poetry, moving from what was basically an oral tradition into a written tradition. The way I figured it, there would be some Native American people who would be interested in it and some Laguna Pueblo people who would be interested in it. There might be other people who are working out of a different cultural tradition but still working with oral material and working in their own art to bring the two together who would be interested. The book is for people who are interested in that relationship between the spoken and the written.

KB: Do you consider yourself a storyteller in a traditional sense?

LS: No, not at all. My friend Mei-mei Berssenbrugge, the poet, spent some time at Laguna Pueblo a few years ago, and she sat in on a kind of a session. I hesitate to call it a storytelling session because they're real spontaneous. It was at my uncle's house, and my uncle's wife Anita and her two sisters were there and some other people. It was in the evening and everyone was feeling jolly and talking. We might have started out with some kind of notorious incident that had happened recently, and pretty soon Mei-mei was sitting there listening to the way people would relate something that happened, and we'd all laugh and then one of Anita's sister's would say, "Well, you remember the time," then the other sister would take over. When the whole session was over, we all went back over to my grandma's house where Mei-mei and I were staying, and Mei-mei said, "They really have a way of telling these stories and incidents and kind of playing off one another." She was really impressed, and I said, "See, I'm not in that class at all." I suppose if I didn't have the outlook of the writer, I might get better at storytelling, but I always say that I'm not good at giving off-the-cuff presentations. Oh, sometimes I have a fine moment. If you really want to hear people who can get rolling in telling, you have to go down to Laguna and kind of fall into the right situation, right feelings and right time.

KB: Was a storyteller a spiritual leader? Was he or she someone who was born into or inherited that role?

LS: It's not like that at all. There is a period of time at the winter solstice when people get together for four days and four nights, and they re-tell all the stories connected with the emergence and the migration of the People. There are people who have to learn and remember those stories and people who have to participate in that telling and re-telling once a year. Those people would probably be designated persons, but they would not be specially designated in any kind of ceremonial or religious way. They wouldn't be called storytellers; they would be called ceremonial religious leaders. The key to understanding storytellers and storytelling at Laguna Pueblo is to realize that you grow up not just being aware of narrative and making a story or seeing a story in what happens to you and what goes on around you all the time, but just being appreciative and delighted in narrative exchanges. When you meet somebody at a post office, he or she says, "How are you, how are you doing?" At Laguna, people will stand there and they'll tell you how they are doing. At Laguna, it's a way of interacting. It isn't like there's only one storyteller designated. That's not it at all. It's a whole way of being. When I say "storytelling," I don't just mean sitting down and telling a once-upon-a-time kind of story. I mean a whole way of seeing yourself, the people around you, your life, the place of your life in the bigger context, not just in terms of nature and location, but in terms of what has gone on before, what's happened to other people. So it's a whole way of being, but there are some people who are willing to be funnier or better storytellers than others, and some people because they are older or they remember better, have a larger repertoire of the *humma-hah* stories. It's not at all like the Irish idea of the bard or the chosen one.

KB: Why are you writing these stories? Are you trying to put the oral tradition in a more stable or lasting form? Do you think anything is lost in the writing down of these stories?

LS: Well, no, I'm not trying to save them, I'm not trying to put them in a stable or lasting form. I write them down because I like seeing how I can translate this sort of feeling or flavor or sense of a story that's told and heard onto the page. Obviously, some things will be lost because you're going from one medium to another. And I use *translate* in the broadest sense. I don't mean translate from the Laguna Pueblo language to English, I mean the feeling or the sense that language is being used orally. So I play with the page and things that you could do on the page, and repetitions. When you have an audience, when you're telling a story and people are listening, there's repetition of crucial points. That's something that on the printed page looks really crummy and is redundant and useless, but in the actual telling is necessary. So I play around with the page by using different kinds of spacing or indentations or even italics so that the reader can sense, say, that the tone of the voice has changed. If you were hearing a story, the speed would increase at certain points. I want to see how much I can make the page communicate those nuances and shifts to the reader. I'm intrigued with that. I recognize the inherent problem; there's no way that hearing a story and reading a story are the same thing; but that doesn't mean that everyone should throw up his hands and say it can't be done or say that what's done on the page isn't catching some of those senses. When I read off the page and read some of the *humma-hah* stories that I wrote down or go through some of the Aunt Susie material, then of course, I think it's more persuasive. In a way, that's not fair; because I'm reading it out loud, I've gone back again. But I think there are some instances where I've been successful so that the reader has a sense of how it might sound if I were reading it to him or her.

KB: In a work like *Storyteller,* are you actually creating something, or are you simply re-telling a myth?

LS: Every time a story is told, and this is one of the beauties of the oral tradition, each telling is a new and unique story, even if it's repeated word for word by the same teller sitting in the same chair. I work to try to help the reader have the sense of how it would sound if the reader could be hearing it. That's original. And no matter how carefully I remember, memory gets all mixed together with imagination. It does for everybody. But I don't change the spirit or the mood or the tone of the story. For some stories, I could just hear Aunt Susie's voice reverberating. The challenge was to get it down so you could have a sense of my Aunt Susie's sound and what it was like. Earlier you said something about writing the stories down in some way that they would be saved. Nobody saves stories. Writing down a story, even tape-recording stories, doesn't save them in the sense of saving their life within a community. Stories stay alive within the community like the Laguna Pueblo community because the stories have a life of their own. The life of the story is not something that any individual person can save and certainly not someone writing it down or recording it on tape or video. That's a nice little idea, and in some places where they've had these kind of archival materials, younger people can go and see or listen to certain stories. But if for whatever reasons the community no longer has a place for a story or a story no longer has a life within that particular period, that doesn't mean that the story no longer has life; that's something that no single person can decide. The old folks at Laguna would say, "If it's important, you'll remember it." If it's really important, if it really has a kind of substance that reaches to the heart of the community life and what's gone before and what's gone later, it will be remembered. And if it's not remembered, the people no longer wanted it, or it no longer had its place in the community.

People outside the community are often horrified to hear some old-timer say, "No, I won't tell my stories to the tape recorder. No, I won't put them on video tape. If these younger folks don't listen and remember from me, then maybe these stories are meant to end with me." It's very tough-minded. It flies in the face of all the anthropologists and people who get moist-eyed over what a good turn they're doing for the Native American communities by getting down these stories. I tend to align myself with the tougher-minded people. The folks at home will say, "If it's important, if it has relevance, it will stay regardless of whether it's on video tape, taped, or written down." It's only the western Europeans who have this inflated pompous notion that every word, everything that's said or done is real important, and it's got to live on and on forever. And only Americans think that America, which has barely been around 200 years, which is a joke, what a short period of time, only Americans think that we'll just continue on. It takes a tremendous amount of stupid blind self-love to think that your civilization or your culture will continue on, when all you have to do is look at history and see that civilizations and people a lot better than people building the MX [missile system] have disappeared. The people at home who say the story will either live or die are just being honest and truthful. But it's a pretty tough statement the western European notion that something just has to live on and on and on. People at home say some things have their time and then things pass. It's like Momaday when he writes about the Kiowa, how the horse came and they became masters of the Plains. He says their great heyday lasted one or two hundred years. It passes and it's gone, you know? You could feel sad about it, but that's the way it is.

KB: In your article, "An Old-Time Indian Attack," you say that the notion that the writer has the power to inhabit any soul, any consciousness, is an idea restricted to the white man. In "Humaweepi," the warrior priest believes that human beings are special, which means they can do anything. If we see the artist as a kind of priest, and this may once again be a white notion, why can't the artist, like Humaweepi, transcend his own experience? Does a person necessarily have to experience something to write about it?

LS: I think that it's possible that the most deeply felt emotions, like the deepest kind of fear or loss or bereavement or ecstasy or joy, those kinds of deep, deep, deep level feelings and emotions, are common in all human beings. But to have a sense of what sorts of things, what sorts of outside stimuli, if you will, or situations or occurrences, will trigger what in whom, then that becomes trickier. That essay was written at a time when there were all of these writers, white male writers, who wanted to be the white shaman. There was a whole white shaman movement, and it was so bogus, it was such a complete joke and a kind of con game. These were like followers of Snyder.* They weren't even working; they couldn't have gotten to a deep level of fear, love, hate. They didn't have the artistic capacity to ever reach that level, even if they'd been writing about themselves and out of their own cultural experience. Again, it was that kind of superficiality, that materialistic notion that if you take the person's line break, or if you take the kind of scanning pattern of the reoccurrences of the bear image or something like that, then you have written something that's equivalent to the healing ceremony of the Chippewas. My friend Geary Hobson, who's a writer—he's a Cherokee—had been savaged by one of these nitwit white shaman, and so the essay was written under those circumstances. The main notion was that those people who were calling themselves white shaman no more had a sense of the deeper level of feeling or what is commonly shared between human beings; they had no more idea than a dog or a cat has an idea of deep levels of human feeling, and yet they were prancing around thinking that they could appropriate that level of experience. The essay was a reaction to that superficiality, and the fact of the matter is that a lot of these so-called white shaman who were kicking around at that time weren't even able to write about themselves or from their particular cultural perspective.

KB: In *Ceremony,* you write about a man's experience. Do you feel like you were going outside of your experience in doing

---

*Editor's note: Gary Snyder is a contemporary poet who has borrowed freely from American Indian traditions. See, for instance, his collection *Turtle Island.* Silko criticizes Snyder and other "white shamans" in "An Old-Time Indian Attack," included in her friend Geary Hobson's collection, *The Remembered Earth.*

this? Is the Native American male's experience much different from the female's?

LS: Well, I don't know if it is or not since I never was a Native American male, you know. But what I do believe is that again, on that deep, deep level, that deep level where we're moved to fear, sorrow, loss, joy, camaraderie, on that deep level, men and women are the same, just like all human beings are. The way the heart pushes in the chest feels the same, whether a woman or a man is experiencing terror. What would trigger it will differ. A woman walking alone at night can be terrified by the sound of other footsteps; it wouldn't necessarily terrify a man, unless an hour before some guys had said, "Look buddy, we're going to get you." Then I think the same physiological response would be there. In *Ceremony*, the male character was dealing with grief and loss and rage and a kind of sickness at heart and loneliness; I have great faith that my consciousness and experience on that level of feeling is true for him.

People have noticed that I write about men and what they did and how they hung out together and so on. That's more complex. In Laguna Pueblo, little girls aren't kept with the women, and little boys aren't kept with the men. Children sort of range freely, and men and women range freely. The division of labor at Laguna Pueblo, especially when I was growing up, was much more flexible. Whoever was strong enough and ready to do a certain task would do it. And it wasn't according to gender. If something needed to be lifted, if there was a big strong Laguna woman, she would be the one that would help lift and not the old shrimpy man. Labor wasn't divided into men's work and women's work. When I was a kid, I got to hang around wherever I wanted to hang around. Of the women in my family, only my great-grandmother was not actively involved in working. Women work very hard, and they work very hard outside of the kitchen or outside of the home in Laguna. Even Grandma Alma, my great-grandmother, who is ninety, would go out and get her own coal and wood.

I had this omnivorous appetite for watching people do things. And I watched how my great-grandmother got down on her knees even when she was old and feeble, but I also watched how men built things. Nobody shooed me away, no one told me girls couldn't watch men build a shed. In the Pueblo, men don't go off as much. It's not like your middle-America, white middle-class man who goes off to work, and work is far away from where the women and children are. In the Pueblo, the men are around. There's all kinds of stuff going on, and people are very busy. I spent a lot of time listening and watching men from the time I was a little girl. And I think that more people, women and men, could write about one another if there wasn't this kind of segregation of the sexes that we have in America. Men can handle writing about women only insofar as they are getting them into or out of bed. But, you know, that isn't because it can't be done, that isn't because only men know what men do, that's because in this particular stupid, great middle-America society, men and women really don't know very much about one another. But that doesn't mean that it is inherent and that it has to be. That's just this one particular place in time.

KB: I'm sure you've been asked this numerous times, but how do you feel about being classified as a minority writer? Ed Abbey recently said that to get published today, you need to be three things: female, minority, and preferably lesbian. How do you react to this?*

LS: Oh, well. That's just Ed Abbey. Ed's always going around poking at hornets' nests, and then he likes to see if he can still run fast enough to get away before he gets stung. What do I think about that? I think you should ask a lesbian ethnic minority woman, who's just trying to get her first novel published or her first book of poems published, if she thinks that that's necessarily true. I disagree. Actually, right now in these Reagan years, Ed Abbey is a little bit off the mark. Right now, the mood is Reaganism, and the emphasis is back on the white male. Actually, there haven't been that many lesbian minority

---

*Editor's note: A self-styled "eco-raider," Edward Abbey is well known for making provocative comments. His collection of nature essays, *Desert Solitaire* (1968), and his radical novel, *The Monkey Wrench Gang* (1975), argue for the necessity of preserving wilderness areas in the southwest; both have been enormously influential.

women who have gotten published. You'd have to ask them what they think about that opportunity. That was the signal of a really bad trend in literature, the bad trending being hopping on a particular bandwagon in order to market books, and so, unfortunately, it would be nice if what Ed said was true, but it really isn't true. It might have been true for a really short period of time before Reaganism and the supremacy of the white male returned and see how many ethnic lesbians got published, and I'm afraid that's just something that Ed made up. Well, no, he didn't make it up, but it's one of those myths like Indians get stipend each month from the U.S. government, that all Indians are being paid off for the stolen land each month, and we're not being paid for the stolen land each month. The land's stolen and we're not being paid, but there are a lot of these things that people believe, and I don't even really think that Ed probably believes that.

KB: Do you think that being a woman and being a minority helped you get the MacArthur Fellowship?

LS: Look at how few women have been chosen. If you looked at how few women and how few ethnic women have gotten the MacArthur, you might conclude that it is just the opposite.

KB: You don't feel it was tokenism?

LS: No, because there have been so few. There's so few women and ethnic women that have gotten MacArthur's, you couldn't even call us tokens. We're not even tokens!

KB: I find the yellow woman, *Kochininako,* particularly interesting. Do you see the myths concerning her as having arisen from the need for escape on the part of the women from a kind of social and sexual domination?

LS: No, not at all. The need for that kind of escape is the need of a woman in middle-America, a white Anglo, the WASP woman. In the Pueblo, the lineage of the child is traced through the mother, so it's a matrilineal system. The houses are the property of the woman, not the man. The land is generally passed down through the female side because the houses belong to the women. One of my early memories was when our house needed to be replastered with the traditional adobe mud plaster. It was a crew of women who came and plastered the house. Why? The women own the houses so the women maintain what they own. The kinds of things that cause white upper-middle-class women to flee the home for awhile to escape or get away from domination and powerlessness and inferior status, vis-a-vis the husband, and the male, those kinds of forces are not operating, they're not operating at all. What's operating in those stories of Kochininako is this attraction, this passion, this connection between the human world and the animal and spirit worlds. Buffalo Man is a buffalo, and he can be in the form of a buffalo, but there is this link, and the link is sealed with sexual intimacy, which is emblematic of that joining of two worlds. At the end of the story, the people have been starving, and the buffalo says, "We will give up our spirits, we will come and die for these people because we are related to them. Kochininako is our sister-in-law." She's a . . . what do you call it in anthropology or sociology, one who shatters the cultural paradigms or steps through or steps out. She does that because there's a real overpowering sexual attraction that's felt. The attraction is symbolized by or typified by the kind of sexual power that draws her to the buffalo man, but the power which draws her to Buffalo Man is actually the human, the link, the animal and human world, those two being drawn together. It's that power that's really operating, and the sexual nature of it is just a metaphor for that power. So that's what's going on there. It doesn't have anything to do with, "Things are really bad at home, so I think I'll run off for awhile." That's not what it's about.

KB: I wanted to ask you a question about the mother figures in some of your work. I was trying to look for a word to describe them. I couldn't quite come up with it. Ambivalent is the wrong word, but you never know quite how to feel about them. For instance, in the very first story in *Storyteller*, the little girl wants corn to eat, and she drowns herself in the lake because her mother won't give it to her. And there's the mother in *Ceremony*. . . .

LS: And then the aunt and the mother's sister. I know what you're talking about. People, women especially, ask me about

57

that and men too. It's a real tough one. The story about the little girl who ran away, that's a story which is very clear in *Storyteller*. It's a story that Aunt Susie liked to tell. In a matrilineal society, in a matriarchy, and especially in this particular matriarchy, the women, as I've already said, control the houses, the lineage of the children, and a lot of the decisions about marriages and so forth. In a sense, the women have called the shots pretty much in the world of relationships and the everyday world. While the Pueblo women were kind of running the show, buying and selling sheep, and of course the Navajos are the same way too, the women making many of the business decisions, the Pueblo men would be taking care of ceremonial matters or maybe out hunting. Although there have been a few Laguna women who were great hunters also. So the female, the mother, is a real powerful person, and she's much more the authority figure. It's a kind of reversal. Your dad is the one who's the soft-touch, and it's the mother's brother who reprimands you. If you're really out of hand and she can't deal with you, it will be your mother's brother, not your father, she goes to. When a man marries, he goes to his wife's house or household or whatever, and his position is one you can feel more of an alliance with . . . more of an alliance with the father because he, in some ways, has less power in that household. So when you have a story like that one, that explains it. But then, how do you explain Tayo's mother who is kind of a lost and unfortunate figure, or how do we explain Auntie? And people have talked about how my male characters have vulnerability and all kinds of complexities and the women . . . they're not as vulnerable. You have to have some vulnerability in a character for readers to be able to establish some kind of link with them. So why don't we see that in my female characters? We have to go back, I suppose, to the women I grew up with. I grew up with women who were really strong, women with a great deal of power, let us say, within the family. And I think about that, and I try to think about my mother: is there something about the way she and I have gotten along, or how we related to one another? But, just remember what the position of the father and the mother would be in Pueblo society. If someone was going to thwart you or frighten you, it would tend to be a woman; you see it coming from your mother, or sent by your mother.

KB: I want to ask you a little bit about the form of your writing. Joseph Bruchac in his interview with Momaday notes the blurring of boundaries between prose and verse in *Ceremony*. Do you write what you think to be prose poems? You seem to be bucking traditional form, and we've already talked about how you want it to look on a page to give the sense of storytellers. Are you working with anything new or unique in doing this type of writing? I mean, this blurring between verse and prose. And why, as in *Ceremony*, where it will break in?

LS: Well, in *Ceremony* the breaks would be the parts that ideally you would hear rather than read. As far as what I'm doing with the blurring of the two, Virgil and the old dudes, the old cats back in the old days, or the Greeks, they didn't worry so much it seems to me, although I'm sure some of the genre definitions and stuff came out of that period of time. In some ways, I feel that it's more valid to have a checklist or a discussion of what constitutes tragedy or comedy than what constitutes poetry or prose. I don't decide I'll take a stance. For my purposes, it's just useless, it's stupid, it doesn't interest me at all. What I'm interested in is getting a feeling or an idea that's part of the story. Getting the story across. And I'm really not particular how it's done. The important thing is that it goes across in a way that I want it to go. I don't waste my time on it. But if other people want to worry over whether what they've just written is a poem or a prose poem, if they want to worry about that or if literary critics want to worry about that, I don't like to tell people what they should spend their time on. I don't spend my time on that.

KB: Have you ever had people say that to you that your poetry isn't poetry at all?

LS: Well, certainly not to my face, but in 1973 I sent five of the Chimney poems to the *Chicago Review*, and that year they gave a prize for all poetry published in all the volumes for the year, and in 1973 I got *Chicago Review's* prize for poetry, which I was really astonished to receive. Then I got the Push-cart prize for poetry, which is even better than the *Chicago Review*'s little poetry award. I must say, it gave me more confidence in what I was doing. The way the Pushcart prize works is all the small magazines nominate one writer's poem that has appeared in their small magazine, and then the Pushcart judges select one piece. I won that over all other poems published, or at least nominated and published, that year. Because of that, if someone says it's not poetry at all, then all I can say is don't argue with me, go fight with people who hand out prizes for poetry.

KB: One of my favorite poems of yours is "Deer Song." There's this line which I really like, "the struggle is the ritual." It seems to me that this line somehow takes in the essence of cooperative existence in the culture. Could you explain that line a little bit more?

LS: Well, on a literal level, there's some intimations that the wolves get the deer. The western European attitude towards things like this is, "Oh, I don't want to see an animal have to die, I don't want to see the blood. Oh, I can eat it, but oh, no, I couldn't kill it!" Well, I've always said if you couldn't kill it, then you better damn well not be eating it. It's sort of puritanical abhorrence of blood and a tremendous fear of death that western European people have; Americans especially. That's why everyone is out jogging and not eating salt because he's so scared of death; those are like amulets to keep death away. So on the literal level, it's not something nasty or awful or horrible or something to avert one's eyes from: *look* at it. It's actually almost like a sacred or ritualistic kind of thing, that giving up of the life. Of course, I also mean for it to transcend that and for people to be able to see that in a struggle to survive, it is again that you will be able to look and see things that are a part of a kind of ritual. Not ritual in a sense of following a set pattern, a form that can never vary, but ritual in a lighter sense that expands our senses. One should be able to see one's own life and lives of other beings as a part of something very sacred and special. Just because it isn't codified or put in a psalm book or a prayer book or just because it isn't a part of a ceremonial chant or something doesn't mean that it isn't valuable, moving, special.

KB: Have you read Galway Kinnell's "The Bear?"

LS: People always ask me that, and I never have yet. But someday I will. Everyone always thinks about that. Momaday is real interested in bears, you know, and his new novel is about a boy who turns into a bear.

KB: I understand that you took a trip to China.

LS: Yes, I was invited to go with a delegation of American writers who were invited by the Chinese Writers Association and the People's Republic. We were in China for three weeks, and we spent a week in Beijing, having a kind of exchange, questions and answers and comments between the Chinese writers of the Chinese Writers Association and ourselves.

KB: You read your poetry over there, then.

LS: Most of the time it was dialogue. It was exchanging questions. Allen Ginsberg asked them about sexual freedom and when was the People's Republic going to say that homosexuality was just as valid as heterosexuality. I think Allen amused the Chinese very much from that regard so it was more dialogue than anything. But one day we did go over to the Beijing Institute, and each person could read for six or seven minutes. You have to remember, especially with poetry, that it is difficult to translate English to Chinese and keep any sense of the music or the whole thing of images and imagery. I think doing very much poetry reading would not have been particularly rewarding. It's real difficult. Some of the material had been translated. But there again, some of the graduate students from the Beijing Institute, who were also assigned to be our interpreters, were studying to be simultaneous interpreters for the U.N. so they had a real good command of going from English to Chinese and Chinese to English. They said they felt that a lot of the translations of poetry were real tough and that they weren't sure that everything was coming across. Of course, you hear that complaint, it works both ways.

KB: Several people have mentioned that the parts you have read from your new novel sound like Toni Morrison's work. Have you thought about that at all or felt any influence?

LS: No, not at all. I had never met Toni before we went to China, and I had never read much of her work before, never. What's funny is I'm always managing to do something that reminds someone of someone else, and he or she will come up and say, "Did you know this and that? Did you read that?" I always say no. I always try not to seem like I'm doing something like someone else. But then that's kind of an inhibition.

KB: I know that you have said in the past that the greatest influence on your writing has been your surroundings. Has there been a single novelist or poet whose work you find particularly inspirational or informational?

LS: You mean working right now?

KB: Not necessarily. I know you have talked about Milton and Shakespeare.

LS: Well, lately, the one person that's meant a lot to me is Wittgenstein. I think his remarks on color turn into some of the most beautiful poetry I've ever read. People call Wittgenstein a philosopher and I call him a poet. I really like reading Wittgenstein right now.

KB: How about influences on your style?

LS: That is for style. You can see the clarity of his remarks on color in one of the last pieces he wrote before he died. With style, I'm like a sponge. I don't consciously look towards anyone. The poetry of my friend Mei-mei Berssenbrugge, I think, influences me. Her writing influences me, my ideas, and some of the things I write about influences her. And I think in terms of my prose style something of what she does with her poetry filters into me and has influenced me, but I couldn't say how exactly. What she does is real important, and so are some of her ideas about her connection with the so-called avant-garde in New York, and so forth. And the kinds of musicians, a lot of her interests have kind of filtered through to me, and I in turn have picked up and taken off that with that in my own directions. My friend Larry McMurtry is a rare book dealer, and he comes across wonderful books in looking for rare expensive books.* He's been breaking me out of the mold of just reading fiction or poetry. For example, H.D.'s *Tribute to Freud* is wonderful.** I like H.D.'s *Tribute to Freud* about a million times more than I like any of her damn poems. I would really not mind if some of H.D.'s magical prose rubbed off on mine; I would not mind that at all.

KB: Paula Gunn Allen has said that reading Momaday's *House Made of Dawn* was a turning point in her life. Has Momaday had the same effect on you as a writer?

LS: I'm trying to think. Turning point? Where was Paula headed before? I don't quite understand. No. I like *The Way to Rainy Mountain* very much, but I would have been doing what I was doing regardless of what Scott had done or not, written or not written.

KB: You've mentioned your novel in progress, *The Almanac of the Dead.* Could you tell us a little bit about that?

LS: It's a very long complex novel, so it's hard to even tell about it. It's got five or six distinct narrative lines, sort of intertwined through it. The "Almanac" in the title refers to the Mayan almanacs or Mayan codices. There are four manuscripts that survived the on-going inquisition and persecution of the Mayan Indian people and all Indian peoples once the Spaniards and the Portuguese arrived. Apparently what happened is early on the priests chose, recruited, captured, whatever, promising young Mayan men, and taught them how to read and write Spanish. This happened very early after the Spaniards went into that area, and these anonymous Mayan people or men used their new knowledge to try to write down what

---

*Editor's note: Larry McMurtry is the author of several western novels, among them *The Last Picture Show* and *Lonesome Dove.*

**Editor's note: H.D. is the pen name for Hilda Doolittle, who helped develop the "Imagist" movement early in her career and wrote long narrative poems later. Her *Tribute to Freud,* based on her psychoanalysis in 1933 and '34, was published in 1944.

had always been in more an oral state or what had been kept with the glyphs, the Mayan glyphs that were carved into stone. Although memory in passing down from person to person had worked before to hold these things, I think they realized that with the cataclysm of the coming of the Europeans, they could no longer count on human memory if humans themselves were being destroyed. So anyway, they wrote down what had, up until then, been kind of the knowledge of the various priests.

The almanacs were literally like a farmer's almanac. They told you the identity of the days, but not only what days were good to plant on, but some days that were extremely dangerous. There were some years that were extremely unfortunate with famine and war. There were other years, even epochs, that would come that would be extremely glorious and fertile. The Mayan people were obsessed with time and knowing each day. They believed that a day was a kind of being and it had a . . . we would maybe say a personality, but that it would return. It might not return again for five thousand or eight thousand years, but they believed that a day exactly as it had appeared before would appear again. It's a view that basically denies a lot of western European notions about linear time, death, simultaneous planes of experience, and so on. Anyway, the Mayan Almanacs or the Mayan codices exist. There's one in Dresden, one in Madrid, one in Paris, and one in Mexico City. I've seen what the fragments were like, and decided that I would like to use the structure of an almanac; it would free me to indulge in different narrative lines. Most of the action takes place in the present day. You get a few glimpses of the remaining fragments. You see, my characters in my novel have a fifth manuscript. There are in fact only four that are known to exist in the world now, but for my purposes, I say there's a fifth fragmentary manuscript, and my characters have it. Every now and then, the reader gets to see a bit of the fragment. The novel centers in Tucson and encompasses Mexico and kind of the edge of Central America. It not only runs through the days when the Spaniards and the Portuguese were taking slaves from the Mayan area and dragging them up to northern Sonora to work in the silver mines until they died, but also, because the Mayan Almanacs were believed to be able to foretell the future, my novel will go a bit into the future. It goes to a time when the struggle which the indigenous peoples are having now in Guatemala and Honduras and Nicaragua spreads north into Mexico. The United States, of course, intervenes and sends troops and tanks and so on into Mexico. And that's as far forward in time as it goes.

KB: You're thinking 1600 pages?

LS: I was thinking 1600. It could be longer. I've got 800 right now.

❑ Critical Essays

A. LaVONNE RUOFF ■

# Ritual and Renewal: Keres Traditions in Leslie Silko's "Yellow Woman"

> "At one time, the ceremonies as they had been performed were enough for the way the world was then. But after the white people came, elements in this world began to shift; and it became necessary to create new ceremonies. I have made changes in the rituals. The people mistrust this greatly, but only this growth keeps the ceremonies strong. . . . That's what the witchery is counting on: that we will cling to the ceremonies the way they were, and then their power will triumph, and the people will be no more."
>
> —BETONIE in *Ceremony*

For Leslie Marmon Silko (Laguna), the strength of tribal traditions is based not on Indians' rigid adherence to given ceremonies or customs but rather on their ability to adapt traditions to ever-changing circumstances by incorporating new elements. Although this theme is most fully developed in her recent novel *Ceremony* (1977), it is also present in her earlier short stories, "The Man to Send Rainclouds," "Tony's Story," from "Humaweepi, Warrior Priest," and "Yellow Woman," included in the volume *The Man to Send Rainclouds: Contemporary Stories by American Indians.*[1]

The history of Silko's own Laguna Pueblo, influenced by many different cultures, provides insight into why she

This essay, which has been condensed with the permission of the author, first appeared as "Ritual and Renewal: Keres Traditions in the Short Fiction of Leslie Silko" in *MELUS* 5:4 (Winter 1978): 2–17.

emphasizes change as a source of strength for tribal traditions. According to their origin legends, the Laguna tribe (in existence since at least 1300), came southward from the Mesa Verde region. Some versions indicate that after pausing at Zia, they were joined by the head of the Parrot clan, who decided to take his people southward with them. After wandering further, first southward from the lake at Laguna and then northward back to the lake, they settled Punyana, probably in the late 1300s. After founding Old Laguna (Kawaik) around 1400, they issued invitations to other pueblos to join them. Those which responded were the Parrot clan from Zia, the Sun clan from Hopi, the Road Runner and Badger clans from Zuni, and the Sun clan from Jemez. The tribe occupied the site of what is now called Laguna by the early 1500s. Additional immigration occurred during the 1690s, when the Lagunas were joined by Indians from the Rio Grande, probably fleeing both drought and the hostility of the Spanish after the Pueblo Rebellion in 1680 and the renewed uprising in 1696. These immigrants came chiefly from Zia, Cochiti, and Domingo, but a few came from Jemez, Zuni, and Hopi. Although some remained to join the Laguna tribe, others returned to their own pueblos when conditions improved. Over the years, a few Navajos intermarried with the tribe, bringing with them the Navajo Sun clan and kachina.[2]

The Spanish first entered the area in 1540, when Francesco de Coronado led an expedition to Zuni and two years later passed through the present site of Laguna on his way back to Mexico. Antonio Espejo, who commanded an expedition to New Mexico in 1582, visited the area in 1583. Between the appointment of Juan de Onate as New Mexico's first governor in 1598 and the Pueblo Rebellion in 1680, there is little historical data on Laguna. Although the pueblo was not subjected to as many attacks from the Spanish as the Rio Grande pueblos, it was forced to surrender in 1692 after an attack by the troops of Governor Diego de Vargas.[3]

Concerning the mixture of people who settled at Laguna, Parsons comments that "it is not surprising that Laguna was the first of the pueblos to Americanize, through intermarriage" (II, 888). Around 1860 and 1870, George H. Pradt [or

Pratt] and two Marmon brothers (Walter and Robert) came to the pueblo, married Laguna women, and reared large families. Silko indicates that her great grandfather Robert and his brother had a government contract to set out the boundary markers for Laguna.[4] Walter, appointed government teacher in 1871, married the daughter of the chief of the Kurena-Shikani medicine men. The chief's son later took his place. According to Parsons, this group led the Americanization faction which was opposed by the pueblo hierarchy. The conservatives removed their altars and sacred objects from Laguna and moved to Mesita; around 1880, part of this group resettled in Isleta. While Robert Marmon served as governor, the two kivas of Laguna were torn down by the progressives and what was left of the sacred objects was surrendered. There were no kachina dances for some time after the Great Split and the laying of the railroad on the edge of the village. When a demand arose later for the revival of the dances, Zuni influences were introduced into Laguna rituals.[5] Parsons closes her description of Laguna with the comment that although the ceremonial disintegration was so marked when she first studied it (around 1920) that it presented an obscure picture of Keresan culture, it now (1939) offered "unrivaled opportunities to study American acculturation and the important role played by miscegenation" (II, 890). Silko herself comments on these changes in her description of the impact of mixed-blood families on Laguna clan systems and the varying attitudes toward these families in the stories of that pueblo:

> People in the main part of the village were our clanspeople because the clan system was still maintained although not in the same form it would have been if we were full blood. . . . The way it changed was that there began to be stories about my great-grandfather, positive stories about what he did with the Laguna scouts for the Apaches. But then after World War One it changed. Soon after that there came to be stories about these mixed blood people, half-breeds. Not only Marmons but Gunns [John] and Pratts too. An identity was being made or evolved in the stories the Lagunas told about these people who had gone outside Laguna, but at the same time of the

outsiders who had come in. Part of it was that the stories were always about the wild, roguish, crazy sorts of things they did. (Evers and Carr, p. 30)

The continuing strength of Laguna traditions and the ability of her people to use alien traditions for their own purposes are strikingly portrayed in Silko's story "The Man to Send Rainclouds." . . . "Tony's Story" deals with the return to Indian ritual as a means of coping with external forces. . . . In "From Humaweepi, Warrior Priest," Silko presents the theme of the transmission of Pueblo religion and ritual through oral tradition.

The continuum of the oral tradition and the importance of storytelling are also demonstrated in Silko's "Yellow Woman." Here, however, the emphasis is on personal renewal, derived from experience outside the pueblo, rather than on mastery of religious ritual. Adapting the traditional "yellow woman" abduction tales to contemporary circumstances, Silko vividly illustrates the influence of these stories on the imagination of a modern Pueblo woman and the usefulness of the genre for explaining why this woman, and generations of women before her, would suddenly disappear with a stranger, only to return later with a story about being kidnapped. Many of the traditional tales emphasize the subsequent benefits which came to the pueblo as a result of these liaisons, as Silko indicates in her summary of them: "Yellow Woman went away with the spirit from the north and lived with him and his relatives. She was gone for a long time, but then one day she came back and brought twin boys."

Boas summarizes the basic elements of the traditional abduction stories as follows: A woman is usually abducted by a dangerous kachina when she goes to draw water.[6] After encountering the abductor, the woman refuses to be taken away because she does not know what to do with her water jar. The abductor then threatens her with death, compels her to place the jar on the ground upside down, and then transports her by various means to his home, where he gives her impossible tasks to perform lest she be killed.[7] In some stories, Yellow Woman is described as the mother of the hero twins Ma'sewi and Uyuyewi, the names given not only to the twin children of the Sun and Yellow Woman but also to all such children of monster kachinas and the women they abducted. The children are usually born miraculously and raised after the death of their mothers.[8] Through bearing twins who subsequently become monster slayers or who simply bring new blood into the pueblo, Yellow Woman becomes a symbol of renewal through liaison with outside forces. In addition to bringing new life to the pueblo, Yellow Woman renews it in other ways. For example, in the tale of "Buffalo Man," Yellow Woman is abducted by him. After she is freed by her husband Arrow Youth, they are pursued by Buffalo Man and his herd. Arrow Youth succeeds in killing the abductor and all the other buffalo. Because she weeps for the death of her buffalo husband, Arrow Youth kills her as well. However, as a result of her abduction and pursuit by Buffalo Man, the pueblo is provided with much-needed meat.[9]

In general, the abductor is an evil force of great power, frequently associated with mountain spirits. Most common among the abductors in the printed accounts are Flint Wing (who lives on a mountain top), Cliff Dweller (who lives on a high mesa), Whirlwind Man (who may be either an evil kachina or who may live among the good kachinas at Wenimatse), Whipper, and Buffalo Man.[10] Although the abductor in Silko's "Yellow Woman" is the contemporary of all these figures, some of the details in her story more closely resemble the accounts of Cliff Dweller (Ma'ctc'Tcowai) than of other abductors. For example, Cliff Dweller is associated with the north, the direction from which Silko says the abductor kachina came. In addition, both Cliff Dweller and the abductor in Silko's story leave their women temporarily to go hunting and bring back meat.[11]

Gunn describes Cliff Dweller as a wayward son who disregarded the teachings and prayers of his mother to become an outlaw and a kidnapper and murderer of women. He never married more than one wife at a time. To get her, he would go into the settlements, marry, and then take his wife to his cliff dwelling; if any refused, he would carry her off by force. When he became dissatisfied with his wife, he would throw her over the cliff and bring home another.[12] In Boas's version, Yellow Woman goes to draw water but is carried away by Cliff

Dweller, who tells her to stand north from him. He rolls the ring (for supporting the water jar on her head) towards her and thus transports her to his house on the cliff. In the versions given by both Boas and Gunn, Yellow Woman is ordered to grind an enormous amount of corn in a short time or else she will be killed. With the help of Spider Woman, Yellow Woman completes the task in the allotted time. After being given other superhuman tasks (which differ in the versions by Boas, Gunn, and Lummis), she realizes that she is going to be killed whether she completes them or not; consequently, she gets Spider Woman to help her escape by weaving a net to let her down from the cliff. In Boas's version, she escapes briefly, only to be killed by Cliff Dweller. Her sons, the hero twins, are born after her death. In Gunn's version, Yellow Woman survives to bear the twins, and Cliff Dweller himself is killed.[13]

Silko's sources for her "Yellow Woman" story are not the published accounts but rather the oral ones passed on by members of her family. As she makes clear in an interview, "I figured that anybody could go to the anthropologists' reports and look at them. I have looked at them myself, but I've never sat down with them and said I'm going to make a poem or story out of this. . . . I don't have to because from the time I was little, I heard quite a bit. I heard it in what would have been passed off now as rumor or gossip. I could hear through all that. I could hear something else, that there was a kind of continuum . . ." (Evers and Carr, p. 30). Silko has also indicated elsewhere that one of her sources was her Great-aunt Alice Little, who used to tell the young Marmon girls stories about Yellow Woman while babysitting for them: "It seemed like, though, you keep hearing the same story all the time."[14]

According to Silko, the river in Laguna, where "Yellow Woman" opens, was always associated with stories as a place to meet boyfriends and lovers: "I used to wander around down there and try to imagine walking around the bend and just happening to stumble upon some beautiful man. Later on I realized that these kinds of things that I was doing when I was fifteen are exactly the kinds of things out of which stories like the Yellow Woman story [came], I finally put the two together: the adolescent longings and the old stories, that plus the stories around Laguna at the time about people who did, in fact just in recent times, use the river as a meeting place" (Evers and Carr, p. 29). She notes that the old adultery stories are better than ever and have become even more intricate, now that indoor plumbing has eliminated some of the excuses for going outside.

Although Silko's "Yellow Woman" is based on traditional abduction tales, it is more than a modernized version. Silko is less concerned with the events involved in Yellow Woman's abduction and her subsequent return home than with the character's confusion about what is real and what is not. Underlying this is the character's identification with Keres legends and her temporary rejection of the confining monotony of life within the pueblo.

Unlike the recorded traditional abduction tales, Silko's story does not begin with Yellow Woman's initial encounter with her abductor. Instead, it begins when Yellow Woman awakes after spending the night with the stranger she met the previous afternoon by the river. As the story opens, Yellow Woman becomes conscious of various strong physical sensations: the dampness with which her thigh clings to that of her abductor, the sight of the brown water birds, the sound of the water, the appearance of her sleeping lover, and the pangs of her own hunger. Indeed, one of the themes of the story is the power which physical sensations and desire have to blot out thoughts of home, family, and responsibility. Following the river southward to where she met her lover, she tries but fails to catch a glimpse of her pueblo. Her failure is one of the first indications that she has been separated from that world, which no longer seems real to her. Her reality consists of immediate physical sensations combined with vague memory of the legends told by her grandfather which her own experience now parallels. The interrelationship between the myth of the past and the experience of the present begins when she touches her lover to tell him she is leaving—an unnecessary act if she really meant to leave. The connection between legend and experience is made explicit when he calls her "Yellow Woman," although he stresses that it was she who suggested the parallel the night before. Now, however, her sense of being part of the myth has weakened: she remembers only the touch of his body and the beauty of the moon.[15] Weakly she insists on her identity and his, separate from the legend. Although the abductor's name is revealed in the story, that of Yellow Woman is not: "I have my own name and I come from the pueblo on the other side of the mesa. Your name is Silva and you are a stranger I met by the river yesterday afternoon." That the stranger is the contemporary counterpart of the mythic abductors is underscored by the fact that his name "Silva" is Spanish for collection or anthology. Despite the young woman's denial that she and Silva are reliving the myth, the mention of it recalls to her the old Yellow Woman stories—not only the abduction tales but also such animal tales as the one about coyote's outsmarting badger when both animals wanted to sleep with Yellow Woman.[16]

In contrast to the abductors in the recorded traditional stories who relied on threats to get Yellow Woman to go with them, Silva relies instead on his psychological dominance and on her physical desire for him. As Silva touches her and as she moves close to him, she is drawn once more into the world of the legend. Clearly she identifies with Yellow Woman when she wonders whether the legendary Yellow Woman had a life and identity outside the myths as she herself does. Her fear of going away with Silva melted away by her pleasure at the warmth of his body, she dimly perceives why the mythic Yellow Woman would go off so quickly with her abductor: "This is the way it happens in the stories, I was thinking, with no thought beyond the moment she meets the ka'tsina spirit and they go." Her resistance to Silva's will that she come with him is limited to her feeble protest that she does not have to go.

Their journey up the mountain intensifies her confusion about what is dream and what is fact. The farther away she goes from home and family, the more powerless she is to prove to herself that she is not Yellow Woman. She hopes to see someone else on the trail so that she can again be certain of her own identity. Although she tries to persuade herself that she cannot be Yellow Woman because the woman of the legend lived in the past and did not experience her modern world, she is nevertheless lured farther and farther into the high country by Silva, who always looks into her eyes and softly sings a mountain song. Only her hunger wrenches her thoughts from him back to her home, where her family would be cooking breakfast and wondering what had happened to her.

The second part of the story takes place high on the mountain where Silva has his home. He does not require her to perform superhuman chores once they arrive, as did the traditional abductors. Instead, he sets her the task of frying some potatoes while he continues to watch her closely. As they eat, her thoughts return to the legend and she asks if he has brought other women here before by telling them also that he was a mountain kachina. He does not answer. After showing her his view of the world (the Navajo reservation, the Pueblo boundaries, and cattle country), he arouses her fears when he matter-of-factly informs her that he is a cattle rustler. Although she wonders about this mountain rustler who speaks Pueblo, she convinces herself that he must be a Navajo because Pueblo men do not do things like that—an allusion to the old Navajo practice of raiding Pueblo settlements for food and women. Once again, he overcomes Yellow Woman's fears through seduction, laughing at her for breathing so hard while he caresses her. When she turns away, he pins her down and warns her "You will do what I want." For the first time she realizes that he could destroy her as other abductors destroyed Yellow Woman in the legends. Nevertheless, her fear turns to tenderness as she watches him sleep.

When she awakens the next morning to find him gone, she is overcome by confusion, vainly seeking some evidence of his presence in the house to prove that he will return or even that he exists. Later in the day, after eating and napping, she awakens again to thoughts about her family. That she is going to remain with Silva is evident from her conclusion that her family (including her baby) will get along without her. She feels the only difference her leaving will make is that a story about her disappearance will be created. Like Yellow Woman and her human counterparts, she will become the source for the continuation of the abduction tale in contemporary oral tradition.

Rather than walk home as she set out to do, she returns to Silva's house, where he has brought home a rustled beef carcass instead of the traditional deer meat. Silva tests her loyalty to him by asking whether she intends to come with him to sell the meat. Her questions as to whether anyone has tried to catch him and why he carried a rifle, reflect her sense of danger; however, still under his spell, she agrees to accompany him.

Part three of the story deals with the confrontation between Silva and an unarmed Anglo rancher, an episode comparable to the tests in the traditional tales in which Yellow Woman's life is threatened or in danger; this time, the danger is indirect rather than direct. After the rancher accuses Silva of rustling, the latter orders Yellow Woman to go back up the mountain with the beef, which she starts to do, hearing at least four shots as she rides quickly away.[17] Reaching a ridge, she tries to see where she left Silva but cannot, just as she was unable to see her pueblo at the beginning of the story before she began the journey up the mountain. Her inability to see what she is seeking signals the end of her interlude with Silva. Unconsciously, she has decided to return home—just as her grandfather had said the legendary Yellow Woman usually did before her.

In the concluding section of the story, Yellow Woman makes her way back on foot to the river where she first met Silva. Although she feels sad about leaving him and is disturbed by his strangeness, her desire for him is rekindled when she comes to the spot where the leaves he trimmed from a willow mark their first meeting place. She convinces herself that she cannot return to him because the mountains are too far away but comforts herself with the belief that he will come back again to the river bank. As she reaches her home, she is brought back to the realities of her own life by the smell of supper cooking and the sight of her mother instructing her grandmother in the Anglo art of making Jell-O.

This acculturation explains why the only member of her family for whom she feels an affectionate kinship is her dead grandfather, who loved the Yellow Woman tales that he passed on to his granddaughter. As her link to the mythological and historical past, he would understand that her disappearance was not a police matter because she had only been stolen by a kachina mountain spirit. For him, this would have been explanation enough; for her family, however, which no longer possesses this sense of unity with the past, she is forced to create the story of being kidnapped by a Navajo. Thus, the grandfather's belief in the tales in which the lives of the Pueblo people were inextricably intertwined with their gods has been transmitted to his granddaughter, who utilizes them as an explanation for her temporary escape from routine. Her conviction that her own experiences will serve the pueblo as a new topic for storytelling and that she herself will have to become a storyteller to explain away her absence indicates that the process will continue.

In all four of these stories, Silko emphasizes the need to return to the rituals and oral traditions of the past in order to rediscover the basis for one's cultural identity. Only when this is done is one prepared to deal with the problems of the present. However, Silko advocates a return to the essence rather than to the precise form of these rituals and traditions, which must be adapted continually to meet new challenges. Through her own stories, Silko demonstrates that the Keres rituals and traditions have survived all attempts to eradicate them and that the seeds for the resurgence of their power lie in the memories and creativeness of her people.

## ☐ *Notes* ∎

1. This volume, edited by Kenneth Rosen (New York: Viking Press, 1974), is an excellent introduction to the work of Silko and of Simon Ortiz (Acoma), who have been widely acclaimed, as well as to the work of writers who are less well known. Both Laguna and Acoma pueblos belong to the Keres language family and their traditional stories are very similar.

2. Florence H. Ellis, "Anthropology of Laguna Pueblo Land Claims," *Pueblo Indians, American Indian Ethnohistory: Indians of the Southwest,* comp. and ed. David A. Horr (New York: Garland Publishing Inc., 1974), III, 1–3, 8–11; Elsie Clews Parsons, *Pueblo Indian Religion* (Chicago: Univ. of Chicago Press, 1939), II, 888–90 (hereafter Parsons). I have followed Ellis's account rather than Parson's, who spent very little time in Laguna, but see also Parsons, *Notes on Ceremonialism at Laguna,* Anthropological Papers of the

American Museum of Natural History, XIX, Pt. 1 (New York: Trustees of the AMNH), 87.

3. Ellis, III, 53; John Gunn, *Schat Chen: History and Traditions and Naratives* [sic] *of the Queres Indians of Laguna and Acoma* (Albuquerque: Albright and Anderson, 1917), pp. 22, 35, 47.

4. Lawrence Evers and Dennis Carr, "A Conversation with Leslie Marmon Silko," *Sun Tracks* 3:1 (Fall 1976), 29.

5. Parsons, II, 888–90; Gunn, p. 96.

6. The kachina [ka'tsina in Keres] spirits as a class are always kind and helpful; they live in the northwest at Wenimatse, a beautiful mountain region where the spirits gamble, dance, hunt, or farm. The term also refers to spirits which can be impersonated by masks. See Parsons, I, 174, 176–77; Franz Boas, ed., *Keresan Texts*, Vol. VIII (New York: Publications of the American Ethnological Society, 1928), Pt. 1, 276–77; and Anthony F. Purley, "Keres Pueblo Concepts of Deity," *American Indian Culture and Research Journal*, I (1974), 31.

7. Boas, VIII, Pt. 1, 218–19. According to Boas, "Yellow Woman" is a generic term used to specify heroines in Keres stories. Parsons points out that Kachina Girl or Yellow Woman (Ko'tchina'ko) is paired with the male kachina and that this supernatural pair is associated with the colors yellow and turquoise. The practice of pairing, whether of the same or opposite sex, carries an assurance of companionship rather than of number (I, 101–02).

8. Boas, VIII, Pt. 1, 107; Gunn, p. 150.

9. Boas, VIII, Pt. 1, 122–27, 261–62; Gunn, pp. 184–89. This story is the subject of Silko's poem "Buffalo Man," read at the MLA–NEH Summer Seminar, June 1977.

10. Boas, VIII, Pt. 1, 104–27; the tales are summarized on pp. 256–62.

11. Although Flint Wing lives on a northern mountain top and goes hunting, the tales about his abduction of Yellow Woman are less similar to Silko's story than are those about Cliff Dweller. See Boas, VIII, Pt. 1, 111–18, 258–59, and Gunn, pp. 122–25.

12. Gunn, p. 143. Cf. the Navajo Cliff or Throwing Monster (tse'neñaxáli'), whose name comes from his habit of catching people in his long sharp claws and throwing them to his children down among the rocks; see Gladys A. Reichard, *Navaho Religion: A Story of Symbolism* (New York: Pantheon Books, 1950), I, 73–4; II, 420.

When Silva says the Navajo people know him too, he may be alluding either to their knowledge of the abduction stories or to the fact that both Cliff Dweller of the Keres legends and Cliff Monster of the Navajo kill by throwing their victims off cliffs.

13. Boas, VIII, Pt. 1, 108; Gunn, pp. 143–52; Lummis, pp. 203–05.

14. Information provided by Leslie Marmon Silko, poetry and prose reading, MLA–NEH Summer Seminar on Contemporary Native American Literature, Flagstaff, Arizona, June 1977.

15. The Moon is female in Keres mythology. See Parsons's chart, I, between 208–09.

16. Cf. the tale recorded by Boas in which Coyote and Badger want to sleep with a brown-haired, light-complexioned Navajo girl, who will permit them to do so only after they bring her rabbits. Each tries to outwit the other (VIII, Pt. 1, 167–69, 271–72). These two animals are very frequently linked in Pueblo stories. See the chapters on "Badger" and "Coyote and Kin" in Hamilton A. Tyler, *Pueblo Animals and Myths* (Norman: University of Oklahoma Press, 1975).

17. The number four appears often in Keres tales. However, Parsons notes that among many Indian peoples, it is the favored numeral. It is used so much, especially in folk tales and ritual where freedom of repetition is unrestricted, that it frequently means no more than "some" or "several." Boas associates it with the characteristic number in individual Laguna families (VIII, Pt. 1, 217).

☐ PAULA GUNN ALLEN ■

# Kochinnenako in Academe: Three Approaches to Interpreting a Keres Indian Tale

I became engaged in studying feminist thought and theory when I was first studying and teaching American Indian literature in the early 1970s. Over the ensuing fifteen years, my own stances toward both feminist and American Indian life and thought have intertwined as they have unfolded. I have always included feminist content and perspectives in my teaching of American Indian subjects, though at first the mating was uneasy at best. My determination that both areas were interdependent and mutually significant to a balanced pedagogy of American Indian studies led me to grow into an approach to both that is best described as tribal-feminism or feminist-tribalism. Both terms are applicable: if I am dealing with feminism, I approach it from a strongly tribal posture, and when I am dealing with American Indian literature, history, culture, or philosophy I approach it from a strongly feminist one.

A feminist approach to the study and teaching of American Indian life and thought is essential because the area has been dominated by paternalistic, male-dominant modes of consciousness since the first writings about American Indians in the fifteenth century. This male bias has seriously skewed our understanding of tribal life and philosophy, distorting it in ways that are sometimes obvious but are most often invisible.

---

From *The Sacred Hoop: Recovering the Feminine in American Indian Traditions* (Boston: Beacon Press, 1986), 222–244.

83

Often what appears to be a misinterpretation caused by racial differences is a distortion based on sexual politics. When the patriarchal paradigm that characterizes western thinking is applied to gynecentric tribal modes, it transforms the ideas, significances, and raw data into something that is not only unrecognizable to the tribes but entirely incongruent with their philosophies and theories. We know that materials and interpretations amassed by the white intellectual establishment are in error, but we have not pinpointed the major sources of that error. I believe that a fundamental source has been male bias and that feminist theory, when judiciously applied to the field, makes the error correctible, freeing the data for reinterpretation that is at least congruent with a tribal perceptual mode.

To demonstrate the interconnections between tribal and feminist approaches as I use them in my work, I have developed an analysis of a traditional Kochinnenako, or Yellow Woman story of the Laguna-Acoma Keres, as recast by my mother's uncle John M. Gunn in his book *Schat Chen*.[1] My analysis utilizes three approaches and demonstrates the relationship of context to meaning, illuminating three consciousness styles and providing students with a traditionally tribal, nonracist, feminist understanding of traditional and contemporary American Indian life.

## Some Theoretical Considerations

Analyzing tribal cultural systems from a mainstream feminist point of view allows an otherwise overlooked insight into the complex interplay of factors that have led to the systematic loosening of tribal ties, the disruption of tribal cohesion and complexity, and the growing disequilibrium of cultures that were anciently based on a belief in balance, relationship, and the centrality of women, particularly elder women. A feminist approach reveals not only the exploitation and oppression of the tribes by whites and white government but also areas of oppression within the tribes and the sources and nature of that oppression. To a large extent, such an analysis can provide strategies for ameliorating the effects of patriarchal colonialism, enabling many of the tribes to reclaim their ancient gynarchical,* egalitarian, and sacred traditions.

At the present time, American Indians in general are not comfortable with feminist analysis or action within the reservation or urban Indian enclaves. Many Indian women are uncomfortable with feminism because they perceive it (correctly) as white-dominated. They (not so correctly) believe it is concerned with issues that have little bearing on their own lives. They are also uncomfortable with it because they have been reared in an anglophobic world that views white society with fear and hostility. But because of their fear of and bitterness toward whites and their consequent unwillingness to examine the dynamics of white socialization, American Indian women often overlook the central areas of damage done to tribal tradition by white Christian and secular patriarchal dominance. Militant and "progressive" American Indian men are even more likely to quarrel with feminism; they have benefited in certain ways from white male-centeredness, and while those benefits are of real danger to the tribes, the individual rewards are compelling.

It is within the context of growing violence against women and the concomitant lowering of our status among Native Americans that I teach and write. Certainly I could not locate the mechanisms of colonization that have led to the virulent rise of woman-hating among American Indian men (and, to a certain extent, among many of the women) without a secure and determined feminism. Just as certainly, feminist theory applied to my literary studies clarifies a number of issues for me, including the patriarchal bias that has been systematically imposed on traditional literary materials and the mechanism by which that bias has affected contemporary American Indian life, thought, and culture.

The oral tradition is more than a record of a people's culture. It is the creative source of their collective and indi-

---

*In a system where all persons in power are called Mother Chief and where the supreme deity is female, and social organization is matrilocal, matrifocal, and matrilineal, gynarchy is happening. However, it does not imply domination of men by women as patriarchy implies domination by ruling class males of all aspects of a society.

vidual selves. When that wellspring of identity is tampered with, the sense of self is also tampered with; and when that tampering includes the sexist and classist assumptions of the white world within the body of an Indian tradition, serious consequences necessarily ensue.

The oral tradition is a living body. It is in continuous flux, which enables it to accommodate itself to the real circumstances of a people's lives. That is its strength, but it is also its weakness, for when a people finds itself living within a racist, classist, and sexist reality, the oral tradition will reflect those values and will thus shape the people's consciousness to include and accept racism, classism and sexism, and they will incorporate that change, hardly noticing the shift. If the oral tradition is altered in certain subtle, fundamental ways, if elements alien to it are introduced so that its internal coherence is disturbed, it becomes the major instrument of colonization and oppression.

Such alterations have occurred and are still occurring. Those who translate or "render" narratives make certain crucial changes, many unconscious. The cultural bias of the translator inevitably shapes his or her perception of the materials being translated, often in ways that he or she is unaware of. Culture is fundamentally a shaper of perception, after all, and perception is shaped by culture in many subtle ways. In short, it's hard to see the forest when you're a tree. To a great extent, changes in materials translated from a tribal to a western language are a result of the vast difference in languages; certain ideas and concepts that are implicit in the structure of an Indian language are not possible in English. Language embodies the unspoken assumptions and orientations of the culture it belongs to. So while the problem is one of translation, it is not simply one of word equivalence. The differences are perceptual and contextual as much as verbal.

Sometimes the shifts are contextual; indeed, both the context and content usually are shifted, sometimes subtly, sometimes blatantly. The net effect is a shifting of the whole axis of the culture. When shifts of language and context are coupled with the almost infinite changes occasioned by Christianization, secularization, economic dislocation from subsistence to industrial modes, destruction of the wilderness and associated damage to the biota, much that is changed goes unnoticed or unremarked by the people being changed. This is not to suggest that Native Americans are unaware of the enormity of the change they have been forced to undergo by the several centuries of white presence, but much of that change is at deep and subtle levels that are not easily noted or resisted.

John Gunn received the story I am using here from a Keres-speaking informant and translated it himself. The story, which he titles "Sh-ah-cock and Miochin or the Battle of the Seasons," is in reality a narrative version of a ritual. The ritual brings about the change of season and of moiety among the Keres. Gunn doesn't mention this, perhaps because he was interested in stories and not in religion or perhaps because his informant did not mention the connection to him.

What is interesting about his rendering is his use of European, classist, conflict-centered patriarchal assumptions as plotting devices. These interpolations dislocate the significance of the tale and subtly alter the ideational context of woman-centered, largely pacifist people whose ritual story this is. I have developed three critiques of the tale as it appears in his book, using feminist and tribal understandings to discuss the various meanings of the story when it is read from three different perspectives.

In the first reading, I apply tribal understanding to the story. In the second, I apply the sort of feminist perspective I applied to traditional stories, historical events, traditional culture, and contemporary literature when I began developing a feminist perspective. The third reading applies what I call a feminist-tribal perspective. Each analysis is somewhat less detailed than it might be; but as I am interested in describing modes of perception and their impact on our understanding of cultural artifacts (and by extension our understanding of people who come from different cultural contexts than our own) rather than critiquing a story, they are adequate.

## Yellow Woman Stories

The Keres of Laguna and Acoma Pueblos in New Mexico have stories that are called Yellow Woman stories. The themes and to a large extent the motifs of these stories are always female-centered, always told from Yellow Woman's point of view. Some older recorded versions of Yellow Woman tales (as in Gunn) make Yellow Woman the daughter of the hocheni. Gunn translates *hocheni* as "ruler." But Keres notions of the hocheni's function and position are an cacique or Mother Chief, which differ greatly from Anglo-European ideas of ruler-ship. However, for Gunn to render *hocheni* as "ruler" is con-gruent with the European folktale tradition.[2]

Kochinnenako, Yellow Woman, is in some sense a name that means Woman-Woman because among the Keres, yellow is the color for women (as pink and red are among Anglo-European Americans), and it is the color ascribed to the Northwest. Keres women paint their faces yellow on certain ceremonial occasions and are so painted at death so that the guardian at the gate of the spirit world, Naiya Iyatiku (Mother Corn Woman), will recognize that the newly arrived person is a woman. It is also the name of a particular Irriaku, Corn Mother (sacred corn-ear bundle), and Yellow Woman stories in their original form detail rituals in which the Irriaku figures prominently.

Yellow Woman stories are about all sorts of things— abduction, meeting with happy powerful spirits, birth of twins, getting power from the spirit worlds and returning it to the people, refusing to marry, weaving, grinding corn, getting wa-ter, outsmarting witches, eluding or escaping from malinten-tioned spirits, and more. Yellow Woman's sisters are often in the stories (Blue, White, and Red Corn) as is Grandmother Spider and her helper Spider Boy, the Sun God or one of his aspects, Yellow Woman's twin sons, witches, magicians, gam-blers, and mothers-in-law.

Many Yellow Woman tales highlight her alienation from the people: she lives with her grandmother at the edge of the village, for example, or she is in some way atypical, maybe a woman who refuses to marry, one who is known for some particular special talent, or one who is very quick-witted and resourceful. In many ways Kochinnenako is a role model, though she possesses some behaviors that are not likely to oc-cur in many of the women who hear her stories. She is, one might say, the Spirit of Woman.

The stories do not necessarily imply that difference is punishable; on the contrary, it is often her very difference that makes her special adventures possible, and these adventures often have happy outcomes for Kochinnenako and for her people. This is significant among a people who value conformity and propriety above almost anything. It suggests that the behavior of women, at least at certain times or under certain circumstances, must be improper or nonconformist for the greater good of the whole. Not that all the stories are graced with a happy ending. Some come to a tragic conclusion, sometimes resulting from someone's inability to follow the rules or perform a ritual in the proper way.

Other Kochinnenako stories are about her centrality to the harmony, balance, and prosperity of the tribe. "Sh-ah-cock and Miochin" is one of these stories. John Gunn prefaces the narrative with the comment that while the story is about a battle, war stories are rarely told by the Keres because they are not "a war like people" and "very rarely refer to their exploits in war."

### Sh-ah-cock and Miochin or the Battle of the Seasons

In the Kush-kut-ret-u-nah-tit (white village of the north) was once a ruler by the name of Hut-cha-mun Ki-uk (the broken prayer stick), one of whose daughters, Ko-chin-ne-nako, became the bride of Sh-ah-cock (the spirit of winter), a person of very violent temper. He always manifested his presence by blizzards of snow or sleet or by freezing cold, and on account of his alliance with the ruler's daughter, he was most of the time in the vicinity of Kush-kut-ret, and as these manifestations continued from month to month and year to year, the people of Kush-kut-ret found that their crops would not mature, and finally they were compelled to subsist on the leaves of the cactus.

On one occasion Ko-chin-ne-nako had wandered a long way from home in search of the cactus and had gathered quite a bundle and was preparing to carry home by singeing off the thorns, when on looking up she found herself confronted by a very bold but handsome young man. His attire attracted her gaze at once. He wore a shirt of yellow woven from the silks of corn, a belt made from the broad green blades of the same plant, a tall pointed hat made from the same kind of material and from the top which waved a yellow corn tassel. He wore green leggings woven from kow-e-nuh, the green stringy moss that forms in springs and ponds. His moccasins were beautifully embroidered with flowers and butterflies. In his hand he carried an ear of green corn.

His whole appearance proclaimed him a stranger and as Ko-chin-ne-nako gaped in wonder, he spoke to her in a very pleasing voice asking her what she was doing. She told him that on account of the cold and drouth, the people of Kush-kut-ret were forced to eat the leaves of the cactus to keep from starving.

"Here," said the young man, handing her the ear of green corn. "Eat this and I will go and bring more that you may take home with you."

He left her and soon disappeared going towards the south. In a short time he returned bringing with him a big load of green corn. Ko-chin-ne-nako asked him where he had gathered corn and if it grew near by. "No," he replied, "it is from my home far away to the south, where the corn grows and the flowers bloom all the year around. Would you not like to accompany me back to my country?" Ko-chin-ne-nako replied that his home must be very beautiful, but that she could not go with him because she was the wife of Sh-ah-cock. And then she told him of her alliance with the Spirit of Winter, and admitted that her husband was very cold and disagreeable and that she did not love him. The strange young man urged her to go with him to the warm land of the south, saying that he did not fear Sh-ah-cock. But Ko-chin-ne-nako would not consent. So the stranger directed her to return to her home with the corn he had brought and cautioned her not to throw away any of the husks out of the door. Upon leaving he said to her, "you must meet me at this place tomorrow. I will bring more corn for you."

Ko-chin-ne-nako had not proceeded far on her homeward way ere she met her sisters who, having become uneasy because of her long absence, had come in search of her. They were greatly surprised at seeing her with an armful of corn instead of cactus. Ko-chin-ne-nako told them the whole story of how she had obtained it, and thereby only added wonderment to their surprise. They helped her to carry the corn home; and there she again had to tell her story to her father and mother.

When she had described the stranger even from his peaked hat to his butterfly moccasins, and had told them that she was to meet him again on the day following, Hut-cha-mun Ki-uk, the father, exclaimed:

"It is Mi-o-chin!"

"It is Mi-o-chin! It is Mi-o-chin!," echoed the mother. "To-morrow you must bring him home with you."

The next day Ko-chin-ne-nako went again to the spot where she had met Mi-o-chin, for it was indeed Mi-o-chin, the Spirit of Summer. He was already there, awaiting her coming. With him he had brought a huge bundle of corn.

Ko-chin-ne-nako pressed upon him the invitation of her parents to accompany her home, so together they carried the corn to Kush-kut-ret. When it had been distributed there was sufficient to feed all the people of the city. Amid great rejoicing and thanksgiving, Mi-o-chin was welcomed at the Hot-chin's (ruler's) house.

In the evening, as was his custom, Sh-ah-cock, the Spirit of the Winter, returned to his home. He came in a blinding storm of snow and hail and sleet, for he was in a boisterous mood. On approaching the city, he felt within his bones that Mi-o-chin was there, so he called in a loud and blustering voice:

"Ha! Mi-o-chin, are you here?"

For an answer, Mi-o-chin advanced to meet him.

Then Sh-ah-cock, beholding him, called again,

"Ha! Mi-o-chin, I will destroy you."

"Ha! Sh-ah-cock, I will destroy you," replied Mi-o-chin, still advancing.

Sh-ah-cock paused, irresolute. He was covered from head to foot with frost (skah). Icycles [*sic*] (ya-pet-tu-ne) draped him round. The fierce, cold wind proceeded from his nostrils.

As Mi-o-chin drew near, the wintry wind changed to a

warm summer breeze. The frost and icycles melted and displayed beneath them, the dry, bleached bulrushes (ska-ra-ru-ka) in which Sh-ah-cock was clad.

Seeing that he was doomed to defeat, Sh-ah-cock cried out:

"I will not fight you now, for we cannot try our powers. We will make ready, and in four days from this time, we will meet here and fight for supremacy. The victor shall claim Kochin-ne-nako for his wife."

With this, Sh-ah-cock withdrew in rage. The wind again roared and shook the very houses; but the people were warm within them, for Mi-o-chin was with them.

The next day Mi-o-chin left Kush Kutret for his home in the south. Arriving there, he began to make his preparations to meet Sh-ah-cock in battle.

First he sent an eagle as a messenger to his friend, Ya-chun-ne-ne-moot (kind of shaley rock that becomes very hot in the fire), who lived in the west, requesting him to come and help to battle Sh-ah-cock. Then he called together the birds and the four legged animals—all those that live in sunny climes. For his advance guard and shield he selected the bat (pickikke), as its tough skin would best resist the sleet and hail that Sh-ah-cock would hurl at him.

Meantime Sh-ah-cock had gone to his home in the north to make his preparations for battle. To his aid he called all the winter birds and all of the four legged animals of the wintry climates. For his advance guard and shield he selected Shro-ak-ah (a magpie).

When these formidable forces had been mustered by the rivals, they advanced, Mi-o-chin from the south and Sh-ah-cock from the north, in battle array.

Ya-chun-ne-ne-moot kindled his fires and piled great heaps of resinous fuel upon them until volumes of steam and smoke ascended, forming enormous clouds that hurried forward toward Kush-kut-ret and the battle ground. Upon these clouds rode Mi-o-chin, the Spirit of Summer, and his vast army. All the animals of the army, encountering the smoke from Ya-chun-ne-ne-moot's fires, were colored by the smoke so that, from that day, the animals from the south have been black or brown in color.

Sh-ah-cock and his army came out of the north in a howling blizzard and borne forward on black storm clouds driven by a freezing wintry wind. As he came on, the lakes and rivers over which he passed were frozen and the air was filled with blinding sleet.

When the combatants drew near to Kush-kut-ret, they advanced with fearful rapidity. Their arrival upon the field was marked by fierce and terrific strife.

Flashes of lightning darted from Mi-o-chin's clouds. Striking the animals of Sh-ah-cock, they singed the hair upon them, and turned it white, so that, from that day, the animals from the north have worn a covering of white or have white markings upon them.

From the south, the black clouds still rolled upward, the thunder spoke again and again. Clouds of smoke and vapor rushed onward, melting the snow and ice weapons of Sh-ah-cock and compelling him, at length, to retire from the field. Mi-o-chin, assured of victory, pursued him. To save himself from total defeat and destruction, Sh-ah-cock called for armistice.

This being granted on the part of Mi-o-chin, the rivals met at Kush-kut-ret to arrange the terms of the treaty. Sh-ah-cock acknowledged himself defeated. He consented to give up Ko-chin-ne-nako to Mi-o-chin. This concession was received with rejoicing by Ko-chin-ne-nako and all the people of Kush-kut-ret.

It was then agreed between the late combatants that, for all time thereafter, Mi-o-chin was to rule at Kush-kut-ret during one-half of the year, and Sh-ah-cock was to rule during the remaining half, and that neither should molest the other.[3]

John Gunn's version has a formal plot structure that makes the account seem to be a narrative. But had he translated it directly from the Keres, even in "narrative" form, as in a storytelling session, its ritual nature would have been clearer.

I can only surmise about how the account might go if it were done that way, basing my ideas on renderings of Keres rituals in narrative forms I am acquainted with. But a direct translation from the Keres would have sounded more like the following than like Gunn's rendition of it:

> Long ago. Eh. There in the North. Yellow Woman. Up north-ward she went. Then she picked burrs and cactus. Then here went Summer. From the south he came. Above there he arrived. Thus spoke Summer. "Are you here? How is it going?" said Summer. "Did you come here?" thus said Yellow Woman. Then answered Yellow Woman. "I pick these poor things because I am hungry." "Why do you not eat corn and melons?" asked Summer. Then he gave her some corn and melons. "Take it!" Then thus spoke Yellow Woman, "It is good. Let us go. To my house I take you." "Is not your husband there?" "No. He went hunting deer. Today at night he will come back."
>
> Then in the north they arrived. In the west they went down. Arrived then they in the east. "Are you here?" Remembering Prayer Sticks said. "Yes" Summer said. "How is it going?" Summer said. Then he said, "Your daughter Yellow Woman, she brought me here." "Eh. That is good." Thus spoke Remembering Prayer Sticks.

The story would continue, with many of the elements contained in Gunn's version but organized along the axis of directions, movement of the participants, their maternal relationships to each other (daughter, mother, mother chief, etc.), and events sketched in only as they pertained to directions and the division of the year into its ritual/ceremonial segments, one belonging to the Kurena (summer supernaturals or powers who are connected to the summer people or clans) and the other belonging to the Kashare, perhaps in conjunction with the Kopishtaya, the Spirits.

Summer, Miochin, is the Shiwana who lives on the south mountain, and Sh-ah-cock is the Shiwana who lives on the north mountain.[4] It is interesting to note that the Kurena wear three eagle feathers and ctc'otika' feathers (white striped) on their heads, bells, and woman's dress and carry a reed flute, which perhaps is connected with Iyatiku's sister, Istoakoa, Reed Woman.

## A Keres Interpretation

When a traditional Keres reads the tale of Kochinnenako, she listens with certain information about her people in mind: she knows, for example, that Hutchamun Kiuk (properly it means Remembering Prayer Sticks, though Gunn translates it as Broken Prayer Sticks)[5] refers to the ritual (sacred) identity of the cacique and that the story is a narrative version of a ceremony related to the planting of corn. She knows that Lagunas and Acomas don't have rulers in the Anglo-European sense of monarchs, lords, and such (though they do, in recent times, have elected governors, but that's another matter, and that a person's social status is determined by her mother's clan and position in it rather than by her relationship to the cacique as his daughter. (Actually, in various accounts, the cacique refers to Yellow Woman as his mother, so the designation of her as his daughter is troublesome unless one is aware that relationships in the context of their ritual significance are being delineated here.)

In any case, our hypothetical Keres reader also knows that the story is about a ritual that takes place every year and that the battle imagery refers to events that take place during the ritual; she is also aware that Kochinnenako's will, as expressed in her attraction to Miochin, is a central element of the ritual. She knows further that the ritual is partly about the coming of summer and partly about the ritual relationship and exchange of primacy between the two divisions of the tribe, that the ritual described in the narrative is enacted by men, dressed by Miochin and Sh-ah-cock, and that Yellow Woman in her Corn Mother aspect is the center of this and other sacred rites of the Kurena, though in this ritual she may also be danced by a Kurena mask dancer. (Gunn includes a drawing of this figure, made by a Laguna, and titled "Ko-chin-ne-nako—In the Mask Dances.")

The various birds and animals along with the forces such as warm air, fire, heat, sleet, and ice are represented in the ritual; Hutchamun Kiuk, the timekeeper or officer who keeps track of the ritual calendar (which is intrinsically related to the solstices and equinoxes), plays a central role in the ritual. The presence of Kochinnenako and Hutchamun Kiuk and the Shiwana Miochin and Sh-ah-cock means something sacred is going on for the Keres.

The ritual transfers the focus of power, or the ritual axis, held in turn by two moieties whose constitution reflects the earth's bilateral division between summer and winter, from the winter to the summer people. Each moiety's right to power is confirmed by and reflective of the seasons, as it is reflective of and supported by the equinoxes. The power is achieved through the Iyani (ritual empowerment) of female Power,[6] embodied in Kochinnenako as mask dancer and/or Irriaku. Without her empowering mediatorship among the south and north *Shiwana,* the *cacique,* and the village, the season and the moiety cannot change, and balance cannot be maintained.

Unchanging supremacy of one moiety/season over the other is unnatural and therefore undesirable because unilateral dominance of one aspect of existence and of society over another is not reflective of or supported by reality at meteorological or spiritual levels. Sh-ah-cock, is the Winter Spirit or Winter Cloud, a *Shiwana* (one of several categories of supernaturals), and as such is cold and connected to sleet, snow, ice, and hunger. He is not portrayed as cold because he is a source of unmitigated evil (or of evil at all, for that matter).

Half of the people (not numerically but mystically, so to speak) are Winter, and in that sense are Sh-ah-cock; and while this aspect of the group psyche may seem unlovely when its time is over, that same half is lovely indeed in the proper season. Similarly, Miochin will also age—that is, pass his time—and will then give way for his "rival," which is also his complement. Thus balance and harmony are preserved for the village through exchange of dominance, and thus each portion of the community takes responsibility in turn for the prosperity and well-being of the people.

A Keres is of course aware that balance and harmony are two primary assumptions of Keres society and will not approach the narrative wondering whether the handsome Miochin will win the hand of the unhappy wife and triumph over the enemy, thereby heroically saving the people from disaster. The triumph of handsome youth over ugly age or of virile liberality over withered tyranny doesn't make sense in a

Keres context because such views contradict central Keres values.

A traditional Keres is satisfied by the story because it reaffirms a Keres sense of rightness, of propriety. It is a tale that affirms ritual understandings, and the Keres reader can visualize the ritual itself when reading Gunn's story. Such a reader is likely to be puzzled by the references to rulers and by the tone of heroic romance but will be reasonably satisfied by the account because in spite of its westernized changes, it still ends happily with the orderly transfer of focality between the moieties and seasons accomplished in seasonal splendor as winter in New Mexico blusters and sleets its way north and summer sings and warms its way home. In the end, the primary Keres values of harmony, balance, and the centrality of woman to maintain them have been validated, and the fundamental Keres principal of proper order is celebrated and affirmed once again.

## A Modern Feminist Interpretation

A non-Keres feminist, reading this tale, is likely to wrongly suppose that this narrative is about the importance of men and the use of a passive female figure as a pawn in their bid for power. And, given the way Gunn renders the story, a modern feminist would have good reason to make such an inference. As Gunn recounts it, the story opens in classic patriarchal style and implies certain patriarchal complications: that Kochinnenako has married a man who is violent and destructive. She is the ruler's daughter, which might suggest that the traditional Keres are concerned with the abuses of power of the wealthy. This in turn suggests that the traditional Keres social system, like the traditional Anglo-European ones, suffer from oppressive class structures in which the rich and powerful bring misery to the people, who in the tale are reduced to bare subsistence seemingly as a result of Kochinnenako's unfortunate alliance. A reader making the usual assumptions western readers make when enjoying folk tales will think she is reading a sort of Robin Hood story, replete with a lovely maid Marian, an evil Sheriff, and a green-clad agent of social justice with the Indian name Miochin.

Given the usual assumptions that underlie European folktales, the Western romantic view of the Indian, and the usual antipatriarchal bias that characterizes feminist analysis, a feminist reader might assume that Kochinnenako has been compelled to make an unhappy match by her father the ruler, who must be gaining some power from the alliance. Besides, his name is given as Broken Prayer Stick, which might be taken to mean that he is an unholy man, remiss in his religious duties and weak spiritually.

Gunn's tale does not clarify these issues. Instead it proceeds in a way best calculated to confirm a feminist's interpretation of the tale as only another example of the low status of women in tribal cultures. In accordance with this entrenched American myth, Gunn makes it clear that Kochinnenako is not happy in her marriage; she thinks Sh-ah-cock is "cold and disagreeable, and she cannot love him." Certainly, contemporary American women will read that to mean that Sh-ah-cock is an emotionally uncaring, perhaps cruel husband and that Kochinnenako is forced to accept a life bereft of warmth and love. A feminist reader might imagine that Kochinnenako, like many women, has been socialized into submission. So obedient is she, it seems, so lacking in spirit and independence, that she doesn't seize her chance to escape a bad situation, preferring instead to remain obedient to the patriarchal institution of marriage. As it turns out (in Gunn's tale), Kochinnenako is delivered from the clutches of her violent and unwanted mate by the timely intervention of a much more pleasant man, the hero.

A radical feminist is likely to read the story for its content vis à vis racism and resistance to oppression. From a radical perspective, it seems politically significant that Sh-ah-cock is white. That is, winter is white. Snow is white. Blizzards are white. Clearly, while the story does not give much support to concepts of a people's struggles, it could be construed to mean that the oppressor is designated white in the story because the Keres are engaged in serious combat with white colonial power and, given the significance of storytelling in tribal cultures, are chronicling that struggle in this tale. Read this way, it would seem to acknowledge the right and duty of the people in overthrowing the hated white dictator, who by this account possesses the power of life and death over them.

Briefly, in this context, the story can be read as a tale about the nature of white oppression of Indian people, and Kochinnenako then becomes something of a revolutionary fighter through her collusion with the rebel Miochin in the overthrow of the tyrant Sh-ah-cock. In this reading, the tale becomes a cry for liberation and a direct command to women to aid in the people's struggle to overthrow the colonial powers that drain them of life and strength, deprive them of their rightful prosperity, and threaten them with extinction. An activist teacher could use this tale to instruct women in their obligation to the revolutionary struggle. The daughter, her sisters, and the mother are, after all, implicated in the attempt to bring peace and prosperity to the people; indeed, they are central to it. Such a teacher could, by so using the story, appear to be incorporating culturally diverse materials in the classroom while at the same time exploiting the romantic and moral appeal Native Americans have for other Americans.

When read as a battle narrative, the story as Gunn renders it makes clear that the superiority of Miochin rests as much in his commitment to the welfare of the people as in his military prowess and that because his attempt to free the people is backed up by their invitation to him to come and liberate them, he is successful. Because of his success he is entitled to the hand of the ruler's daughter, Kochinnenako, one of the traditional Old World spoils of victory. Similarly, Sh-ah-cock is defeated not only because he is violent and oppressive but because the people, like Kochinnenako, find that they cannot love him.

A radical lesbian separatist might find herself uncomfortable with the story even though it is so clearly correct in identifying the enemy as white and violent. But the overthrow of the tyrant is placed squarely in the hands of another male figure, Miochin. This rescue is likely to be viewed with a jaundiced eye by many feminists (though more romantic women might be satisfied with it, since it's a story about an Indian woman of long ago), as Kochinnenako has to await the coming of a handsome stranger for her salvation, and her fate is decided by her father and the more salutary suitor Miochin. No one asks Kochinnenako what she wants to do; the reader is informed that her marriage is not to her liking when she admits to Miochin that she is unhappy. Nevertheless, Kochinnenako acts like any passive, dependent woman who is exploited by the males in her life, who get what they want regardless of her own needs or desires.

Some readers (like myself) might find themselves wondering hopefully whether Miochin isn't really female, disguised by males as one of them in order to buttress their position of relative power. After all, this figure is dressed in yellow and green, the colors of corn, a plant always associated with Woman. Kochinnenako and her sisters are all Corn Women and her mother is, presumably, the head of the Corn Clan; and the Earth Mother of the Keres, Iyatiku, is Corn Woman herself. Alas, I haven't yet found evidence to support such a wishful notion, except that the mask dancer who impersonates Kochinnenako is male, dressed female, which is sort of the obverse side of the wish.

### A Feminist-Tribal Interpretation

The feminist interpretation I have sketched—which is a fair representation of one of my early readings from what I took to be a feminist perspective—proceeds from two unspoken assumptions: that women are essentially powerless and that conflict is basic to human existence. The first is a fundamental feminist position, while the second is basic to Anglo-European thought; neither, however, is characteristic of Keres thought. To a modern feminist, marriage is an institution developed to establish and maintain male supremacy; because she is the ruler's daughter, Kochinnenako's choice of a husband determines which male will hold power over the people and who will inherit the throne.[7]

When Western assumptions are applied to tribal narratives, they become mildly confusing and moderately annoying from any perspective.[8] Western assumptions about the nature of human society (and thus of literature) when contextualizing a tribal story or ritual must necessarily leave certain elements unclear. If the battle between Summer Spirit and Winter Spirit is about the triumph of warmth, generosity, and kindness over coldness, miserliness, and cruelty, supremacy of the good over the bad, why does the hero grant his antagonist rights over the village and Kochinnenako for half of each year?

The contexts of Anglo-European and Keres Indian life differ so greatly in virtually every assumption about the nature of reality, society, ethics, female roles, and the sacred importance of seasonal change that simply telling a Keres tale within an Anglo-European narrative context creates a dizzying series of false impressions and unanswerable (perhaps even unposable) questions.

For instance, marriage among traditional Keres is not particularly related to marriage among Anglo-European Americans. As I explain in greater detail in a later essay, paternity is not an issue among traditional Keres people; a child belongs to its mother's clan, not in the sense that she or he is owned by the clan, but in the sense that she or he belongs within it. Another basic difference is the attitude toward conflict; the Keres can best be described as a conflict-phobic people, while Euro-American culture is conflict-centered. So while the orderly and proper annual transference of power from Winter to Summer people through the agency of the Keres central female figure is the major theme of the narrative from a Keres perspective, the triumph of good over evil becomes its major theme when it is retold by a white man.

Essentially what happens is that Summer (a mask dancer dressed as Miochin) asks Kochinnenako permission, in a ritual manner, to enter the village. She (who is either a mask dancer dressed as Yellow Woman, or a Yellow Corn Irriaku) follows a ritual order of responses and actions that enable Summer to enter. The narrative specifies the acts she must perform, the words she must say, and those that are prohibited, such as the command that she not "throw any of the husks out of the door." This command establishes both the identity of Miochin and constitutes his declaration of his ritual intention and his ritual relationship to Kochinnenako.

Agency is Kochinnenako's ritual role here; it is through her ritual agency that the orderly, harmonious transfer of primacy between the Summer and Winter people is accomplished. This transfer takes place at the time of the year that Winter goes north and Summer comes to the pueblo from the south, the time when the sun moves north along the line it makes with the edge of the sun's house as ascertained by the hocheni calendar keeper who determines the proper solar and astronomical times for various ceremonies. Thus, in the proper time, Kochinnenako empowers Summer to enter the village. Kochinnenako's careful observance of the ritual requirements together with the proper conduct of her sisters, her mother, the priests (symbolized by the title Hutchamun Kiuk, whom Gunn identifies as the ruler and Yellow Woman's father, though he could as properly—more properly, actually—be called her mother), the animals and birds, the weather, and the people at last brings summer to the village, ending the winter and the famine that accompanies winter's end.

A feminist who is conscious of tribal thought and practice will know that the real story of Sh-ah-cock and Miochin underscores the central role that woman plays in the orderly life of the people. Reading Gunn's version, she will be aware of the vast gulf between the Lagunas and John Gunn in their understanding of the role of women in a traditional gynecentric society such as that of the western Keres. Knowing that the central role of woman is harmonizing spiritual relationships between the people and the rest of the universe by empowering ritual activities, she will be able to read the story for its western colonial content, aware that Gunn's version reveals more about American consciousness when it meets tribal thought than it reveals about the tribe. When the story is analyzed within the context to which it rightly belongs, its feminist content becomes clear, as do the various purposes to which industrialized patriarchal people can put a tribal story.

If she is familiar with the ritual color code of this particular group of Native Americans, a feminist will know that white is the color of Shipap, the place where the four rivers of life come together and where our Mother Iyatiku lives. Thus she will know that it is appropriate that the Spirit of Woman's Power/Being (Yellow Woman) be "married" (that is, ritually connected in energy-transferring gestalts) first with Winter who is the power signified by the color white, which informs clouds, the Mountain Tse-pina, Shipap, originating Power, Koshare, the north and northwest, and that half of the year, and then with Summer, whose color powers are yellow and green, which inform Kurena, sunrise, the growing and ripening time of Mother Earth, and whose direction is south and southeast and that portion of the year.

A feminist will know that the story is about how the Mother Corn Iyatiku's "daughter," that is, her essence in one of its aspects, comes to live as Remembering Prayer Sticks' daughter first with the Winter people and then with the Summer people, and so on.

The net effect of Gunn's rendition of the story is the unhappy wedding of the woman-centered tradition of the western Keres to patriarchal Anglo-European tradition and thus the dislocation of the central position of Keres women by their assumption under the rule of the men. When one understands that the hocheni is the person who tells the time and prays for all the people, even the white people, and that the Hutchamun Kiuk is the ruler only in the sense that the Constitution of the United States is the ruler of the citizens and government of the United States, then the Keres organization of women, men, spirit folk, equinoxes, seasons, and clouds into a balanced and integral dynamic will be seen reflected in the narrative. Knowing this, a feminist will also be able to see how the interpolations of patriarchal thinking distort all the relationships in the story and, by extension, how such impositions of patriarchy on gynocracy disorder harmonious social and spiritual relationships.

A careful feminist-tribal analysis of Gunn's rendition of a story that would be better titled "The Transfer of Ianyi (ritual power, sacred power) from Winter to Summer" will provide a tribally conscious feminist with an interesting example of how colonization works, however consciously or unconsciously to misinform both the colonized and the colonizer. She will be able to note the process by which the victim of the translation process, the Keres woman who reads the tale, is misinformed because she reads Gunn's book. Even though she knows that something odd is happening in the tale, she is not likely to apply sophisticated feminist analysis to the rendition; in the absence of real knowledge of the colonizing process of story-changing, she is all too likely to find bits of the Gunn tale sticking in her mind and subtly altering her perception of herself, her role in her society, and her relationship to the larger world.

The hazard to male Keres readers is, of course, equally great. They are likely to imagine that the proper relationship of women to men is subservience. And it is because of such a shockingly untraditional modern interpretation, brought on as much by reading Gunn as by other, perhaps more obvious societal mechanisms, that the relationships between men and women are so severely disordered at Laguna that wife-abuse, rape, and battery of women there has reached frightening levels in recent years.

## Political Implications of Narrative Structure

The changes Gunn has made in the narrative are not only changes in content; they are structural as well. One useful social function of traditional tribal literature is its tendency to distribute value evenly among various elements, providing a model or pattern for egalitarian structuring of society as well as literature. However, egalitarian structures in either literature or society are not easily "read" by hierarchically inclined westerners.

Still, the tendency to equal distribution of value among all elements in a field, whether the field is social, spiritual, or aesthetic (and the distinction is moot when tribal materials are under discussion), is an integral part of tribal consciousness and is reflected in tribal social and aesthetic systems all over the Americas. In this structural framework, no single element is foregrounded, leaving the others to supply "background." Thus, properly speaking, there are no heroes, no villains, no chorus, no setting (in the sense of inert ground against which dramas are played out). There are no minor characters, and foreground slips along from one focal point to another until all the pertinent elements in the ritual conversation have had their say.

In tribal literatures, the timing of the foregrounding of various elements is dependent on the purpose the narrative is intended to serve. Tribal art functions something like a forest in which all elements coexist, where each is integral to the being of the others. Depending on the season, the interplay of various life forms, the state of the overall biosphere and psy-chosphere, and the woman's reason for being there, certain plants will leap into focus on certain occasions. For example, when tribal women on the eastern seaboard went out to gather sassafras, what they noticed, what stood out sharply in their attention, were the sassafras plants. But when they went out to get maple sugar, maples became foregrounded. But the foregrounding of sassafras or maple in no way lessens the value of the other plants or other features of the forest. When a woman goes after maple syrup, she is aware of the other plant forms that are also present.

In the same way, a story that is intended to convey the importance of the Grandmother Spirits will focus on grand-mothers in their interaction with grandchildren and will con-vey little information about uncles. Traditional tales will make a number of points, and a number of elements will be present, all of which will bear some relationship to the subject of the story. Within the time the storyteller has allotted to the story, and depending on the interest and needs of her audience at the time of the storytelling, each of these elements will receive its proper due.

Traditional American Indian stories work dynamically among clusters of loosely interconnected circles. The focus of the action shifts from one character to another as the story unfolds. There is no "point of view" as the term is generally understood, unless the action itself, the story's purpose, can be termed "point of view." But as the old tales are translated and rendered in English, the western notion of proper fictional form takes over the tribal narrative. Soon there appear to be heroes, point of view, conflict, crisis, and resolution, and as western tastes in story crafting are imposed on the narrative structure of the ritual story, the result is a western story with Indian characters. Mournfully, the new form often becomes confused with the archaic form by the very people whose tra-dition has been re-formed.

The story Gunn calls "Sh-ah-cock and Mi-o-chin or The Battle of the Seasons" might be better termed "How Kochin-nenako Balanced the World," though even then the title would be misleading to American readers, for they would see Kochin-nenako as the heroine, the foreground of the story. They would see her as the central figure of the action, and of course that would be wrong. There is no central figure in the tale, though there is a central point. The point is concerned with the proper process of a shift in focus, not the resolution of a conflict. Kochinnenako's part in the process is agency, not heroics; even in Gunn's version, she does nothing heroic. A situation presents itself in the proper time, and Yellow Woman acts in accordance with the dictates of timing, using proper ritual as her mode. But the people cannot go from Winter into Summer without conscious acceptance of Miochin, and Yellow Woman's invitation to him, an acceptance that is encouraged and supported by all involved, constitutes a tribal act.

The "battle" between Summer and Winter is an accurate description of seasonal change in central New Mexico during the spring. This comes through in the Gunn rendition, but because the story is focused on conflict rather than on balance, the meteorological facts and their intrinsic relationship to human ritual are obscured. Only a non-Indian mind, accustomed to interpreting events in terms of battle, struggle, and conflict, would assume that the process of transfer had to occur through a battle replete with protagonist, antagonist, a cast of thousands, and a pretty girl as the prize. For who but an industrialized patriarch would think that winter can be vanquished? Winter and Summer enjoy a relationship based on complementarity, mutuality, and this is the moral significance of the tale.

## Tribal Narratives and Women's Lives

Reading American Indian traditional stories and songs is not an easy task. Adequate comprehension requires that the reader be aware that Indians never think like whites and that any typeset version of traditional materials is distorting.

In many ways, literary conventions, as well as the conventions of literacy, militate against an understanding of traditional tribal materials. Western technological-industrialized minds cannot adequately interpret tribal materials because they are generally trained to perceive their entire world in ways that are alien to tribal understandings.

This problem is not exclusive to tribal literature. It is one that all ethnic writers who write out of a tribal or folk tradition face, and one that is also shared by women writers, who, after all, inhabit a separate folk tradition. Much of women's culture bears marked resemblance to tribal culture. The perceptual modes that women, even those of us who are literate, industrialized, and reared within masculinist academic traditions, habitually engage in more closely resemble inclusive-field perception than excluding foreground-background perceptions.

Women's traditional occupations, their arts and crafts, and their literature and philosophies are more often accretive than linear, more achronological than chronological, and more dependent on harmonious relationships of all elements within a field of perception than western culture in general is thought to be. Indeed, the patchwork quilt is the best material example I can think of to describe the plot and process of a traditional tribal narrative, and quilting is a non-Indian woman's art, one that Indian women have taken to avidly and that they display in their ceremonies, rituals, and social gatherings as well as in their homes.

It is the nature of woman's existence to be and to create background. This fact, viewed with unhappiness by many feminists, is of ultimate importance in a tribal context. Certainly no art object is bereft of background. Certainly the contents and tone of one's background will largely determine the direction and meaning of one's life and, therefore, the meaning and effect of one's performance in any given sphere of activity.

Westerners have for a long time discounted the importance of background. The earth herself, which is our most inclusive background, is dealt with summarily as a source of food, metals, water, and profit, while the fact that she is the fundamental agent of all planetary life is blithely ignored. Similarly, women's activities—cooking, planting, harvesting, preservation, storage, homebuilding, decorating, maintaining, doctoring, nursing, soothing, and healing, along with the bearing, nurturing, and rearing of children—are devalued as blithely. An antibackground bias is bound to have social costs that have so far remained unexplored, but elite attitudes toward workers, nonwhite races, and women are all part of the price we pay for overvaluing the foreground.

In the western mind, shadows highlight the foreground. In contrast, in the tribal view the mutual relationships among shadows and light in all their varying degrees of intensity create a living web of definition and depth, and significance arises from their interplay. Traditional and contemporary tribal arts and crafts testify powerfully to the importance of balance among all elements in tribal perception, aesthetics, and social systems.

Traditional peoples perceive their world in a unified-field fashion that is very different from the single-focus perception that generally characterizes western masculinist, monotheistic modes of perception. Because of this, tribal cultures are consistently misperceived and misrepresented by nontribal folklorists, ethnographers, artists, writers, and social workers. A number of scholars have recently addressed this issue, but they have had little success because the demands of type and of analysis are, after all, linear and fixed, while the requirements of tribal literatures are accretive and fluid. The one is unidimensional, monolithic, excluding, and chronological while the other is multidimensional, achronological, and including.

How one teaches or writes about the one perspective in terms of the other is problematic. This essay itself is a pale representation of a tribal understanding of the Kochinnenako tale. I am acutely aware that much of what I have said is likely to be understood in ways I did not intend, and I am also aware of how much I did not say that probably needed to be said if the real story of the transfer of responsibility from one segment of the tribe to the other is to be made clear.

In the end, the tale I have analyzed is not about Kochinnenako or Sh-ah-cock and Miochin. It is about the change of seasons and it is about the centrality of woman as agent and empowerer of that change. It is about how a people engage themselves as a people within the spiritual cosmos and in an ordered and proper way that bestows the dignity of each upon all with careful respect, folkish humor, and ceremonial delight. It is about how everyone is part of the background that shapes the meaning and value of each person's life. It is about propriety, mutuality, and the dynamics of socioenvironmental change.

## ☐ Notes ∎

1. John M. Gunn, *Schat Chen: History, Traditions and Narratives of the Queres Indians of Laguna and Acoma* (Albuquerque: Albright and Anderson, 1917; reprint, New York: AMS, 1977). Gunn, my mother's uncle, lived among the Lagunas all his adult life. He spoke Laguna (Keres) and gathered information in somewhat informal ways while sitting in the sun visiting with older people. He married Meta Atseye, my great-grandmother, years after her husband (John Gunn's brother) died and may have taken much of his information from her stories or explanations of Laguna ceremonial events. She had a way of "translating" terms and concepts from Keres into English and from a Laguna conceptual framework into an American one, as she understood it. For example, she used to refer to the Navajo people as "gypsies," probably because they traveled in covered wagons and the women wear long, full skirts and head scarves and both men and women wear a great deal of jewelry.

2. His use of the term may reflect the use by his informants, who were often educated in Carlisle or Menaul Indian schools, in their attempt to find an equivalent term that Gunn could understand to signify the deep respect and reverence accorded the hocheni tyi'a'muni. Or he might have selected the term because he was writing a book for an anonymous non-Keres audience, which included himself. Since he spoke Laguna Keres, I think he was doing the translations himself, and his renderings of words (and contexts) was likely influenced by the way Lagunas themselves rendered local terms into English. I doubt, however, that he was conscious of the extent to which his renderings reflected European traditions and simultaneously distorted Laguna-Acoma ones.

Gunn was deeply aware of the importance and intelligence of the Keresan tradition, but he was also unable to grant it independent existence. His major impulse was to link the western Keres with the Sumerians, to in some strange way demonstrate the justice of his assessment of their intelligence. An unpublished manuscript in my possession written by John Gunn after *Schat Chen* is devoted to his researches and speculations into this idea.

3. Gunn, *Schat Chen,* pp. 217–222.

4. Franz Boas, *Keresan Texts,* Publications of the American Ethnological Society, vol. 8, pt. 1 (New York: American Ethnological Society, 1928), writes, "The second and the fourth of the shiwana appear in the tale of summer and winter. . . . Summer wears a shirt of buckskin with squash ornaments, shoes like moss to which parrot feathers are tied. His face is painted with red mica and flowers are tied on to it. . . . Winter wears a shirt of icicles and his shoes are like ice. His shirt is shiny and to its end are tied turkey feathers and eagle feathers" (p. 284).

5. Boas, *Keresan Texts,* p. 288. Boas says he made the same mistake at first, having misheard the word they used.

6. When my sister Carol Lee Sanchez spoke to her university Women's Studies class about the position of centrality women hold in our Keres tradition, one young woman, a self-identified radical feminist, was outraged. She insisted that Sanchez and other Laguna women had been brainwashed into believing that we had power over our lives. After all, she knew that no woman anywhere has ever had that kind of power; her feminist studies had made that fact quite plain to her. The kind of cultural chauvinism that has been promulgated by well-intentioned but culturally entranced feminists can lead to serious misunderstandings such as this and in the process become a new racism based on what becomes the feminist canon. Not that feminists can be faulted entirely on this—they are, after all, reflecting the research and interpretation done in a patriarchal context, by male-biased researchers and scholars, most of whom would avidly support the young radical feminist's strenuous position. It's too bad, though, that feminists fall into the patriarchal trap!

7. For a detailed exposition of what this dynamic consists of, see Adrienne Rich, "Compulsory Heterosexuality and Lesbian Existence," *Signs: Journal of Women in Culture and Society,* vol. 5, no. 4 (Summer 1980).

8. Elaine Jahner, a specialist in Lakota language and oral literature, has suggested that the western obsession with western plot in narrative structure led early informant George Sword to construct narratives in the western fashion and tell them as Lakota traditional stories. Research has shown that Sword's stories are not recognized as Lakota traditional stories by Lakotas themselves; but the tribal

narratives that are so recognized are loosely structured and do not exhibit the reliance on central theme or character that is so dear to the hearts of western collectors. As time has gone by, the Sword stories have become a sort of model for later Lakota storytellers who, out of a desire to convey the tribal tales to western collectors have changed the old structures to ones more pleasing to American and European ears. Personal conversations with Elaine Jahner.

Education in western schools, exposure to mass media, and the need to function in a white-dominated world have subtly but perhaps permanently altered the narrative structures of the old tales and, with them, the tribal conceptual modes of tribal people. The shift has been away from associative, synchronistic, eventcentered narrative and thought to a linear, foreground-centered one. Concurrently, tribal social organization and interpersonal relations have taken a turn toward authoritarian, patriarchal, linear, and misogynist modes—hence the rise of violence against women, an unthinkable event in older, more circular, and tribal times.

# Whirlwind Man Steals Yellow Woman

Kochinnenako, Yellow Woman, was grinding corn one day with her three sisters. They looked into the water jars and saw that they were empty. They said, "We need some water." Kochinnenako said she would go, and taking the jars made her way across the mesa and went down to the spring. She climbed the rockhewn stairs to the spring that lay in a deep pool of shade. As she knelt to dip the gourd dipper into the cool shadowed water, she heard someone coming down the steps. She looked up and saw Whirlwind Man. He said, "Guwatzi, Kochinnenako. Are you here?"

"Da'waa'e," she said, dipping water calmly into the four jars beside her. She didn't look at him.

"Put down the dipper," he said. "I want you to come with me."

"I am filling these jars with water as you can see," she said. "My sisters and I are grinding corn, and they are waiting for me."

"No," Whirlwind Man said. "You must come and go with me. If you won't come, well, I'll have to kill you." He showed her his knife.

Kochinnenako put the dipper down carefully. "All right," she said. "I guess I'll go with you." She got up. She went with Whirlwind Man to the other side of the world where he lived with his mother, who greeted her like his wife.

The jars stayed, tall and fat and cool in the deep shade by the shadowed spring.

---

From *Spider Woman's Granddaughters* (Boston: Beacon Press, 1989), 187–188.

That was one story. She knew they laughed about Kochinnenako. Brought her up when some woman was missing for awhile. Said she ran off with a Navajo, or maybe with a mountain spirit, "Like Kochinnenako." Maybe the name had become synonymous with "whore" at Guadalupe. Ephanie knew that Yellow was the color of woman, ritual color of faces painted in death, or for some of the dances. But there was a tone of dismissal, or derision there that she couldn't quite pin down, there anyway. No one told how Kochinnenako went with Whirlwind Man because she was forced. Said, "Then Whirlwind Man raped Kochinnenako." Rather, the story was that his mother had greeted Yellow Woman, and made her at home in their way. And that when Kochinnenako wanted to return home, had agreed, asking only that she wait while the old woman prepared gifts for Kochinnenako's sisters.

Ephanie wondered if Yellow Woman so long ago had known what was happening to her. If she could remember it or if she thought maybe she had dreamed it. If they laughed at her, or threw her out when she returned. She wondered if Kochinnenako cried.

⬜ PATRICIA CLARK SMITH with
PAULA GUNN ALLEN ■

# Earthy Relations, Carnal Knowledge: Southwestern American Indian Women Writers and Landscape

Last year the pinons were plentiful

It took only a late night phone call
listening and laughing in the bedroom dark
(her husband was laying right there
but one-sided conversations never make sense).

And it made no sense right from the beginning
(the blue moonlight slid down the long center curve of
his back as he got up to take a drink of water).

After the phone call,
she had snow-laced dreams
where she was trying to catch the dark horse
and the other watched, chuckling under his breath.
She smelled chamisa when she woke and knew what
had happened
 far away the other was going to feed the horses
 beneath Toadlena mountains,
 the air was heavy with rainscent,
 sage and rabbitbrush.
But here the morning light bolted into the room in streaks
where her nightgown was a rumpled heap under the bed
and she remembered only the phone call

and the time she followed him into the trading post,
a skinny dog at her heels.
He bought her a Coke and they sat on
the dusty steps outside, not even talking.

---

From *The Desert Is No Lady: Southwestern Landscapes in Women's Writing and Art,* ed. Vera Norwood and Janice Monk (New Haven: Yale University Press, 1987), 174–196.

115

The sun was hot and sticky, fine dirt settling on them.
That was when he said:
    It's better here in the spring.
    Maybe you'll come back then.
As she drove off, she saw him in the rear-view mirror
mounting the dark horse.
That was how it was that day.

Here she cleaned the house thoroughly
and at noon, he called again saying:
    Come on out,
    the clouds are still real low in the mornings
    but it warms up.
    We can ride over the mountain if you want,
and she did.
I have no choice, she told herself,
leaving her nightgown on the floor
and her husband waiting at lunch.
    She took the next Trailways to Gallup
    a radio and a can of coffee.

    People saw them at the trading post at Newcomb
    reading the bulletin board.
    They left on the dark horse toward Two Grey Hills
    late in the afternoon
    and weren't seen again that spring.

It doesn't make sense, her husband said,
she seemed happy.
But happiness had nothing to do with it
    and years from now
    her grandchildren will understand saying:

    Back then, those things always happened.

That was last year,
the piñons were large
and the winter—so cold, so cold

      beneath Toadlena mountain,
      the white desert
      shining with snow.[1]
                    —LUCI TAPAHONSO

Long before *context* became an academic buzz word, it was a
Spider Woman word. It speaks of things woven together, and

of understanding the meaning of a thread in terms of the whole piece of goods. For southwestern American Indians, that whole is the land in its largest sense. The land is not only landscape as Anglo writers often think of it—arrangements of butte and bosque, mountain and river valley, light and cloud shadow. For American Indians, the land encompasses butterfly and ant, man and woman, adobe wall and gourd vine, trout beneath the river water, rattler deep in his winter den, the North Star and the constellations, the flock of sandhill cranes flying too high to be seen against the sun. The land is Spider Woman's creation; it is the whole cosmos.[2]

American Indian people—even urban dwellers—live in the context of the land. Their literature thus must be understood in the context of both the land and the rituals through which they affirm their relationship to it. Women and female sexuality are at the center of many of these rituals. The wilderness, American Indian women, ritual, and American Indian women's writing are inextricably woven together. I begin by looking at the relationship between American Indian literature and ritual and then go on to speak of how women and wilderness are part of these.

Like the songs and stories from their ongoing oral tradition, contemporary American Indians' literature is connected with ritual. Even contemporary American Indian jokes often rely on a knowledge of ritual:

Q. What's a seven-course dinner on the Sioux Reservation?
A. A six-pack and a puppy.

To get the full savor of the joke (or the puppy), you need to understand that puppy meat was valued more highly than dog, as veal is thought tastier than beef, and the Sioux used to serve puppy only as a special treat on ceremonial occasions. A seven-course dinner, including fine wine or champagne, is a white way of marking a special occasion. But contemporary Indians, for cultural and economic reasons, are more likely to pop the top of a beer can than the cork on a bottle of Dom Perignon. Alcoholism is common on reservations. The joke takes in all of this knowledge, and it is, among other things, a reflection both wry and poignant on a lost richness and a present deprivation. But to make the joke at all is to reaffirm the richness of American Indian life and humor, to recall a connection with ritual, with "the way," at the same time as one acknowledges what one contemporary American Indian woman poet, nila northSun, calls "the way things are."[3] Like the joke, contemporary American Indian literature reflects to a certain degree ritual understandings.

American Indian literature involves ritual; ritual is ceremonial action that reaffirms people's connection with the land. Nontribal people often perceive the land as an object, as something faintly or greatly inimical, to be controlled, reshaped, painted, or feared.[4] Tribal people see it as something mysterious, certainly beyond human domination, and yet as something to be met and spoken with rather than confronted. For them, the land is not just collection of objects you do things *to,* nor is it merely a place you do things *in,* a stage-set for human action. Rather, it is a multitude of entities who possess intelligence and personality. These entities are active participants with human beings in life processes, in thoughts and acts simultaneously mundane and spiritual. People and the land hold dialogue within the structure of ritual, in order to ensure balance and harmony. Ritual is the means by which people, spirits, rocks, animals, and other beings enter into conversation with each other. One major part of people's ritual responsibility is to speak with these nonhuman entities and to report the conversation; American Indian literature records echoes of that ongoing dialogue.

In this literature, that dialogue, the ritual interplay between people and the land, is often presented in sexual terms. Of course, the sexual metaphor for expressing some sort of relationship between people and land is not unique to Native Americans: scholars have remarked the inclination of early European male colonists to speak of the American earth in terms of sexual conquest, envisioning themselves taming and possessing a virgin land or being seduced away from civilization by the wilderness. But as Annette Kolodny has pointed out, imagery that casts the land as a rape victim, a seductress of men, or a compliant virgin ripe for taming by "husbandry" was understandably uncomfortable for colonial women on the Eastern frontiers, even though they, like their menfolk, dreamed

118

of transforming the landscape. Instead of using overtly sexual metaphors, eighteenth-century colonial women wrote about their hopes and plans for sweetly *domesticating* wilderness, for grafting native stock, for planting gardens. Later, when white women found themselves in the open prairies rich with wild-flowers, they spoke enthusiastically of discerning natural park-lands and gardens ready to respond gratefully to their care.[5]

Eighteenth- and nineteenth-century women's letters and travel diaries, on the subject of the land, recall certain shared archetypes from popular literature, and it is not only biblical passages about *Judea capta* and Goshen that come to mind. One thinks as well as Pamela and Jane Eyre taming, respectively, the wildernesses in Mr. B—— and Rochester; of the Peggottys and their friends reclaiming Little Em'ly and Martha into the family circle—of all the good men and women of the popular literature of the time who cajole and encourage their sexually undisciplined friends into comfortable, useful, temperate domesticity.

Subduing or training a wild landscape into a kitchen garden one can tend and view with satisfaction through the window is much like Jane's assisting at Mr. Rochester's trans-formation from an unpredictable creature of passionate en-ergy into a loving (if handicapped) husband, upon whose lap she can perch familiarly as she combs the snarls from his "shaggy black mane." Both acts, even though they suppress the wilder aspects of sexuality, are really assertions of sexual dominance; the domesticator proves more powerful than the now tamed wild thing. Productivity and fertility are not neces-sarily diminished by either act; domesticated plants arranged in orderly rows bear fruit, even as the Rochesters, we are told, produce children.

And yet something is lost. Though fertile and easier to live with, both the tamed Rochester and the domesticated plants are oddly defused of a particular charge of sexual en-ergy that was at once frightening and intoxicating and quintes-sential. Rochester and the garden-grown plant are no longer completely themselves. Readers and gardeners alike sense that loss, however dimly. (When I first read *Jane Eyre,* Rochester's blindness and humility disturbed me deeply. And even when my family's loamed beds were thick with hybrid June strawberries, my mother and I walked the field beyond the garden, parting the grasses to find the small, sparse wild fruit. The wild strawberries weren't ours the way the garden ones were; we couldn't control their growth, couldn't take them for granted, but they were incomparably sweet.)

Southwestern American Indian cultures do not approach wilderness as something to be either raped or domesticated, but they do associate wilderness with sexuality. Indeed, they see wilderness and sexuality as identical. In both traditional and contemporary literatures, wilderness often appears not as mere landscape-backdrop, but as a spirit-being with a clearly sexual aura. That being, who always embodies some aspect of the land, may be either male or female. A male being may abduct a human woman, or a female being may seduce a human man, but subjugation is not the dynamic of either event. In the instances of spirit-men abducting human women, what happens is not a Zeus-style rape, not the ravishing of some hapless girl who's had the dubious luck to encounter a swan or a bull with a knowing leer in his not-quite-animal eyes.

In such comings-together of persons and spirits, the land and the people engage in a ritual dialogue—though it may take the human participant a while to figure that out. The ultimate purpose of such ritual abductions and seductions is to transfer knowledge from the spirit world to the human sphere, and this transfer is not accomplished in an atmosphere of control or domination.

In old stories like the Keres Yellow Woman stories, or in Leslie Silko's contemporary "Yellow Woman," based upon them, the human woman makes little attempt either to resist or to tame the spirit-man who abducts her. Nor do men, in stories where they are seduced by spirit women, attempt to control or dominate them. The human protagonists usually engage willingly in literal sexual intercourse with the spirits who simultaneously walk the land and embody it. This act brings the land's power, spirit, and fecundity in touch with their own, and so ultimately yields benefit for their people.

If their full nuances are taken into account, *to have intercourse with* and *to know* convey something of the sense of what really goes on in those bushes beyond the light of the village fires, of what really happens up there, far to the north where the Ka'tsina has taken you. Unlike Yeats's Leda, the human protagonist does, without question, put on both knowledge and power through the sexual act. Furthermore, the act channels the awesome power and energy of our human sexuality—the preserve of wilderness in human beings—into socially useful channels. The coming together of person and spirit may lead to the birth of magical children, the discovery of rich sources of food or water, or the gift of a specific ceremony.

I want to turn now to two Navajo stories about the connections between the people and the land. The great Navajo chant *Beauty Way* deals with a fruitful coming-together of an earth-surface person—a human being—and a spirit; the *Beauty Way* ceremony itself, which incorporates the story, is given to the Navajo people as a consequence of that event. "The Snake-man," a contemporary short story by Luci Tapahonso, a young Navajo writer, movingly echoes elements of the *Beauty Way* story.

*Beauty Way* concerns the adventures of two sisters, White Corn Girl and Yellow Corn Girl, during the Navajo-Taos Pueblo wars. Corn Man, their uncle, has promised to marry them to the best warriors, but to his dismay the men who prove to be the most skillful in battle are two strange, sickly-looking elders enlisted as volunteers on the Navajo side. Instead of sticking to his promise, Corn Man tells his nieces to choose husbands for themselves at the victory celebration dance. But, as in the stories of many other cultures, promises have a way of keeping themselves once they are made.

At the dance, the Corn Girls grow overheated and stray away from the dance circle into the cool darkness, where they smell a strangely alluring odor, the sweet pipe smoke of two handsome young men encamped at some distance from the Navajo. The men obligingly share their intoxicating tobacco with the Corn Girls, and each sister falls asleep beside one of the strangers. When the sisters awake, they discover to their dismay that they have not been lying with a pair of handsome young warriors after all, but with the two mysterious old codgers to whom they were originally promised. Their relatives track them down but then, in disgust, leave the two women to the elderly husbands they appear to have chosen for themselves. Unbeknownst to either the Corn Girls or their family, the two old ones are actually Big Bear Man and Big Snake Man.

Finding themselves seduced and abandoned by their family, the Corn Girls run away together from their husbands, covering much of the Navajo country in their flight and pursued from afar by Big Bear Man and Big Snake Man. Eventually, at the Rio Grande, the two girls are separated. Here, the myth branches into what will become *Mountain Way* and *Beauty Way*. The former concerns White Corn Girl, Elder Sister, who eventually finds herself among her husband's Bear People. *Beauty Way* follows Yellow Corn Girl, Younger Sister, who finally arrives ragged and thirsty at a pool atop Black Rock, near Canyon de Chelly. There, a handsome stranger offers her sanctuary beneath the earth. She accepts and slips through a crevice to the underground world—the domain of her in-laws, the Snake People.

In the lower world, the Snake People initially appear to Younger Sister in human form. She does not guess their identity at first, even though they address her kindly as "daughter-in-law" and hold target practice with lightning arrows—a sure clue, for the Snake People are closely associated with weather. Younger Sister's adventures now assume a pattern. Her in-laws give her tasks or set her prohibitions which she bungles each time out of ignorance, absent-mindedness, or impetuous curiosity. Each time, when the Snake People confront her with her errors, she puts up a remarkably realistic adolescent defense, presenting herself as a hapless, put-upon innocent stumbling through life, a girl from whom little should reasonably be expected. "I am someone who's just traveling any old place," she says.

Each time they are confronted with this defense, the Snake People reply, with great forbearance and mild sarcasm, "Yes, we can see that." Their treatment of Younger Sister is delightful in its wise restraint. Even though they often suffer more than she does from her irresponsibility, they and other beings always help her out of her predicaments and are satisfied to let her be punished by the natural consequences of her actions, trusting experience to teach her what she needs to know.

For example, on her first night among them, she is warned not to rekindle the fire once it goes out. The Snake People additionally caution her that, should she catch a clear sight of them, she must remember that their ugliness lies only in their shape. Of course she rekindles the fire, and its light reveals her benefactors as a family of snakes. Younger Sister leaps wildly among them in panic before she fearfully resigns herself to bedding down again in their midst. In the morning, the Snake People complain that they're sore from being trampled upon, but all Younger Sister suffers is a case of swollen joints, although she's run away from their kinsman and literally walked all over them. Their continuing care of her is the best evidence of their true nature; Snake People, contrary to the old cliché of the Western matinee, do not speak with forked tongues, and that is the lesson she must begin with.

Younger Sister next is entrusted with jars containing wind, hail, male and female rain, and mist. On successive days, when the Snake People are gone about their business, she disobeys instructions and meddles with each jar in turn, unleashing the different kinds of weather. The Snake People are treated to a week of dust storms, floods, hailstones, and pea-soup fog, but each night they sigh "what can we expect?" and again leave her to care for the jars the following morning.

Younger Sister is being gently and skillfully socialized, learning by example the wisdom and forbearance of the Snake People, learning to respect the power of the elements and the need for great care and scrupulous attention to ritual in their presence. Unlike Ulysses and Pandora, her ancient Greek counterparts who against orders let things out of bags or boxes, Younger Sister is given room to err in order to prepare her eventually to take full charge of the weather.

Off and on during Younger Sister's underworld sojourn among the Snake People, she glimpses a shadowy figure who bears some resemblance to the elderly man she has fled, but Big Snake Man stays in the background, allowing his family to socialize his bride. He does not directly enter Younger Sister's experience again until the end of her time among his people, when she is cautioned not to stray from the Snake

People's territory. Of course, her eager curiosity moves her to test those prohibitions, with disastrous results. In this, her last forbidden venture, she wanders to the north and joins some rock wrens in a rock-rolling game. Younger Sister, a clumsy novice, is crushed beneath the stones. By the time her body is recovered only her bones remain, but Big Snake Man sings over her and restores her to life.

After all her trials and errors, Younger Sister is at last deemed ready to begin learning *Beauty Way* for herself—though in a sense she has been learning it all along. After a four-year apprenticeship, she masters all the songs and prayers and sand paintings and is entrusted with the ritual paraphernalia of the great chant. At the end of that time, Big Snake Man, now revealed as her husband, performs the full nine-day ceremony for her. But she is told that Big Snake Man will no longer be considered her husband, for neither he nor earth-surface people may perform chants for their own kin. (Elder Sister, who has been having parallel adventures all this time among various spirits who live in the mountains, is simultaneously learning *Mountain Way*.)

After her *Beauty Way* ceremony, Younger Sister leaves the Snake People and the two Corn Girls, reunited, go back to their human family long enough for them to sit their younger brother down between them and teach him both *Beauty Way* and *Mountain Way*. When they have passed on the ceremonies, the sisters return to the wilderness—Elder Sister to the mountains, and Younger Sister to the realm of the Snakes—to take their places among the Holy People. Back among the Snake People, Younger Sister is again given charge of the jars of weather.[6]

It is important to understand this story and similar ones, like the Keres stories of Yellow Woman, as stories about the relationship between human women and the land and its various embodiments.[7] As a consequence of her initial erotic experience, Younger Sister is socialized but not suppressed; she fares far better than most of the European folk-tale heroines who stray away from their families into the forests. Her encounters with the spirits of the land teach her what she needs to know in order to be an adult woman: to live within a family, to understand and respect the forces of nature, and maintain a ritual relationship with them. The preserve of wilderness within her—her energy, curiosity, sexuality—is not forcibly repressed, as if it were shameful and unnatural, but brought into contact with the outer wilderness. Both inner and outer wilderness are natural and beautiful sources of energy and fertile supply, but the outer wilderness is balanced, and it operates in harmony; balance is what Younger Sister must learn from her time among the snakes. Over a long period of experimentation, she learns to draw on her own inner wilderness and to channel it usefully.

In the story, Big Snake Man is indeed threatening at times, and he remains unfathomably mysterious. But even before he comes together with Younger Sister, he appears as an anonymous benefactor of her people. His alliance with her may involve a little deception, but it is hardly rape. When she flees him, he pursues her at a discreet distance—shooing her, so to speak, in the direction she needs to go, allowing her to find her own adventure. Through most of her time in the lower world, he remains a shadowy figure, working his healing magic when it is needed.

The sisters are not a pair of passive princesses badgered into submissiveness by their husbands and in-laws. They are strongly bonded with one another, and each makes choices that, even when they are in error, result in the getting of wisdom and power. In this story, a woman's exploration of her inner wilderness, and her dalliance with an embodiment of the outer wilderness, do not result in expulsion from paradise or in the unleasing of a stinging swarm of evils. Rather, her adventures end in the gift of a healing ceremony, the knowledge to use that ceremony rightly, and the power to pass it on to her own people. It must make a great difference for a child to grow up with the story of Younger Sister, rather than the stories of Eve and Pandora, as part of her heritage, and such a story must strongly shape her visions both of wilderness and of what it means to be a woman.

Younger Sister's story is a beautiful and useful paradigm for the way many contemporary American Indian women writers deal with the theme of women and the land. As Leslie Silko tells us:

> You should understand
> the way it was
> back then
> because it is the same
> even now.[8]

"Even now"—in a contemporary Christian boarding school on the Navajo Reservation—the story goes on. "The Snake-man," by Luci Tapahonso, subtly incorporates aspects of Younger Sister's wilderness experience.[9] *Beauty Way* permeates and enriches this brief and seemingly artless short story about little girls who innocently thwart an institution designed to socialize them out of the Navajo way into the white world. In this gentle tale of resistance, the land, embodied in two spirit-beings, one male and one female, helps the children preserve their Navajo identity against great odds.

Tapahonso's loose, easy narrative unselfconsciously shifts tenses and plot order, recalling the style of much American Indian oral literature and giving a strong sense of non-linear time to the story. What's happening at a given moment to the little girls is of a piece with what often happens, and what has happened before in old-story time. The tale is at once a piece of psychological and sociological realism; though set in modern times, it is an old story, or part of one.

"The Snake-man" centers on the nighttime doings of homesick little girls quartered in a third-floor dormitory room, allowed to see their families only on weekends, who long wistfully "to go to public school, and eat at home every day." The dorm mother sleeps in a separate room down the hall, and her "mothering" amounts to policing them. She is mostly a nuisance to be circumvented, effective neither as a mother nor as a disciplinarian. The institution, though sterile and isolating, does not wholly strip the children of either family or ritual life, for these little girls create both for themselves. Within their barren room, far away from their families, they mother one another, the big girls taking charge of the smaller ones, and pass on what comfort, philosophy, and knowledge they can to one another. When they grow frightened, "They all [sleep] two-to-a-bed, and the big girls [make] sure all the little girls [have] someone bigger with them."

The calmest and most mature girl is an orphan whose parents are buried in the school cemetery. Each night she sneaks down the fire escape to rendezvous at the edge of the graveyard with her mother's ghost. The other children stand guard at the window during her walks and question her eagerly about her mother when she returns. The child draws strength from her trips to the graveyard and sleeps peacefully once she's back in the dorm. The others huddle together in the dark and enjoy scaring themselves with talk about ghosts and about *"how the end of the world was* REALLY *going to be."* Their speculations muddle Navajo, Christian, and comic-book eschatology, reflecting their cultural confusions, as they talk of the time when "all the dinosaurs and monsters that are sleeping in the mountains will bust out and eat the bad people— no one can escape, either." When she hears this, the little girl who is nurtured by her dead mother only says quietly, "No one can be that bad."

Apart from the benign mother-ghost, the main spirit-person in the little girls' world is a male figure, the Snake-man, said to live in the attic. "There was a man in there, they always said in hushed voices, he always kept the attic door open just a little, enough to throw evil powder on anyone that walked by. . . . Once they even heard him coming down the attic stairs to the door." The Snake-man isn't visible, "cause he's sort of like a blur, moves real fast and all you can see is a black thing go by"—but he steals jewelry from them and "has a silver bracelet that shines and if he shines it on you, you're a goner."

Once, when the girl is in the graveyard and the others are standing guard, they hear a scratching noise outside. Certain *"he"* is making the sound, they rush to the windows trying to catch sight of him, "to get a description of him in case someone asks them," and they station someone on the fire escape "in case he tries to get up here." When the girl returns from the graveyard, the others hysterically tell her about the lurking presence outside. She calmly suggests it's "probably somebody's father trying to see his daughter." This settles the other children down; eventually, after more discussion, they agree the shadowy visitor is most likely the boyfriend of one of the junior high girls on the lower floor. They return to speculating about the Snake-man and finally drift off to sleep, all but one: "The bigger girls slept with the littler ones, and they prayed that God wouldn't let . . . the snake man come to them, and that the world wouldn't end until after their moms came to visit. As the room got quiet and the breathing became even and soft, the little girl got up, put on her house-coat and slid soundlessly down the fire escape."

The children of Tapahonso's story need to learn how to become Navajo women. They must learn, first, to head complex households; second, to deal with their own sexuality; third, to understand and perform their ritual obligations—the same things the two sisters of *Beauty Way* and *Mountain Way* must learn. Consciously or subconsciously, the children are trying to carry out their learning tasks, even within the sterile enclosure of the dormitory. In "The Snake-man," we see them being socialized toward Navajo womanhood, aided, as their Corn Girl ancestors are, by spirit-people who embody different faces of the wilderness.

The spirit figures, the mother-ghost and Snake-man, surround the dormitory and keep alive the connection between the children and the land. Ironically, the walls of the institution are no walls at all; the children bring the frightening power of wilderness right into the dorm attic, and one of them secretly ventures outside each night to encounter its benign, nurturing presence.

The gentle mother-figure is unusual, in that Navajo ghosts of the sort who manifest themselves around graveyards are generally considered threatening; Tapahonso herself has written a number of poems that deal with the notorious ghosts of accident victims who haunt the shoulders of New Mexico Route 666, inflicting their hostile half-lives on unwary travelers. No sane person deliberately seeks them out.[10]

The unseen spirits of dead relatives, however, can be absorbed back into the natural world and become helping presences in people's lives. In "A Spring Poem-Song," Tapahonso tells her children to go outside early in the morning and greet them:

They hover waiting
in front of the house
   by the doors
   above the windows
They are waiting to give us their blessing
   waiting to give us protection
go out and receive them
The good spirits in the gentle-bird morning
They hover singing, dancing in the clear morning
They are singing    They are singing [11]

The mother-ghost of "The Snake-man" is this sort of spirit, taken back into the natural world and seeing to her orphaned daughter's blessing and protection, even though she takes specific visible form. Moreover, she seems to take on aspects of one of the great Mothering spirits of the Navajo world, Changing Woman, perhaps, or Spider Woman. Certainly, she embodies the nurturing powers of wilderness. The little girl describes her mother waiting outside "at the edge of the cemetery by those small, fat trees. She's real pretty. . . . She waves at me like this: 'Come here, shi yashii, my little baby.' She always calls me that. She's soft, and smells so good." There in the dark of the trees, away from the confining walls—a place a child might normally find terrifying—she gives her daughter knowledge of her roots, destiny, and right conduct, talking to her lovingly "about when I was a baby, and what I'll do when I get big. She always worries if I'm being good or not."

Through her daughter's mediation, the mother-spirit's teaching and tenderness extend to the other girls who remain within the dorm. The Mother's stabilizing presence, among other things, enables the children to confront Snake-man and all he represents. A bogeyman in an Anglo story is often said to be a means for children to objectify and confront their sexual fears; indeed, probably Snake-man *does* have a great deal to do with male potency—a phenomenon doubly mystifying to little girls in a sexually segregated boarding school. Like all snakes, he is phallic—not just because he's longer than he is wide, but also because he is capable of astonishing feats of shape-shifting and sneaking up on you. According to the children, he's also intent on "throwing evil powder on you." This detail may be a displaced image of ejaculation, but it may also derive from Navajo stories about skinwalkers of both sexes, who witch people with corpse powder. Certainly, in his physical movements, Snake-man reminds one of archetypal males in many cultures—a back-door man, a dark blur easing out of sight round a dark corner, a Navajo C. C. Rider, or Speedy Gonzales. When the children seek a "rational" explanation for him, they connect him with sexual males; first they think he's a divorced father, and finally they choose the explanation that is most interesting to them—he's the boyfriend of one of the older girls on a forbidden tryst.

Snake-man, then, in part represents the men the little girls must eventually encounter in their lives as women. But Snake-man is more than any Freudian explanation suggests. He is an embodiment of the wilderness, and his sexuality goes beyond the human, although he encompasses it, for he embodies the wilderness outside people as well as within them. As in *Beauty Way*, he is the agent through which the little girls experience the land, or aspects of it. His presence keeps them alive to the awesome and potentially threatening force of wilderness. It is in part through him that they learn the art of being a family, of nurturing, and of being in a ritual community, for the thrilling fear he excites impels them to bond together and to invent as best they can private rituals that keep them safe without reducing his mystery and power.

In this simple and moving story of resistance, the children create their own nurturing community to substitute for the tribal life they have been denied; the one in touch with her dead mother becomes a kind of clan mother to the others. The institutional walls do not shut out the wilderness the children must keep touching if they are to learn to be women. Instinctively, they bring the wilderness inside and go forth to meet it in the spirit-figures who directly and indirectly communicate the knowledge the children need most.

Even a story like "The Snake-man," then, which seems to contain little landscape and says little about the land, may center on the relationship between people and wilderness. Certainly one of the most distinctive themes in contemporary Southwestern Indian literature by women is the retelling of the traditional women-abducted-by-wilderness-spirit stories.

130

Interestingly, this is a theme that these writers' contemporary male counterparts do not choose to retell. American Indian male writers do use images of the Southwestern land that suggest her as female; they address her as "our mother" and convey a clear sense of land as a living entity. Their poems and stories contain human lovers and mothers, daughters and grandmothers, witches and medicine women. But, despite the wealth of old stories about male heroes encountering spirit-women as lovers or platonic helpers, the tales of Grandmother Spider or Changing Woman giving crucial advice to questing heroes are not the tales contemporary men choose to retell.

The figure from oral literature about whom American Indian men of the Southwest write most fondly is Coyote, who appears frequently as a hell-raising buddy or alter ego, or as the symbol of the dogged will to survive—the continuance, despite the odds, of both the wilderness and the tribes.[12] That symbolism is legitimate and moving. But in the last ten years or so, Coyote seems to have become especially an emblem of *male* bonding, *male* clan, *male* cussedness and creativity and survival. Indian women writers in the Southwest, on the other hand, seem far more open to depicting encounters with spirit-figures of both sexes.

This may simply be a reflection of a present-day uneasiness on the part of men toward powerful women that cuts across cultures; after all, few contemporary Anglo men have written modern versions of *She;* there is no musical about The Blessed Virgin Mary Superstar. It may not be a comfortable time for male writers in any segment of American culture to deal with supernatural women of power. But American Indian women writers in the Southwest continue to center some of their finest work on direct encounters with the land in the form of the spirits who embody it, whether Snake-man or Grandmother Spider, Coyote or the angry entity who has been speaking up lately through Mount St. Helen's voice. These women bring astonishingly varied emphases to that common theme; their diversity is not surprising, given their different tribal affiliations and upbringings, ranging from Tapahonso's traditional reservation family life, to the Hopi poet Wendy Rose's adolescence in 1960s Berkeley, to the military-base childhood of Chickasaw writer Linda Hogan. It is that diversity I want to speak of now, and how the encounter with the land is presented in the works of three women writers—Luci Tapahonso (Navajo), Leslie Silko (Laguna Pueblo), and Joy Harjo (Creek).

Tapahonso is the youngest of the three women and had the most traditional upbringing, as one of eleven children born to Navajo-speaking farming people who still live on the mesa north of Shiprock. Some of her early schooling was off-reservation, at what is now Navajo Academy in Farmington, New Mexico—an experience she draws on for "The Snakeman"—much of her adult life has been spent in urban Phoenix and Albuquerque. As Geary Hobson notes in a recent review, her work often centers on "coming back home to visit . . . or thinking about going back home, or . . . about not being able to go back home, even when one knows that would be the best possible medicine."[13] In her biographical note for her first collection of poetry, she writes, "I know I cannot divide myself or separate myself from that place—my home, my land, my people."[14]

Tapahonso's characters cannot separate themselves from the land, whether they abandon the city, or continually affirm their identity with points west, or simply understand the Albuquerque cityscape as somehow an extension of

> the whole empty
> navajo spaces past
> Many Farms      Round Rock[15]

In the city, they continue to perform ceremonial actions that seal their connections with the land. In the early morning they greet the spirits of relatives, whose presence mingles with the cheerful voices of sparrows on the lawn.[16] They sprinkle cornmeal on the threshold of a daughter's first-grade classroom:

> remember now, my clear-eyed daughters,
> remember now, where this pollen,
>     where this cornmeal is from
>     remember now, you are no different
>     see how it sparkles
>     feel this silky powder

> it leaves a fine trail skyward
> as it falls
>     blessing us
>     strengthening us [17]

It is important and restorative for Tapahonso's urban Indians to remember that, beyond the city and within it, beneath and between the pavement, the earth remains herself. After a thunderstorm, a woman expects rainwater to pool in the folds of heavy plastic draped over the family's bikes, but she is pleased instead to see the rain making its way to its natural destination, sliding in streams off the plastic, "absorbed instantly / by the dirt / dirt thirsty in winter." [18]

For Tapahonso, kinship with the land is more than a question of affectionate memory and respect, and it is far more than metaphor. This comes through clearly in "A Breeze Swept Through," about the births of her two daughters, Lori Tazbah and Misty Dawn, who are the earth's daughters as well:

> The first born of dawn woman
> slid out amid crimson fluid streaked with stratus clouds
>     her body glistening August sunset pink
>     light steam rising from her like rain on warm rocks
>         (A sudden cool breeze swept through
>         the kitchen and Grandpa smiled then
>         sang quietly, knowing the moment.)
> She came when the desert day cooled
> and dusk began to move in
> in that intricate changing of time
>     she gasped and it flows from her now
>     with every breath     with every breath.
>     She travels now
>         sharing scarlet sunsets
>         named for wild desert flowers
>         her smile a blessing song.
> And in mid-November
> early morning darkness
> after days of waiting pain,
>     the second one cried     wailing.

133

Sucking first earth breath,
separating the heavy fog,
she cried and kicked      tiny brown limbs.
     Fierce movements as
     outside the mist lifted as
     the sun is born again.
         (East of Acoma, a sandstone boulder
         split in two—a sharp, clean crack.)
         She is born of damp mist and early sun.
         She is born again      woman of dawn.
         She is born knowing the warm smoothness of rock.
         She is born knowing her own morning strength.[19]

The babies bear strong family resemblance to the "Navajo spaces" of their mother and, in the case of the younger child, to her father's Acoma spaces as well; their own small bodies at birth echo the land's appearance at that very moment. Their arrivals are acknowledged not only by their human relatives, but by the land herself, who welcomes them as flesh of her flesh with a breeze of annunciation, a rock splitting clearly in two. The children are named for the land, whose power flows through them in the cycles of their breath.

The characters in Tapahonso's poems can easily lose touch with the blood connections they were born knowing; her poems encompass humorous and tragic glimpses of people, on or off reservation, who are divided, uncentered, helpless, and speak unflinchingly of bars and parking lots, alcoholism, abused women, wrecked cars, and abandoned children. But Tapahonso's great theme is the connection with family and land, or the rediscovery of it. In "Last year the piñons were plentiful," she chooses the oldest form of story to talk about that relationship, the story of the erotic coming-together of a woman and the land. "It is the same even now" for this woman as it was in the Corn Girls' time, even though the mysterious male figure who inspires her dreams of "the air heavy with rainscent / sage and rabbitbrush" can use Mountain Bell to awaken her need for wilderness, even though she leaves her clean house and steady husband on a Trailways bus.

Her husband is puzzled at her leaving an apparently happy life, but indeed "happiness [has] nothing to do with it."

When she rides with the man on the dark horse toward Two Grey Hills and the Chuska Mountains, it is an old-time ritual wedding with the land she has chosen. Whatever happens after we lose sight of them will result in grandchildren who understand her actions better than her husband does. More immediately, what comes of her elopement is a winter that is all a high-desert winter should be—trees heavy with piñon, deep snow to melt in time and ensure more growth, and icy breathtaking beauty.

A better-known and more-sophisticated writer than Tapahonso (though not, I think, a more powerful one), Leslie Marmon Silko is of mixed Laguna, Hispanic, and Anglo ancestry. Many members of her family were educated in Indian schools like Carlisle and Sherman Institute, and as a child she attended a private day-school in Albuquerque. Her work reflects the mixed-blood's sense of dwelling at the edges of communities: "We are . . . Laguna, Mexican, White—but the way we live is like Marmons, and if you are from Laguna Pueblo, you will understand what I mean. All those languages, all those ways of living are combined, and we live somewhere on the fringes of all three."[20] That experience of growing up around Laguna life without being fully immersed in it gives Silko's work a certain doubleness, a flexible narrative point of view. At times there's a distance, an ironic edge, a sense that she is writing *about* a tradition as much as *out* of it. Her narratives are more self-conscious than Tapahonso's in that they call more attention to their sources. In "Yellow Woman," a modern heroine thinks about one of the old-time Yellow Woman stories, even as Silva, the man she has met by the river, makes love to her:

> He touched my neck and I moved close to him to feel his breathing and to hear his heart. I was wondering if Yellow Woman had known who she was—if she knew that she would become part of the stories. Maybe she'd had another name that her husband and relatives called her so that only the ka'tsina from the north and the storytellers would know her as Yellow Woman. But I didn't go on; I felt him all around me, pushing me down into the white river sand. . . .
>
> "Do you know the story?"

"What story?" He smiled and pulled me close to him as he said this. . . . This is the way it happens in the stories, I was thinking, with no thought beyond the moment she meets the ka'tsina spirit and they go.

This flexible viewpoint enables Silko to take old tales like the ones of woman-abducted-by-wilderness-spirit and treat them simultaneously, or in successive retellings, with high humor, irony, and reverence. This does not always sit well with her critics, white and Indian alike, some of whom seem to expect all American Indian literature to be as pomp-ously solemn as *Billy Jack* or *Hanta Yo*. But Silko knows that the real stories are large and true enough to contain many stories, to bear many interpretations. In her collection *Story-teller*, Silko juxtaposes a number of pieces that treat very differently the theme of a woman leaving home for the wilder-ness. "Cottonwood" is a fairly straight retelling of two Yellow Woman stories. In the first, Yellow Woman goes out around the fall equinox to meet the Sun himself:

> She left precise stone rooms
> that hold the heart silently
> She walked past white corn
> hung in long rows from roof beams
> the dry husks rattled in a thin autumn wind.
>
> She left her home
>    her clan
>    and the people
>       (three small children
>       the youngest just weaned
>       her husband away cutting firewood)
>                 (64)

Her rendezvous with the sun, her willingness to join him, ensures that he will come out of his Sun House; he will not leave the earth locked forever in winter. The second part of the poem deals with her abduction by Buffalo Man; both the Buffalo People and she herself are finally slain by her jeal-ous husband, Arrow Boy, once he discovers that she does not especially want to be rescued, but the end result is the gift of buffalo meat as food in time of drought,

> all because
> one time long ago
> our daughter, our sister Kochininako
> went away with them.
>
> (76)

*Storyteller* also contains "Yellow Woman," a masterfully ambiguous story, whose heroine, like Yellow Woman, meets a man by the river, a man named Silva (forest, in Spanish), who may be a Navajo cattle thief or the ka'tsina he laughingly tells her he is—or both. Many details in the story parallel the old Keres tales of Yellow Woman and Whirlwind Man or Buffalo Man. But what is most important in the story is the heroine's awakened consciousness of her own sexuality and her acute sensual awareness of the man, the river, and the mountain terrain they travel: "And again he was all around me with his skin slippery against mine, and I was afraid because I understood that his strength could hurt me. I lay underneath him and I knew that he could destroy me. But later, while he slept beside me, I touched his face and I had a feeling—the kind of feeling that overcame me that morning along the river. I kissed him on the forehead and he reached out for me" (58). In letting herself open to Silva, she lets herself open to wilderness in all its wonder, its threat and vulnerability. The description fits her experience of both the man and the mountain.

"Yellow Woman" ends ambiguously. Silva may or may not get shot by a rancher, and he may or may not be a ka'tsina who will one day return for the heroine. Though she decides finally to tell her family only that she's been kidnapped by "some Navajo," what stays with her—and with the reader—is the lyrical evocation of Silva and his terrain: ants swarming over pine needles, the "mountain smell of pitch and buck brush," the danger and beauty she has experienced on those heights.

The heroine of "Yellow Woman" at times admits that hers is an unlikely story, but on the whole both she and the reader are inclined toward the belief in Silva as mountain spirit. Still, we understand there might be ways, in current parlance, to deconstruct that interpretation. Indeed, Silko does not need a critic to perform that task for her, just as the obscene and irreverent antics of Pueblo sacred clowns in a sense "deconstruct" ceremonies without the help of anthropologists.[21] Her poem "Storytelling" begins with a straight-faced recap of the Yellow Woman and Buffalo Man tale, then proceeds in a rapid verbal montage:

> "You better have a damn good story,"
> her husband said,
> "about where you have been for the past
> ten months and how you explain these
> twin baby boys."
> . . . . . . . . . . . . .
> It was
> in the summer
> of 1967.
> T.V. news reported
> a kidnapping.
> Four Laguna women
> and three Navajo men
> headed north along
> the Rio Puerco River
> in a red '56 Ford
> and the FBI and
> state police were
> hot on their trail
> of wine bottles and
> size 42 panties
> hanging in bushes and trees
> all along the road.
>
> "We couldn't escape them," he told police later.
> "We tried, but there were four of them and
> only three of us."
> . . . . . . . . . . . . .
> It was
> that Navajo
> from Alamo,

you know,
the tall
good-looking
one.

He told me
he'd kill me
if I didn't
go with him
And then it
rained so much
and the roads
got muddy.
That's why
it took me
so long
to get back home.

My husband
left
after he heard the story
and moved back in with his mother.
It was my fault and
I don't blame him either.
I could have told
the story
better than I did.

(95–98)

Whether deeply moving and ceremonial or slapstick, whether a woman abandons her water jar or her size 42 panties, whether she goes off with Whirlwind Man or the good-looking Navajo from Alamo, Silko conveys the sense that all these stories somehow concern an inevitable human need to go forth and experience wilderness—and the sexual wildness that it encompasses.

There is not space here to do justice to Silko's fine, complex novel *Ceremony;* Paula Allen has already spoken extensively of its treatment of woman and the land.[22] But, if male writers have been reluctant to retell for themselves the old stories of human men and the spirit-women who embody the land, in *Ceremony* Silko does it for them. As part of a healing ceremony that begins long before his birth and his spiritual illness, Tayo, a half-breed Laguna veteran of World War II, must "close the gap between isolate human beings and lonely landscape" brought about through old witchery that has led not only to Tayo's illness but also to World War II, strip-mining, nuclear weapons, racism, and a drought-plagued land. Witchery, not white people, has set a loveless, fearful, mechanistic, death-bent force loose in the world.

Silko does a wonderful job of making us see the Laguna landscape as the nexus of all modern history. The original witches' convention takes place near Laguna; on Bataan, Tayo sees the remote ancestors of his own people dying in the jungle mud; Laguna land encompasses the uranium fields; Los Alamos lies to the north and Trinity Site to the south. Tayo is not a single shell-shocked veteran suffering from flashbacks but a figure at the geographic and spiritual center of a cosmic illness.

The ceremony to counter the effects of the witchery must face the infectious force of people, both Anglo and Indian, who unbeknownst to themselves are witchery's victims. These people dismiss all ceremony and traditions, whether European or American Indian, as superstition, and they treat the land and one another as objects. The ceremony turns in large part on Tayo's coming together with Ts'eh, a beautiful, mysterious woman he encounters in the mountains beyond the Pueblo. Ts'eh, she tells him, is a "nickname." We know, and Tayo eventually figures out, that it is short for Tse-pi'na—in Keres, "Woman Veiled in Clouds"—the Laguna name for Mount Taylor. She is, she says, "a Montano," and a member of "'a very close family. . . . I have a sister who lives down that way. She's married to a Navajo from Red Lake. . . . Another lives in Flagstaff. My brother's in Jemez.' She stopped suddenly, and she laughed."[23]

She is a mountain spirit, like her brothers and sisters—sacred mountains all. Though she and Tayo are lovers, in scenes among the most erotic in American literature, her sexuality extends far beyond the act of intercourse—she is healer, nurturer, plotter, planter, and she schemes for the good of people and plants and animals. When she spreads her black storm-pattern blanket, snow falls; she folds it up again—in time to keep the snow-laden branches of fruit trees from breaking—the sky clears. When she bundles up her blue silk shawl with her damp laundry and seedlings and balances it atop her head, Pueblo style, she is Mount Taylor, its blue summit swathed in clouds. She collects, sorts, and transplants herbs and wildflowers, teaching Tayo something of her lore as she works. "She sat flat on the ground and bent close over the plants, examining them for a long time, from the petals, sprinkled with pollen, down the stem to each leaf, and finally to the base, where she carefully dug the sand away from the roots. 'This one contains the color of the sky after a summer rainstorm. I'll take it from here and plant it in another place, a canyon where it hasn't rained for a while'" (235). When she leaves Tayo, she charges him to help carry on her work, to gather a plant that won't be ready for harvesting before she moves on. At the climax of the novel, after he has resisted a brutal final temptation to perpetuate the witchery, Tayo immediately turns his thoughts to her work: "He would go back there now, where she had shown him the plant. He would gather the seeds for her and plant them with great care in places near sandy hills. . . . The plants would grow there like the story, strong and translucent as stars" (266). From Ts'eh, Tayo learns to nurture; through her, he learns to love the land and to recognize the depth of its love for him.

The Ts'eh and Tayo episodes of *Ceremony* are among the most powerful modern recreations of the old stories of women and the land, just as the novel itself is among the most acute evocations of New Mexico landscape. That landscape can be not only mountain and river bottom, but a barroom floor in Gallup, seen through a child's eyes:

> He lay on his belly with his chin on the wooden floor and watched the legs and the shoes under the tables. . . . He searched the floor until he found a plastic bar straw, and then he played with piles of cigarette butts. When he found chewing gum stuck beneath the tables, he put it in his mouth and tried to keep it, but he always swallowed it. . . . He played for hours under the tables, quiet, watching for someone to drop a potato-chip bag or a wad of gum. He learned about coins, and

141

searched for them, putting them in his mouth when he found them.

(114–115)

This child, or one very like him, will grow up to be Tayo—who knows, even before he meets Ts'eh, how to watch the land with the same intimacy, the same sense of the importance of the small change others might not think worth noticing and treasuring, the same careful regard for the things and creatures others would call trash.

Tayo's sensitivity of eye and heart and his care for the life in things compensate for the precise ceremonial knowledge he has never been given, as a half-outsider. Even before the war, his illness, and his awareness of the ceremony that centers on him, Tayo knows how to see and understands that ritual means holding intercourse with the land. During the prewar drought he seeks out a spring his uncle has shown him, a spring that never runs dry, even in the dust-bowl years. He does not know the proper Laguna way to pray for rain, but, like the little girls in Tapahonso's "The Snake-Man," he does what he can. He "imagine[s] with his heart" the right rituals and simply shakes pollen over the spring and asks for rain. Then he just sits and watches the pool at the source. What he sees suggests the keenness of his sight and insight, the receptivity of his eye: "The spider came out first. She drank from the edge of the pool, careful to keep the delicate egg sacs on her abdomen out of the water. She retraced her path, leaving faint crisscrossing patterns in the fine yellow sand. He remembered stories about her. She waited in certain locations for people to come to her for help" (98).

Tayo is ready to meet Ts'eh; even before their coming together, he knows that the land is alive and beautiful. She awakens his knowledge that the land is not merely alive but endowed with personality and intelligence and capable of evoking and giving back a love that is infinitely personal.

At times Tapahonso and Silko skillfully depict the urban Indian experience, but their work seldom strays much farther than Gallup, Albuquerque, or Phoenix.[24] Joy Harjo's particular poetic turf is cities, especially from the point of view of an Indian woman traveling between them. Her poems are full of planes, cars, pick-ups, borders, and white center-lines; she writes not only of the Oklahoma of her childhood and New Mexico, where she's spent many of her adult years, but of Iowa and Kansas, Calgary and East Chicago, Anchorage and New Orleans, and corrugated tunnels in airports, "a space between leaving and staying."[25] Her work traces the modern Pan-Indian trails criss-crossing the country, no longer trade routes in the old way, but circuits—the pow-wow circuit, the academic-feminist lecture circuit, the poetry-reading circuit. The primacy of travel in her works probably makes her, of the three women I've discussed, the most typical of contemporary American Indian writers. In and out of the Southwest, as Paula Gunn Allen remarks, wandering is an old custom among many tribes.[26] This is perhaps especially true of Oklahoma tribal people, whose wanderings have not always been voluntary. In an interview, Harjo said, "maybe the people of Oklahoma always have this sense that somehow we're going to have to move again. . . . Somehow, it's not settled, even though we've all lived there since about 1830."[27]

Harjo is also different from Tapahonso and Silko in two other ways. First, her work is more openly concerned than theirs with feminist themes. Second, she has a strong interest in the occult or metaphysical traditions of cultures besides the American Indian: she is an adept Tarot reader and a visionary.

Harjo does have a strong home-base, an acute sense of the red earth and the red people that the name Oklahoma simultaneously signifies. The literal earth is part of her early memory: "I love language, sound, how emotions, images, dreams are formed in air and on the page," she writes. "When I was a little kid in Oklahoma, I would get up before everyone else and go outside to a place of rich dark earth next to the foundation of the house. I would dig piles of earth with a stick, smell it, form it. It had sound. Maybe that's when I first learned to write poetry, even though I never really wrote until I was in my early twenties."[28]

An early poem, "The Last Song," especially affirms that

strong childhood bond with a particular patch of southwestern earth that "has sound," that speaks and nurtures:

> how can you stand it
> he said
> the hot oklahoma summers
> where you were born
> this humid thick air
> is choking me
> . . . . . . . . . . . .
> it is the only way
> i know how to breathe
> an ancient chant
> that my mother knew
> came out of a history
> woven from wet tall grass
> in her womb
> and i know no other way
> than to surround my voice
> with the summer songs of crickets
> in this moist south night air
>
> oklahoma will be the last song
> i'll ever sing [29]

Here, the land is a mother and a mother of mothers; a singer who gives human singers their songs. This is the poem of a woman who grew up not only playing in the soil, but listening to it. Most of Harjo's poetry does not center specifically on her Creek heritage—or not yet: Geary Hobson speculates that "oklahoma will be the last song / i'll ever sing" may be a promise of the theme Harjo will turn to in time. [30] Meanwhile, the land does not manifest itself in her poetry in spirit-figures out of her particular tribal tradition, like Tapahonso's Snake-man or Silko's mountain ka'tsinas. What does pulse throughout Harjo's work is a sense that all landscape she encounters is endowed with an identity, vitality, and intelligence of its own. This sense of life and intelligence in the land is quite different from the human emotions an Anglo poet might *project* upon landscape; the life in Harjo's landscapes makes poems written out of the pathetic fallacy indeed seem pathetic by comparison.

"Kansas City" illustrates Harjo's sense of the individual identities of natural things. In that poem, Noni Daylight (a kind of alter ego who appears often in Harjo's works) elects to remain

> in Kansas City, raise the children
> she had by different men,
> all colors. Because she knew
> that each star rang with separate
> colored hue, as bands of horses,
> and wild
>         like the spirit in her . . .[31]

Her children of different colors are comparable, in their beautiful singularity, to the each-ness of stars and horses. Noni's children, Noni's men, and Noni herself are singular and vitally connected with that natural universe of stars and horses. Even though they live in Kansas City, they are not alienated from or outside of nature.

Moreover, in Harjo's poems the land acknowledges its connection to people. In "Leaving," the speaker wakes as her roommate gets up to answer a late-night phone call:

> Her sister was running way from her boyfriend and
> was stranded in Calgary, Alberta. Needed money
> and comfort for the long return back home.
>
> I dreamed of a Canadian plain, and warm arms around me,
> the soft skin of the body's landscape. And I dreamed
> of bear, and a thousand-mile escape homeward.

> (28)

Even the imagined landscape of the Canadian plain, usually considered harsh country and certainly radically different from Harjo's Oklahoma, is like the sisters and friends earlier in the poem who warm and sustain one another. Both the women and the land are soft, comforting, erotic, familiar, associated with the healing and power of the totemic bear, and with home.

Harjo turns to the theme of human erotic connections with spirit figures who embody the land in her many poems about the moon. In them, the moon appears not as symbol and certainly not as background lighting, but as a full, intelligent female person. That the moon should be so important in Harjo's work makes sense given her womancenteredness and her representation of herself as a woman on the move. The womanness of the moon is in almost all cultures, and she can be there for the wanderer in Anchorage or Hong Kong; like Harjo, she is a traveler too. The moon, that medieval emblem of instability for Western Europeans, is a stable comforter for Harjo; in "Heartbeat," Noni Daylight drops acid and drives through Albuquerque with a pistol cradled in her lap. In the middle of this nighttown horror, "Noni takes the hand of the moon / that she knows is in control overhead." The poem concludes, "It is not the moon, or the pistol in her lap / but a fierce anger / that will free her" (37). Even so, given that Noni has yet to find that anger, the moon is the only entity who remains steady, who reaches out to Noni in a time when "these nights, she wants out."

And yet the comforting moon Harjo knows is also as completely herself and as mysterious as Snake-man or mountain ka'tsinas. Harjo conveys this moon's wildness and independent life beautifully in "Moonlight": "I know when the sun is in China / because the night-shining other-light / crawls into my bed. She is moon." Harjo imagines the other side of the world,

> in Hong Kong. Where someone else has also
> awakened, the night thrown back and asked,
> "Where is the moon, my lover?"
> And from here I always answer in my dreaming,
> "The last time I saw her, she was in the arms
> of another sky."
>
> (52)

What matters most about Harjo's moon is her ability as a living spirit to enter into the sort of dialogue with people that

146

reassures them, no matter where they are, of their own lives and their connection with wilderness. In "September Moon," as Harjo and her children try to cross Albuquerque's Central Avenue in the midst of State Fair traffic, she encounters the moon rising out of the trapped air of the urban Rio Grande Valley:

> I was fearful of traffic
> trying to keep my steps and the moon was east,
> ballooning out of the mountain ridge, out of smokey clouds
> out of any skin that was covering her. Naked.
> Such beauty.
> > Look.
> We are alive. The woman of the moon looking
> at us, and we are looking at her, acknowledging
> each other.
>
> > > (60)

The land and the person acknowledging each other as living beings, sensate and sensual, their lives inextricably woven together in Spider Woman's web—this is what lies at the heart of American Indian ritual and southwestern American Indian women's writing.

## ☐ *Notes* ■

This chapter was conceived and outlined with Paula Gunn Allen, and we jointly drafted the first few pages. When other commitments made it necessary for Allen to withdraw from the project, I went on to write the bulk of the essay, and responsibility for errors rests with me. But the ideas here derive from our initial collaboration.

1. Luci Tapahonso, "Last year the piñons were plentiful," in "A Sense of Myself" (M.A. thesis, University of New Mexico, 1983), 9.

2. I focus here on traditional and contemporary material from southwestern American Indians, but my broader observations about the relations between human beings and wilderness apply to most American Indian cultures. The best book on American Indian

religion is Peggy V. Beck and Anna L. Waters, *The Sacred: Ways of Knowledge, Sources of Life* (Tsaile [Navajo Nation], Arizona: Navajo Community College Press, 1977). Two good anthologies of essays on the subject are *Seeing with a Native Eye,* ed. Walter Holden Capps (New York: Harper and Row, 1976) and *Teachings from the American Earth: Indian Religion and Philosophies,* ed. Barbara Tedlock and Dennis Tedlock (New York: Liveright, 1975).

    3. nila northSun, "the way and the way things are," *diet pepsi and nacho cheese* (Fallon, Nevada: Duck Down Press, 1977), 13.

    4. *Often* is, of course, a key qualifying word in this sentence; certainly there are and have been non-Indian people able to perceive the land as something other than an object.

    5. See Annette Kolodny, *The Lay of the Land* (Chapel Hill: University of North Carolina Press, 1975), and *The Land Before Her* (Chapel Hill: University of North Carolina Press, 1984).

    6. My principle sources for *Beauty Way* are Father Berard Haile, O.F.M., and Lelan C. Wyman, *Beautyway* (New York: Pantheon, 1957) and Clyde Benally, *Diné jí Nkéé? Naahane'; A Utah Navajo History* (Salt Lake City: University of Utah Press, 1982). There are several versions of *Beauty Way,* and this essay contains only a summary of a sacred text of great complexity and beauty.

    7. Yellow Woman (Kochinako, or Kochininako), in Keres tradition "the mother of us all," is closely associated with the north, with hunting, and with rain; she is often described as an intercessory figure. In many of the stories, she appears as a human woman who makes alliances with male spirit figures, from whom she obtains gifts that benefit her people. See John M. Gunn, *Schat-Chen: History, Traditions, and Narratives of the Queres Indians of Laguna and Acoma* (Albuquerque, 1917), 184–189; Franz Boas, *Keresan Texts* (New York: Publications of the American Ethnological Society, no. 7, pts. 1–2, 1928), 56–59; Hamilton A. Tyler, *Pueblo Animals and Myths* (Norman: University of Oklahoma Press, 1975), 28–29, 100, 105–106, 213, 227, 229. Of contemporary authors, Leslie Silko draws most often on the Yellow Woman stories.

    8. Leslie Silko, "Storytelling," *Storyteller* (New York: Seaver, 1981), 94. Hereafter this volume cited parenthetically in the text.

    9. Luci Tapahonso, "The Snake-man," in *The Remembered Earth.* ed. G. Hobson (Albuquerque: University of New Mexico Press, 1981), 308–310.

148

10.   . . . They say
            you should never pick up
      strangers or injured animals
      on dark reservation roads

      you'll be safe if
      you do not brake for animals
            on lone moonlight nights
      They say
      the deeds of day
      have no disguise from
            the darkness of night and truth
      so they say
      never leave the pollen behind and
            always know a medicineman.

Tapahonso: "This is a warning," in *One More Shiprock Night* (San Antonio: Texas Art Press, 1981), 90. For other Tapahonso road-ghosts, see "She Sits on the Bridge," in *Earth Power Coming*, ed. Simon J. Ortiz (Tsaile, Arizona: Navajo Community College Press, 1983), 222; and "They Are Together Now," "A Sense of Myself," 24.

11. Tapahonso, "A Spring Poem-Song," in "A Sense of Myself," 30.

12. See Patricia Clark Smith, "Coyote Ortiz: Canis latrans latrans in the Poetry of Simon Ortiz," *Studies in American Indian Literature*, ed. Paula Gunn Allen (New York: Modern Language Association, 1983), 192–210.

13. Geary Hobson, "Blood Connections," *Contact II* 6, nos. 30–31 (1983–1984), 64.

14. Tapahonso, *One More Shiprock Night*, 94.

15. Tapahonso, "For Earl and Tsaile April Nights," in "A Sense of Myself," 7.

16. Tapahonso, "A Spring Poem-Song."

17. Tapahonso, "For Misty Starting School," in "A Sense of Myself," 27.

18. Tapahonso, "The lightening awoke us," ibid., 12.

19. Tapahonso, "A Breeze Swept Through," ibid., 16.

20. Leslie Silko, "Contributors' Biographical Notes," in *Voices of the Rainbow: Contemporary Poetry by American Indians*, ed. Kenneth Rosen (New York: Seaver, 1975), 230.

21. "The sacred Clowns of North American tribal people are

direct evidence that the sacred ways of tribal people are not inflexible, self-important and without humor." Beck and Walters, "Sacred Fools and Clowns," in *The Sacred*, 306. See also Barbara Tedlock, "The Clown's Way," in *Teachings from the American Earth*, 105–118.

22. Paula Gunn Allen, "The Feminine Landscape of Leslie Marmon Silko's *Ceremony*," in *Studies in American Indian Literature*, 127–133.

23. Leslie Marmon Silko, *Ceremony* (New York: Viking, 1977), 234. Hereafter cited parenthetically in the text.

24. The major exception is Silko's brilliant short story "Storyteller," which grew out of time spent in Ketchikan, Alaska.

25. Joy Harjo, "White Bear," *She Had Some Horses* (Chicago: Thunder's Mouth Press, 1983), 27.

26. Paula Gunn Allen, review of Harjo's *What Moon Drove Me to This?* in *The Greenfield Review* 9, nos. 3–4 (Winter 1981–82): 12.

27. Joy Harjo, in conversation with Paula Gunn Allen, August 1983.

28. Harjo, "Biopoetics Sketch," *The Greenfield Review* 9, nos. 3–4 (Winter 1981–82): 8.

29. Harjo, "The Last Song," *What Moon Drove Me to This?* (New York: Reed, 1979), 67.

30. Geary Hobson, review of *What Moon Drove Me to This?* in *Greenfield Review* 9, nos. 3–4 (Winter 1981–82): 15–16.

31. Harjo, "Kansas City," *She Had Some Horses*, 33. Hereafter this volume cited parenthetically in the text.

☐ BERNARD A. HIRSCH ■

# "The Telling Which Continues": Oral Tradition and the Written Word in Leslie Marmon Silko's *Storyteller*

"I was never tempted to go to those things . . . ," said Leslie Marmon Silko of the old BAE [Bureau of American Ethology] reports. ". . . I . . . don't have to because from the time I was little I heard quite a bit. I heard it in what would be passed now off as rumor or gossip. I could hear through all that. I could hear something else, that there was a kind of continuum. . . ."[1] That continuum provides both the structural and thematic basis of *Storyteller*. Comprised of personal reminiscences and narratives, retellings of traditional Laguna stories, photographs, and a generous portion of her previously published short fiction and poetry, this multigeneric work lovingly maps the fertile storytelling ground from which her art evolves and to which it is here returned—an offering to the oral tradition which nurtured it.[2]

Silko has acknowledged often and eloquently the importance of the oral tradition to her work and tries to embody its characteristics in her writing. This effort, as she well knows, is immensely difficult and potentially dangerous, and this awareness surfaces at several points in *Storyteller*. She recalls, for instance, talking with Nora, whose "grandchildren

From *American Indian Quarterly* 12 (Winter 1988): 1–26.

had brought home / a . . . book that had my 'Laguna coyote' poem in it":

> "We all enjoyed it so much [says Nora]
> but I was telling the children
> the way my grandpa used to tell it
> is longer."
> "Yes, that's the trouble with writing," I said.
> "You can't go on and on the way we do
> when we tell stories around here."
>
> (110)[3]

"The trouble with writing," in the context Silko here establishes for it, is twofold: first, it is static; it freezes words in space and time. It does not allow the living story to change and grow, as does the oral tradition. Second, though it potentially widens a story's audience, writing removes the story from its immediate context, from the place and people who nourished it in the telling, and thus robs it of much of its meaning.[4] This absence of the story's dynamic context is why, in writing, "You can't go on the way we do / when we tell stories around here."

But Nora does a wonderful thing. She uses Silko's poem to create a storytelling event of her own. In this sense Silko's poem itself becomes a part of the oral tradition and, through Nora's recollection of her grandfather's telling, a means of advancing it as well. The conversation with Nora is important in *Storyteller* because it reminds us of the flexibility and inclusiveness of the oral tradition.[5] Even writing can be made to serve its ends.

*Storyteller* helps keep the oral tradition strong through Silko's masterful use of the written word, and the photographs, to recall and reestablish its essential contexts. The photographs are important because they reveal something of the particular landscape and community out of which Laguna oral tradition is born, and of specific individuals—of Aunt Susie, Grandma A'mooh, Grandpa Hank, and all those storytellers who have accepted responsibility for "remembering a portion . . . [of] the long story of the people." The photographs, however, as Silko uses them, do more than provide a survival record. As we shall see, they involve the reader more fully in the storytelling process itself and, "because they are part of many of the stories / and because many of the stories can be traced in the photographs," they expand the reader's understanding of individual works and also suggest structural and thematic links between them.

The photographs also are arranged to suggest the circular design of *Storyteller,* a design characteristic of oral tradition. The merging of past and present are manifest in the book's design, as is the union of personal, historical, and cultural levels of being and experience, and through such harmonies—and their periodic sundering—the ongoing flux of life expresses itself. The opening photograph, for instance, is of Robert G. Marmon and Marie Anaya Marmon, Silko's great-grandparents, "holding [her] grandpa Hank." The second picture, three pages later, is of Aunt Susie—of whom Silko is the "self-acknowledged, self-appointed heir"[6]—and Leslie Silko herself as child. These photographs do not merely locate Silko within a genealogical context or even that of an extended family, but within a continuous generational line of Laguna storytellers as well. The last three photographs in the book bring us full circle. The first of these comes at the end of the book's written text; it is of the adult Silko and was taken among the Tucson Mountains where she now lives. The second is of Grandpa Hank as a young man after his return from Sherman Institute, and the third is of three generations preceding her, including her father as a boy, Grandpa Hank's brother, and her great-grandfather. Though there is clearly an autobiographical dimension to *Storyteller,* Silko's arrangement of photographs at the beginning and end of the book subordinates the individual to the communal and cultural. Her life and art compels us, as does the literature itself, to acknowledge the ongoing power of Laguna oral tradition in her writing.

This cyclic design, of course, is not merely a function of the arrangement of photographs. It derives primarily from the episodic structure of *Storyteller* and the accretive process of teaching inherent in it. Each individual item is a narrative episode in itself which relates to other such episodes in various ways. Oral storytelling, Walter J. Ong tells us, "normally and naturally operated in episodic patterning . . . episodic structure was the natural way to talk out a lengthy story line if only because the experience of real life is more like a string of episodes than it is like a Freytag pyramid"; [7] and it is real life, "the long story of the people," that is Silko's concern. Moreover, the telling of her portion of the story, and of the individual stories which comprise it, involves, like all oral storytelling, a teaching process, one in which the varieties of genre and voice Silko uses are essential.

In *Storyteller,* the reader learns by accretion. Successive narrative episodes cast long shadows both forward and back, lending different or complementary shades of meaning to those preceding them and offering perspectives from which to consider those that follow. Such perspectives are then themselves often expanded or in some way altered as the new material reflects back upon them. This kind of learning process is part of the dynamic of oral tradition. Silko uses it in *Storyteller* to foster the kind of intimacy with the reader that the oral storyteller does with the listener. Such a relationship is born of both the powerful claims of the story, in whole and in part, on the reader's attention and the active engagement by the accretive process of the reader's imagination. This process in effect makes the reader's responses to the various narrative episodes a part of the larger, ongoing story these episodes comprise while simultaneously allowing the episodes to create the contexts which direct and refine these responses. In this way the stories continue; in this way both the story and the reader are renewed.

It is impossible within the limits of this paper to explore the workings of this process over the entire length of *Storyteller,* yet the interrelationships between the various narrative episodes and photographs throughout is so rich and intricate that any attempt to formally divide the work into sections or categories would be arbitrary at best, of necessity reductive, and at worst misleading. Still, there are groups of narrative episodes that seem to cluster around particular themes and cultural motifs which I believe can be meaningfully seen as representative of the overall design and method of the book.

## II

N. Scott Momaday has said: "We are what we imagine. Our very existence consists in our imagination of ourselves. . . . The greatest tragedy that can befall us is to go unimagined."[8] It is apparent throughout *Storyteller* that Silko would agree, and she reminds us that in the oral tradition, "sometimes what we call 'memory' and what we call 'imagination' are not so easily distinguished" (227). In "The Storyteller's Escape," the old storyteller's greatest fear as she waits for death is that she will go unremembered—unimagined. *Storyteller* itself is a self-renewing act of imagination/memory designed to keep storytellers as well as stories from so tragic a fate. The book's opening section, which I will arbitrarily call the "Survival" section (pp. 1–53), establishes this particular concern.[9] Embracing five reminiscences, four photographs, two traditional Laguna stories, the short stories "Storyteller" and "Lullaby," and the poem "Indian Song: Survival," this section explores from various angles the dynamics and meaning of survival, both personal and cultural, for tribal people in contemporary America.

Silko visually establishes continuity through the photographs. The first two, described earlier, reveal in their depiction of three generations of Silko's family genealogical continuity, but especially important in primarily the second and third photos is the idea of cultural transmission. Such transmission involves more than the passing of stories from generation to generation, essential as that is. It involves the entire context within which such passing occurs, and this includes both the land and the relationship, beyond blood ties, between teller and hearer. That is why, to tell the story correctly, Silko must bring us into the storytellers' presence, to let us somehow see them, learn something of their histories, and most of all, to hear them tell their stories.

These elements are certainly present in the book's title story, "Storyteller," which is at the hub not only of the "Survival" section but of the book as a whole. Explaining, in Silko's words, "the dimensions of the process" of storytelling, this tale, set not in Laguna but in Inuit country near Bethel, Alaska,[10] is at once dark and hopeful, embracing all that has come before it in the book and establishing both the structure and primary thematic concerns of what follows. It is a tale of multiple journeys that become one journey expressed through multiple stories that become one story. At its center is a young Eskimo girl, orphaned, living with a lecherous and dying old man, the village storyteller, and his wife, victimized by Gussuck and "assimilated" Eskimo men, and determined to avenge herself against the Gussuck storekeeper responsible for her parents' death.

Speaking of his use of "three distinct narrative voices in *The Way to Rainy Mountain*—the mythical, the historical, and the immediate"—Momaday says: "Together, they serve, hopefully, to validate the oral tradition to an extent that might not otherwise be possible."[11] A similar mix of voices occurs in "Storyteller"—indeed, throughout the book as a whole—and to similar effect. Against the backdrop of the prophesied coming of a "final winter," the girl comes of age and the old man, the mythic voice, begins his story of the great bear pursuing the lone hunter across the ice.

He tells the story lovingly, nurturing every detail with his life's breath, because it is the story that makes his death meaningful. The story is an expression of sacred natural processes, ancient and unending, of which his death is a part, processes Silko will treat later in the book in such works as "The Man to Send Rain Clouds" and the poem "Deer Song." But most importantly the story, in the intensely beautiful precision of the old man's telling, becomes the girl's legacy, a powerful vision by which she can unify the disparate aspects of her experience to create herself anew in profoundly significant cultural terms.

She recalls having asked her grandmother, the old man's wife, about her parents, and her grandmother told how the Gussuck storeman traded them bad liquor. The grandmother is the historical voice. Her story and that of the giant bear become linked in the girl's imagination. Once, while listening "to the old man tell the story all night," she senses her grandmother's spirit. "It will take a long time," the old woman tells her, "but the story must be told. There must not be any lies." At first, she thinks that the spirit is referring to the bear story. She "did not know about the other story then."

This "other story" is in truth the conclusion of her grand-mother's story, a conclusion that will make it the girl's story. As it stands, in the inaction of civil and religious authorities and in the storeman's continued existence, the story of her parent's death has not been properly told. The story is life and in life it must be completed. And the story of the giant bear "stalking a lone hunter across the Bering Sea ice" tells her how. "She spent days walking on the river," getting to know the ice as precisely as the old man had described it in his story, learning "the colors of ice that would safely hold her" and where the ice was thin. She already knew that the storeman wanted her and thus it is easy for her to lure him out onto the river and to his death. Though he appeared to chase her out onto the ice, it was she who was the bear.

The attorney wants her to change her story, to tell the court that "it was an accident," but she refuses, even though to follow his advice would mean freedom. Hers is the "imme-diate" voice, the voice that carries the old stories into the pres-ent and locates the present within the cycle of mythic time. Through the story, life derives purpose and meaning and ex-perience becomes comprehensible; also through the story, and through her fidelity to it, the girl recreates herself from the fragments of her own history.

Her emergence whole and intact from her experience is, in this respect, like Tayo's emergence in Silko's 1977 novel *Ceremony,* a victory for her people;[12] given the immediate context in which the title story is placed in *Storyteller,* it is, like all stories in the oral tradition, a ritual. The girl's role as a culture-bearer, for example, receives significant emphasis from the surrounding material.

Following "Storyteller" there is a picture of Marie Ana-yah Marmon, Grandma A'mooh, reading to two of her great granddaughters, Silko's sisters. She is reading, apparently, from *Brownie the Bear,* a book, we later learn, she read many times, not only to her great-granddaughters but to Silko's un-cles and father. Accompanying this photograph is a reminis-cence about Grandma A'mooh, whose name Silko, as a child, deduced from the woman's continual use of "'a'moo'ooh' / . . . the Laguna expression of endearment / for a young child / spoken with great feeling and love" (34). That love is evident on the faces of the old woman and the little girls; it is also clear that although she is not in this captured moment telling a story from the oral tradition, she has turned the occasion, much as Nora did with the printed version of Silko's coyote poem, into a rich oral storytelling experience.

We come to the title story by way of several other narrative episodes, beginning with Silko's brief reminiscence and history of Aunt Susie, her father's aunt. Aunt Susie

> was of a generation,
> the last generation here at Laguna,
> that passed down an entire culture
> by word of mouth
> an entire history
> an entire vision of the world.
>
> (4–6)

In its rhythms and repetitions, Silko's telling here assumes the quality of a chant and in this she reinforces not only Aunt Susie's role as culture-bearer but her own as Aunt Susie's cultural heir. Their relationship provides a necessary context within which to consider the girl and the old man in the title story. That relationship is complicated in several ways, but this context, along with the photograph that follows "Storyteller," highlights her role as the storyteller-successor to the old man.

For Silko, how a story is told is inseparable from the story itself. The old man's bear story exerts its hold on the girl's imagination through his intensely precise, chant-like, dramatic telling and retelling of it. Silko recalls a child's story Aunt Susie told about a "little girl who ran away," and she insists that we hear it as Aunt Susie told it: "She had certain phrases, certain distinctive words/she used in her telling. / I write when I still hear / her voice as she tells the story" (7). In her own telling Silko uses poetic form with varying line-lengths, stresses, and enjambment to provide some of the movement and drama of oral storytelling. She also provides several italicized expository passages to evoke the digressive mode of traditional storytellers and the conversational texture of their speech. When the little girl asks for "yashtoah," for example, we are told that

"Yashtoah" is the hardened crust on corn meal mush
that curls up.
The very name "yashtoah" means
it's sort of curled up, you know, dried,
just as mush dries on top.

(8)

"This is the beauty of the old way," Silko has said. "You can stop the storyteller and ask questions and have things explained." [13]

Aunt Susie's story, in some respects, is a sad one about a little girl who, feeling unloved because she does not get what she wants, decides to drown herself. Attempts by a kindly old man and her mother to save her fail and the child drowns. Grieving, the mother returns to Acoma where, standing on a high mesa, she scatters the girl's clothes to the four directions—and "they all turned into butterflies— / all colors of butterflies." This is a child's story and whatever truths it may teach it should evoke the child's capacity for wonder and delight. Aunt Susie succeeded brilliantly in this respect. She brought the characters to life, the mother's tenderness and the prophetic foreboding of the old man "that implied the tragedy to come":

But when Aunt Susie came to the place
where the little girl's clothes turned into butterflies
then her voice would change and I could hear the
    excitement and wonder
and the story wasn't sad any longer.

(15)

The child learns something of pain through such a story, but she learns too of life's perpetuity, that from death itself can emerge beautiful life. She learns of the delicate balance in which all things exist, a balance forever threatened and forever renewed.

But harsh realities, having been delicately yet honestly prepared for by Aunt Susie's story, dominate, appropriately enough, the two recollections leading directly into "Storyteller." The first offers a brief history of Silko's great-grandparents, and we learn that Robert G. Marmon married a Pueblo woman and "learned to speak Laguna"; but "when great-grandpa went away from Laguna / white people who knew / sometimes called him 'Squaw Man.'" The second recollection is of the Albuquerque hotel incident in which Marmon's two young sons, because they are Indians, were not permitted in the hotel.

"Storyteller," is fed by the various motifs and concerns of the narratives leading into it and it recasts them in new ways. In that sense it is as much a retelling as an original telling. It is not merely a story of survival but, like the bear story within it, a survival story itself. It is unsparing in its treatment of the nature and consequences of discrimination and unqualified in its vision of the capacity of oral tradition not merely to survive discrimination but to use it as a source of power. However, as the narratives that follow "Storyteller" suggest, the oral tradition is only as strong—or as fragile—as the memories that carry it and the relationships that sustain it.

Silko's remembrance of Grandma A'mooh, which follows "Storyteller," is warm and moving, yet painful as well. Grandma A'mooh, as her name suggests, was love itself to Silko. She loved the land, her people, her granddaughters, and the stories that evolved from them, yet it was thought best, in her later years, to remove her from all that sustained her and have her live with her daughter in Albuquerque. The daughter had to work, so much of the time Grandma A'mooh was alone—"she did not last long." Silko tells us, "without someone to talk to."

"Indian Song: Survival," like the narrative episodes which precede it, concerns what survival is and what is needed to survive, but it considers these ideas from a somewhat different perspective than the others. It is in the first-person and this heightens the intimacy of the sustaining relationship of the individual with the land the poem explores. The poem moves in a sequence of spare yet sensual images which express at once the elemental and regenerating power of this relationship, and Silko's versification, like that of most of the poetry in *Storyteller,* is alive with motion and the subtle interplay of sound and silence. It is a "desperation journey north" she describes, but it is marked by neither panic nor haste.

"Mountain lion," Silko writes, "shows me the way." He

is her guide as he has been for Laguna hunters throughout
the time, and his presence helps to establish the true nature
of this journey. It is a journey to reestablish old ties, ties essential to survival in any meaningful sense. As the journey
continues the "I" becomes more inclusive as the speaker becomes increasingly able to merge with the nature around her.
Asked at poem's end "if I still smell winter / . . . I answer:"

> taste me
>   I am the wind
> touch me,
>   I am the lean brown deer
> running on the edge of the rainbow.
>                              (37)

The "desperation journey" has become a journey of self-
discovery, of finding one's being entire in the land. Now she
can travel spirit roads.

The wholeness of the relationship emerging from "Indian Song: Survival" enhances our understanding of what,
precisely, the young girl in "Storyteller" accomplishes. Her life
has been a desperate journey and her final awakening involves
the reestablishment of a vital, intimate connection to the land.
This is what the bear story requires of her. The poem also intensifies further the poignancy of Grandma A'mooh's last days
by compelling us to learn again the value of what, for her own
"good," had been taken from her.

Silko follows "Indian Song: Survival" with a painfully
enigmatic story from Aunt Susie, a Laguna "flood" story in
which a little girl and her younger sister return home to their
village after a day's play only to find it abandoned except for
"the old people / who cannot travel." Their mother and the
others went to the high place to escape the coming flood. If
"Indian Song: Survival" concerns the establishment of vital
relationships, this story tells of their being sundered. There
is a beauty in the girl's devotion to her sister as there is pain
in their mother's leaving them and these elements, devotion
and separation, are central to the short story, "Lullaby," which
follows.

If, as Momaday said, the greatest tragedy is to go unimagined, the title of Silko's "Lullaby" is in one sense bitterly ironic. Having been robbed of her grandchildren, Ayah, the old Navajo woman at the heart of the story, sings a song for them, a song that she remembers having been sung by her mother and grandmother. It is a beautiful song expressing with delicate economy the world view in which she was raised, and its closing words doubtlessly provide some consolation:

> We are together always
> We are together always
> There never was a time
> when this
> was not so.
>
> (51)

But we cannot forget that there are no children to hear it and, though Ayah's "life had become memories," those memories seem dominated now by the loss of children—of her son Jimmie in the war and the babies to the white doctors. For Silko, to go unremembered is to go unimagined, and in that sense Ayah's is a tragic story. Grandma A'mooh, in her last years, was taken from her grandchildren but she does not go unremembered. Such a fate, though, seems likely to befall Ayah, for her babies are taken not simply to make them well, but to make them white.

The "Survival" section, however, does not end on a hopeless note. Ayah's "lullaby" expresses a timeless harmony and peace which are reflected in the photograph which closes the section, taken from the sandhills a mile east of Laguna. The land seems whole and eternal here, and where that is so the people, and the oral tradition, will survive.

### III

But today, even the land is threatened. A photograph in what I will call the "Yellow Woman" section of *Storyteller* is of the Anaconda company's open-pit uranium mine. "This photograph," Silko tells us, "was made in the early 1960s. The mesas and hills that appear in the background and foreground are gone now, swallowed by the mine." This photograph deep-

162

ens our understanding of many things in *Storyteller*: of the importance of the photographs to the stories, for one thing, and of Silko's father's love of photography for another. "He is still most at home in the canyons and sandrock," she says, "and most of his life regular jobs / have been a confinement he has avoided." Some might think less of him for this, but Silko stifles this tendency—first by the story of Reed Woman and Corn Woman that precedes the reminiscence about her father and second by his photographs themselves, one of which is that of the now vanished mesas and hills. Moreover, his photography intensified his love of the land and enabled him to relate to it in new and fulfilling ways. We learn, for instance, that

> His landscapes could not be done
> without certain kinds of clouds—
>> some white and scattered like river rock
>> and others
>> mountains rolling into themselves
>> swollen lavender before rainstorms.
>
> (161)

Clouds, as we know, are a source of life itself to the land, and for Lee H. Marmon they bring to it a profound and varied beauty as well. Essential to the continuity of physical life, the clouds are no less essential to his spirit in that they help him express through his art his particular vision of the land and by so doing, to define himself in terms of it. Equally important, in these times, is that his artistry can help others, be they Indians removed from the land or people who have never known it, to develop a richer, more meaningful sense of the land than is held by such as those who run Anaconda. It is precisely the development of such a relationship—to the land, to the spirits that pervade it, and to the stories that derive from it—that occupies the "Yellow Woman" section of *Storyteller*.

The "Yellow Woman" section, comprised of the short story "Yellow Woman," four poems, poetic retellings of two traditional stories, four reminiscences, four photographs, and two "gossip stories,"[14] is framed by "Yellow Woman" and "Storytelling," a poem consisting of six brief vignettes based on the abduction motif of the traditional Yellow Woman stories. As does "Storyteller" in the "Survival" section, "Yellow Woman," and the traditional stories from which Silko's version evolves, establish the primary structural and thematic concerns of this section.

Based on the traditional stories in which Yellow Woman, on her way to draw water, is abducted by a mountain kachina, Silko's "Yellow Woman" concerns the development of the visionary character. This is hinted at in the story's epigram, "What Whirlwind Man Told Kochininako, Yellow Woman":

> I myself belong to the wind
> and so it is we will travel swiftly
> this whole world
> with dust and with windstorms. [15]

Whirlwind Man will take her on a journey beyond the boundaries of time and place, a journey alive with sensation and danger which promises a perspective from which she can see the world new and entire. This in effect is what happens in the story. Like the prophets and visionaries of many cultures, Indian and non-Indian, the narrator travels to the mountain where she learns to see beyond the range of mundane experience. She recalls that, at Silva's mountain cabin,

> I was standing in the sky with nothing around me but the wind that came down from the blue mountain peak behind me. I could see faint mountain images in the distance miles across the vast spread of mesas and valleys and plains. I wondered who was over there to feel the mountain wind on those sheer blue edges—who walks on the pine needles in those blue mountains.
> "Can you see the pueblo?" Silva was standing behind me.
> I shook my head. "We're too far away."
> "From here I can see the world."

The pueblo, which comprised her whole world before, is, from the perspective of the mountain, but a barely discernible part of a much larger whole. With Silva, on the mountain, she has entered the more expansive and truer realm of imagination and myth.

When we can see imaginatively, William Blake has said, when we can see not merely with but through the eye, "the whole creation will appear infinite and holy whereas it now appears finite and corrupt. This will come to pass by an improvement of sensual enjoyment" (*The Marriage of Heaven and Hell*, plate 14).[16] This is the narrator's experience. She follows a strong impulse in running off with Silva; desire moves her to leave the familiar, secure world of the pueblo and her family to walk a new and daring road. She opens her story in the morning, after she and Silva first made love:

> My thigh clung to his with dampness, and I watched the sun rising up through the tamaracks and willows. . . . I could hear the water, almost at our feet where the narrow fast channel bubbled and washed green ragged moss and fern leaves. I looked at him beside me, rolled in the red blanket on the white river sand.

She does not awaken to the proverbial harsh light of morning awash in guilt, but to a newly, more vibrantly alive world of sensation within and around her. But this is a world which, like Silva himself, is as frightening in its strength and intensity as it is seductive, and when Silva awakens she tells him she is leaving:

> He smiled now, eyes still closed. "You are coming with me, remember?" He sat up now with his bare dark chest and belly in the sun.
> "Where?"
> "To my place."
> "And will I come back?"
> He pulled his pants on. I walked away from him, feeling him behind me and smelling the willows.
> "Yellow Woman," he said.
> I turned to face him, "Who are you?" I asked.

Last night, he reminds her, "you guessed my name, and you knew why I had come." Their lovemaking made her intuitively aware of another, more vital level of being, one which had been within her all along, nurtured since childhood by her grandfather's Yellow Woman stories—and she knew she was Yellow Woman and her lover the dangerous mountain ka'tsina who carries her off.

But imaginative seeing on this morning after is threatening to the narrator, for seeing oneself whole demands eradication of those perceptual boundaries which offer the security of a readily discernible, if severely limited, sense of self. The narrator clings to that historical, time-bound sense of self like a child to her mother's skirts on the first day of school. "I'm not really her," she maintains, not really Yellow Woman. "I have my own name and I come from the pueblo on the other side of the mesa." It is not so much "confusion about what is dream and what is fact"[17] that besets her here as it is the fear of losing that reality which has heretofore defined her—and him. As they walk she thinks to herself:

> I will see someone, eventually I will see someone, and then I will be certain that he [Silva] is only a man—some man from nearby—and I will be sure that I am not Yellow Woman. Because she is from out of time past and I live now and I've been to school and there are highways and pickup trucks that Yellow Woman never saw.

Jim Ruppert is right, I think, when he says that the narrator "struggles to . . . establish time boundaries and boundaries between objective reality and myths,"[18] and that struggle is part of the learning process she undergoes in the story. Newly awakened to her own imaginative potential, she has yet to discern the proper relationship between experiential reality and the timeless, all-inclusive mythic reality of her grandfather's stories.

Her desire, however, is stronger than her fear. After they reach his cabin, eat, and she looks out over the world from the mountain, Silva unrolls the bedroll and spreads the blankets. She hesitates, and he slowly undresses her. There is compulsion, this time, on his part, and fear on hers, but she is held to him more by her own passion than by his force. When she does leave, during their confrontation with a rancher who, rightly, accuses Silva of stealing cattle, it is at his command. "I felt sad at leaving him," she recalls, and considers going back, "but the mountains were too far away now. And I told myself, because I believe it, that he will come back sometime and be waiting again by the river."

She returns home. Yellow Woman stories usually end that way. And as she approaches her house, A. Lavonne Ruoff tells us, "she is brought back to the realities of her own life by the smell of supper cooking and the sight of her mother instructing her grandmother in the Anglo art of making Jell-O."[19] The details here suggest a world governed more by routine than by passion, a world somewhat at odds with itself, as mother instructing grandmother suggests, and a world no longer receptive to the wonder and wisdom of the old stories. Having sensed this, she "decided to tell them that some Navajo had kidnapped me." But the unnamed narrator here, like the unnamed Eskimo girl in "Storyteller," keeps the oral tradition alive by going on her own journey of self-discovery—a journey born of acknowledging the rightful demands of passion and imagination—and by intuitively accepting the guidance of her grandfather's stories. He life itself has become part of a visionary drama to be completed by Silva's return, and within that context it has gained fullness and meaning. Her recognition, in the story's final sentence, that hers is a Yellow Woman story—and that she is Yellow Woman—reveals as much. She has come to see herself, in Momaday's words, "whole and eternal"[20] and like Momaday when, on his journey, he came out upon the northern plains, she will "never again . . . see things as [she] saw them yesterday or the day before."[21]

*Cottonwood,* which follows "Yellow Woman," is in two parts, each a poetic rendering of a Laguna Yellow Woman story; taken together, these poems and Silko's story provide a richer, more inclusive perspective than they do separately on both the relationship between oral tradition and the written word and Silko's use of the Yellow Woman character.

The focus in "Yellow Woman" is on the unnamed woman narrator. She tells her own story, which concerns her evolving consciousness of who she is, and though that story has definite communal implications, its focus is interior and personal. *Cottonwood,* however, though undeniably Silko's creation, derives directly from the oral tradition and retains that tradition's communal perspective.[22] Neither "Story of Sun House" nor "Buffalo Story," the poems that comprise *Cottonwood,* deal with character development or internal conflict any more than do the stories on which they are based. Rather each poem underscores the communal consequences of Yellow Woman's action, and in each case those consequences are positive. Given the narrator's references within "Yellow Woman" to the grandfather's Yellow Woman stories—indeed, Silko's story ends with such a reference—the *Cottonwood* poems, placed where they are, suggest that however offensive her actions may be to conventional morality, the narrator brings from her journey with Silva a boon for her people.

"Story of Sun House" ends as follows: "Cottonwood, / cottonwood. / So much depends / upon one in the great canyon." It is this tree, "among all the others" where Yellow Woman came to wait for the sun. Like the lone cottonwood, Yellow Woman too has been singled out, and much depends upon her as well. She is called by the Sun to journey to Sun House, and this involves the loss of what is familiar and secure and dear:

> She left precise stone rooms
> that hold the heart silently
> She walked past white corn
> hung in long rows from roof beams
> the dry husks rattled in a thin autumn wind.
>
> She left her home
>         her clan
>         and the people
>                 (three small children
>                 the youngest just weaned
>                 her husband away cutting firewood). . .
>                                         (64)

The sacrifice is great, and in the spare yet powerfully evocative images of these lines Silko conveys the intense pain of separation. Her versification here, with "home," "clan," and "people" isolated in separate lines and children and husband further isolated in parentheses to the right, makes such pain

168

almost palpable, as does the southeastward movement of the verse as it mirrors her journey toward the sun. Such "drastic things," however, "must be done / for the world / to continue." Harmony between the people and the spirit powers of the universe is necessary to existence and, through her marriage to the Sun, Yellow Woman perpetuates this harmony. The "people may not understand" her going; the visionary is invariably misunderstood. But that does not deter her, for she goes "out of love for this earth."

The narrator in "Yellow Woman," too, restores an essential harmony through her going—a going which is also likely to be misunderstood. Her experience in living the reality revealed in her grandfather's stories has shown her the oneness of past and present, of historical and mythic time, and of the stories and the people. More, she has given the people another story and that, too, "must be done / for the world / to continue."

Yellow Woman brings about good in "Buffalo Story" as well, and in a sense its link with Silko's short story is even stronger than that of "Story of Sun House." Like "Sun House," it enriches the short story by locating it for the reader within the necessary cultural and communal context, but "Buffalo Story" is itself enriched by the individualistic perspective cast forward upon it by "Yellow Woman." "Buffalo Story" follows the abduction storyline somewhat more closely than does "Story of Sun House" and evokes the sexual aspects of the traditional Yellow Woman stories more insistently. During a time of drought, when game is scarce and crops cannot grow, Yellow Woman, looking for water for her family, comes to a churning, muddy pool. At first she fears that a great animal had fouled the water. Then

> she saw him.
> She saw him tying his leggings
> drops of water were still shining on his chest.
> He was very good to look at
> and she kept looking at him
> because she had never seen anyone like him.
> It was Buffalo Man who was very beautiful.
> (69)

She has ventured far from her village, as has the narrator in
"Yellow Woman," and the intense sexual pull Buffalo Man has
on her here recalls that of Silva on the narrator. When Arrowboy, her husband, finds her asleep and calls to her to run to
him so that they might escape the Buffalo People, to whose
country Buffalo Man had abducted her, "She seemed to / get
up a little slowly / but he didn't think much of it then." Her
slowness here, he later learns, is not due to fatigue. After he
kills all the Buffalo People, he tells Yellow Woman to go tell the
people that there is meat, but she refuses to come down from
the cottonwood which they had climbed to escape the Buffalo
People's pursuit. Arrowboy sees that she is crying and asks her
why:

> "Because you killed them,"
> > she said.
> "I suppose you love them,"
> > Estoy-eh-muut [Arrowboy] said,
> "and you want to stay with them."
> And Kochininako nodded her head
> and then he killed her too.
> > (75)

Paula Gunn Allen, while acknowledging the underlying centrality of oral tradition in the lives of tribal people, nonetheless
maintains that "the oral tradition is often deceptive in what it
makes of the lives of women." She says that

> so cleverly disguised are the tales of matricide, abduction and
> humiliation that the Indian woman is likely to perceive con-
> sciously only the surface message of the beauty, fragility, and
> self-sacrificing strength of her sisters though she cannot help
> but get the more destructive message that is the point of
> many tribal tales.[23]

Such a "destructive message" is at least potentially present in
the "Buffalo Man" story in Boas' *Keresan Texts*, but Silko casts
the killing of Yellow Woman in "Buffalo Story" in a much different light. In Boas's version, when Arrowboy explains to

170

Yellow Woman's father why he killed her, the Chief says, "Indeed? . . ." "All right," said he, "never mind." His response seems to justify the killing.[24] In "Buffalo Story" her father, though implicitly accepting the justice of what was done, cries and mourns. Moreover, in Silko's rendering we are told that "It was all because / one time long ago / our daughter, our sister Kochininako / went away with them" that the people were fed and buffalo hunting began. Yellow Woman here is not an adultress who deserted her people but rather remains "our daughter, our sister" whose journey, like her journey in "Story of Sun House," brought good to her people.[25]

The context here established by the written word— Silko's short story—is essential in helping us to see Yellow Woman more completely than do the traditional stories alone, just as those stories in turn provide the necessary cultural context for "Yellow Woman." Through the narrator's telling in Silko's story, the individual dimension predominates and personal longings are shown to be as powerful and worthwhile as communal needs. Silko well knows, as the *Cottonwood* poems make clear, that individual sacrifice is at times crucial to community survival. But, as "Yellow Woman" reveals, individual fulfillment can be equally important to a tribal community, especially in the modern world where acculturation pressures are perhaps greater than ever before. Silko shows us, in this opening sequence of the "Yellow Woman" section, that personal and communal fulfillment need not be mutually exclusive—that they in fact enhance each other. And, by extension, the same is true of oral tradition and the written word as ways of knowing and of expression. To attain this harmony requires a powerful and inclusive vision, one receptive both to internal and external demands and the diverse languages which give them meaning. The development of such a vision, and of the network of relationships to the land, the people, the stories, and oneself it fosters, is, as I have said, the controlling idea of what I have called the "Yellow Woman" section of *Storyteller*, and it is expressed in various ways in the narrative episodes that follow.

The five short pieces that follow "Yellow Woman" and the *Cottonwood* poems focus on learning to see the land

rightly and developing the proper relationship to it. This learning process is implicit in the narrator's experience in "Yellow
Woman," both in her journey with Silva up the mountain and
in the precise, evocative detail in which she describes particular aspects of the landscape; it becomes refined and expanded
in these brief narratives. In the first one, a poem entitled "The
Time We Climbed Snake Mountain," the narrator is a teacher
who knows the mountain intimately and knows that "Somewhere around here / yellow spotted snake is sleeping": "So /
please, I tell them / watch out, / don't step on the spotted yellow snake / he lives here. / The mountain is his" (77). "Them"
are never identified, but that is unimportant because this kind
of teaching has been going on for thousands of years. It is a
simple lesson in perspective and respect.

What follows is a personal reminiscence which in a different way reinforces this lesson. It is of Silko's girlhood when
she first learned to hunt, and through her telling we learn
something of how she began to acquire the wisdom she hands
down in "The Time We Climbed Snake Mountain." Hunting
alone one day Silko saw, or thought she saw, a "giant brown
bear lying in the sun below the hilltop. Dead or just sleeping,
I couldn't tell." She "knew there were no bears that large on
Mt. Taylor; I was pretty sure there were no bears that large
anywhere," and she also knew "what hours of searching for
motion, for the outline of a deer, for the color of a deer's hide
can do to the imagination." Almost paralyzed with caution and
curiosity, eager to examine the bear up close but unsure if it
is dead or is just sleeping or is at all, she walks, "as quietly and
as carefully as I probably will ever move," away from it. As she
goes she looks back, still unsure of what she has seen, and
"the big dark bear remained there. . . ." "I never told anyone
what I had seen," Silko laughingly recalls, "because I knew
they don't let people who see such things carry .30-30s or hunt
deer with them" (78).

That the bear impressed itself deeply on her imagination, however, is apparent as she recalls another hunting trip
which took place two years after the first one. Her uncle had
killed a big mule deer, and, as Silko went to help him, she
realized that it was the same time of day as when she saw, or
thought she saw, the bear:

I walked past the place deliberately.
I found no bones, but when a wind moved through the
light yellow grass that afternoon I hurried around the
hill to find my uncle.
Sleeping, not dead, I decided.

(79)

At this point, there is no longer any doubt in her mind that the
bear was real; and her use of poetic form further suggests that
this place where she saw the great bear has become part of an
inner as well as an outer landscape. Through an act of imagination she has learned a profound truth from the land which
intensifies her bond to it.

The photograph which separates these two reminiscences reinforces this idea. In it, laid out on the porch of the
old cabin in which Silko and her hunting party stayed on
Mt. Taylor, are five mule deer bucks, prayer feathers tied to
their antlers, Silko herself, and her Uncle Polly. She and her
uncle had just finished "arranging the bucks . . . so they can
have their pictures taken." Given the "special significance" of
photographs to her family and to the people of Laguna, the
careful arrangement of the deer, and the prayer feathers, we
are prepared for the subtle revelation in her second reminiscence. Her vision of the bear, like the deer, was a gift to help
the people survive. It was the intimate expression of the land
to her imagination of its own spiritual integrity and that of its
creatures. Through the mystery and wonder of her seeing, the
land impressed itself indelibly upon her memory.

Two photographs follow the second bear reminiscence.
The first, discussed earlier, is of hills and mesas that no longer
exist and, placed where it is in *Storyteller,* the photograph
movingly conveys the need, more important now than ever
before, for all people to know the land as the place that gives
us being and the source of our profoundest wisdom. It reminds
us, as does *Storyteller* as a whole, about the oral tradition—of
the fragility of what was once thought whole and eternal and
of how much all life ultimately depends on imagination and
memory. The second photo, taken from the east edge of Laguna looking toward the west, enhances this idea by showing
us the place from which the stories in *Storyteller,* old and

173

contemporary, arise. What follows is a series of such stories and reminiscences unified not by subject or theme but by the shared landscape that nurtured them. They express the richness, diversity, playfulness and humor of Laguna oral tradition. Like the first of these two photographs, they also express its fragility.

The first story which follows these photographs is a poetic retelling of a hunting story Silko, when a child of seven, heard from her Aunt Alice. It flows smoothly out of the photograph of Laguna in that it endows a particular portion of the land with mystery and wonder, and by so doing makes it a gift of and to the imagination. Though she heard this story six years before she saw the great bear on a hunting trip, the story flows out of her recollection of this experience as well; and by using cyclic rather than chronological structure, she more strikingly evokes, as with the "Yellow Woman" and *Cottonwood* sequence, the timeless significance of the oral tradition to the understanding of human experience. Told, as are other such stories in the book, in the conversational accents and occasional expository digressions of the traditional storyteller, the story is again of Yellow Woman, here a young girl and a fine hunter who, having gotten seven big rabbits in a morning's hunting, comes upon "a great big animal" who asks for one of her rabbits, which he immediately devours. The animal's demands escalate with his appetite and they are rendered by Silko in a compellingly dramatic sequence as the animal, having demanded and received all the girl's rabbits and weapons, insists upon her clothes as well. Rightly fearful that she herself will be next, little Yellow Woman fools the animal into letting her remove her clothes in a cave too small for him to enter. Knowing, however, that her escape is at best temporary, she calls upon the twin Brothers, Ma'see'wi and Ou'yu'ye'wi, who kill the animal with their flint knives. They then cut the animal open, pull out his heart, and throw it. At this point in the telling the legend melds with contemporary reality, myth enters experience, as we are told that the heart landed "right over here / near the river / between Laguna and Paguate / where the road turns to go / by the railroad tracks / right around / from John Paisona's place— / that big rock there /

looks just like a heart, / . . . and that's why / it is called / Yash'ka / which means 'heart'" (87–88).

By telling this story to her seven-year-old niece, who is disappointed at not having been allowed to join her parents on a hunting trip, Aunt Alice both entertains and teaches. She raises the child's self-esteem by showing her that young girls can be skillful and clever hunters, alerts the prospective young hunter to the unexpected dangers that at times confront a hunter, reassures her that such obstacles, however dangerous, may be overcome, and perhaps most importantly, helps her niece to see the land with the same sense of wonder and joy with which she heard the story. A part of the landscape heretofore ordinary and unremarked has by means of the story been made precious to the child. Six years later, when she sees the giant bear, Silko will have her own hunting story to tell—and Aunt Alice's story will be recalled anew, recreated as it is here, richer and truer than ever.

The story told by a loving aunt of a special place engenders a reminiscence of another place which is special because of the woman who may, or may not, be buried there. With this reminiscence Silko shifts her focus from the land per se to the people—more precisely, to how people get remembered. This reminiscence concerns two women. Silko's great-grandmother, Helen, was born of an old traditional family, and Silko recalls that "even as a very young child / I sensed she did not like children much and so I remembered her / from a distance . . ." (88). Much dearer to memory is a woman Silko never knew, old Juana, of whom Silko learned from the stories of Grandma Lillie, one of Helen's daughters. Juana, who "raised Grandma Lillie and her sisters / and brothers," was not born into a "genteel tradition" as was Grandma Helen. A Navajo, "Juana had been kidnapped by slavehunters / who attacked her family." Stripped of her family, of whom no trace remained, her language, and her heritage, Juana "continued with the work she knew" and was eventually hired by Silko's Grandpa Stagner to care for his family. Silko recalls going on Memorial Day with Grandma Lillie to take flowers to Juana's grave. The graveyard where she was buried was old and the "small flat sandstones" which served as grave markers were mostly broken or covered over; as a result Grandma Lillie could never be certain if they found her grave—"but we left the jar of roses and lilacs we had cut anyway." Juana's actual presence, like the giant bear's in the earlier hunting story, is ultimately irrelevant. As the bear lives in Silko's imagination, so Juana lives in her, and in Grandma Lillie's heart, where they have more perfect being.[26] Though orphaned young, Juana is restored through the stories to a family, language, and heritage.

Juana is remembered for her loving kindness, but that is not the only way people get remembered. The tone shifts rather suddenly from the reminiscence about Juana to two "gossip" stories, both of them rich in humor and irony. The first story, of a man caught en flagrante in a cornfield by his wife and her two sisters, and Silko's telling of it—in which she uses the storyteller's conversational tone and shifts the point of view from the two lovers to the wife and sisters and then to the man alone—express a delicious comic blend of conspiracy, anticipation, antagonism and resignation. She dramatically sets the scene: "His wife had caught them together before / and probably she had been hearing rumors again / the way people talk" (89). The lovers planned to meet in the afternoon, when it was so hot that "everyone just rested" until evening, when it was cool enough to return to work. "This man's wife was always / watching him real close at night / so afternoon was / the only chance they had" (90). When they were caught the woman left, and the man had to take the inevitable chastisement alone. His "wife would cry a little," her sisters would comfort her, "and then they would start talking again / about how good their family had treated him / and how lucky he was. / He couldn't look at them / so he looked at the sky / and then over at the hills behind the village" (91). Though the man's inability to look at the women may suggest guilt, his wandering gaze has something of boredom in it, as if he were merely playing a role in an ancient and rather tiresome domestic ritual. His manhood is not spared, as the women are quick to remind him that his lover "had a younger boyfriend / and it was only afternoons that she had any use / for an old man":

> So pretty soon he started hoeing weeds again
> because they were ignoring him

>like he didn't matter anyway
>now that
>that woman was gone.
>
>(92)

The irony here is rich. The man, it seems, is important to his wife and relatives, and perhaps to the community as a whole, only by virtue of his infidelity. It is this by which he lives in a communal memory, enriches the storytelling life of the people, and gains mythic dimension. Apart from that context he "didn't matter."

"Then there was the night," Silko gleefully continues, whetting our appetite for the story of old man George who, on a trip to the outhouse, "heard strange sounds / coming from one of the old barns / below." Checking, "just in case some poor animal / was trapped inside," the old man is shocked to discover Frank.

>so respectable and hard-working
>and hardly ever drunk—
>well there he was
>naked with that Garcia girl—
>you know,
>the big fat one.
>And here it was
>the middle of winter
>without their clothes on!
>
>(92–93)

Silko's tone here expresses two points of view simultaneously. George, to say the least, is surprised to find a man like Frank in this situation and Silko, as storyteller, relishes the irony. Further, she creates the proper context here by giving us, through her "you know" aside, a sense of her immediate audience—another young person, perhaps, to whom Frank would be cited by conventional morality as an example to follow. "Poor old man George / he didn't know what to say," and his befuddlement is comically rendered in the story's closing lines: "so he just closed the door again / and walked back home— / he even forgot where he was going / in the first place." But he'll remember Frank and the Garcia girl.

It may at first glance seem strange that these stories are followed by a brief recollection of Grandma A'mooh and the way she read the children's book *Brownie the Bear* to her great-granddaughters, especially since "Storytelling," which follows, consists of six vignettes largely in the same vein as the "gossip" stories. This reminiscence, however, mentioned earlier in another context, is wonderfully appropriate here. Taken in conjunction with the "gossip" stories that surround it, it reminds us again of the variety and inclusiveness of the oral tradition. It also underscores Silko's intent throughout *Storyteller* to convey the dynamic relationship between the oral tradition and the life it expresses. The life of a community, or of an individual, does not arrange itself into precise categories, literary or otherwise, nor does it follow neat, unbroken lines of development; and Silko, by juxtaposing different kinds of narratives and subjects, helps us to see vital, rewarding connections that might otherwise go unnoticed. Remember, too, that her emphasis in the "Grandma A'mooh" reminiscence is on how a story is told. A good story cannot exist apart from a good storyteller. Much of the fun of the "gossip" stories, as we have seen, is in Silko's manner of telling them. Grandma A'mooh.

> always read the story with such animation and expression
> changing her tone of voice and inflection
> each time one of the bears spoke—
> the way a storyteller would have told it.

(93)

Her telling makes the story live, recreates it in effect with each repetition. This is what Silko, in the "gossip" stories as well as in others, tries to do, to give a sense of the flux and immediacy of life lived. Too, it is her telling which links Grandma A'mooh to past generations of storytellers—as it does Silko.

The six vignettes in "Storytelling," all variations on the Yellow Woman abduction stories, bring what I have called the "Yellow Woman" section of *Storyteller* full circle. The first of

178

these is Silko's abbreviated rendering of the opening of the "Buffalo Story," when Yellow Woman goes for water:

> "Are you here already?"
> "Yes," he said.
> He was smiling.
> "Because I came for you."
> She looked into the
> shallow clear water.
> "But where shall I put my water jar?"
> (95)

In this version Yellow Woman is apparently expecting Buffalo Man, and though coercion might be implied when he says he came for her, her response is willing, even coy and playful. The tone of the fifth vignette is quite similar:

> Seems like
> its always happening to me.
> Outside the dance hall door
> late Friday night
> in the summertime.
> and those
> brown-eyed men from Cubero,
> smiling.
> They usually ask me
> "Have you seen the way the stars shine
> up there in the sands hills?"
> And I usually say "No. Will you show me?"
> (97)

Silko alerts us as "Storytelling" begins that we "should understand / the way it was / back then, / because it is the same / even now" (94). The traditional stories, Silko is saying, both here and throughout *Storyteller,* offer profound and necessary insights into contemporary experiences. Specifically, the "Yellow Woman" stories, especially Silko's renderings of them, are among other things open, unqualified expressions of woman's sexuality. This is not to say that, because the traditional stories are abduction stories, Silko is dealing in rape fantasies. Quite the contrary. In her versions the coercive element, though present, is not the controlling one. Yellow Woman is at all times in charge of her own destiny. She understands and accepts her sexuality, expresses it honestly, and is guided by her own strong desire. We see this in Silko's short story, "Yellow Woman," in the *Cottonwood* stories, and again in these two "Storytelling" vignettes. By focusing in these little narratives not on the lovemaking but on the prelude to it, Silko establishes the sexual integrity of both the mythic and contemporary Yellow Woman, and conveys with playful subtlety the charged eroticism between them and Buffalo Man and "those / brown-eyed men from Cubero" respectively.

Yellow Woman's sexual integrity gets a broadly comic touch in the fourth vignette, where Silko inverts the traditional abduction motif. The F.B.I. and state police in the summer of 1967 pursued a red '56 Ford with four Laguna women and three Navajo men inside. A kidnapping was involved, and the police followed a trail "of wine bottles and / size 42 panties / hanging in bushes and trees / all along the road." When they were caught, one of the men explained: "'We couldn't escape them' . . . / 'We tried, but there were four of them and / only three of us'" (96).

But sexual honesty, especially a woman's, is, as we have seen, likely to be misunderstood. In the first *Cottonwood* poem, "Story of Sun House," the Sun tells Yellow Woman that even though their union is necessary for the world to continue, "the people may not understand"; and the narrator in "Yellow Woman" must make up a story for her family about being kidnapped by a Navajo. In fact, the abduction motif of the Yellow Woman stories proves useful, or almost so, in a number of situations. "No! that gossip isn't true," says a distraught mother in the third "Storytelling" vignette: "She didn't elope / She was *kidnapped* by / that Mexican / at Seama Feast. / You know / my daughter / isn't / *that* kind of girl" (95–96). As was stated earlier, however, there cannot be a good story without a good storyteller, as the contemporary Yellow Woman of the sixth vignette learns. "It was / that Navajo / from Alamo, / you know, / the tall / good-looking / one," she tells her husband. "He told me / he'd kill me / if I didn't / go with him." That, rain, and muddy roads, she said, are why "it took me / so long / to get back home." When her husband leaves her, she blames herself: "I could have told / the story / better than I did" (97–98).

In a *Sun-Tracks* interview, Silko said of "these gossip stories": "I don't look upon them as gossip. The connotation is all wrong. These stories about goings-on, about what people are up to, give identity to a place."[27] What she argues for here is in effect what the "Yellow Woman" section is all about: a new way of seeing. Seen rightly, such stories are neither idle rumor nor trivial chatter, but are rather another mode of expression, a way in which people define themselves and declare who they are. Thus it is fitting that the "Yellow Woman" section, and this essay, conclude with a photograph taken of some of the houses in Laguna. Here, after all, is where the people live their lives and it is this sense of life being lived, of life timeless and ongoing, changing and evolving, contradictory and continuous, that Silko expresses with grace and power through her melding of oral tradition and the written word in *Storyteller.*

## ☐ *Notes* ■

Much of the work for this study was done with the generous support of the University of Kansas General Research Fund.

1. Larry Evers and Denny Carr, "A Conversation with Leslie Marmon Silko," *"Sun Tracks,* vol. 3, no. 1 (Fall 1976), 30.

2. Speaking to students at Laguna-Acoma High School, Silko said, "Our greatest natural resource is stories and storytelling. We have an endless, continuing, ongoing supply of stories." Per Seyersted, "Two Interviews with Leslie Marmon Silko," *American Studies in Scandinavia* 13 (1981), 21.

3. All quotations from *Storyteller* are taken from the 1981 Seaver edition.

4. The Navajo, for example, "believe that the life and power of their mythology depends upon its being retained in the memory of the people and that to record the mythology is . . . to take away its vitality." Sam D. Gill, *Sacred Words: A Study of Navajo Religion and Prayer,* Contributions in Intercultural and Comparative Studies 4 (Westport, Connecticut: Greenwood Press, 1981), 49.

5. Silko mentions this conversation with Nora in Evers and Carr, 31.

6. Priscilla Wald, rev. of Leslie Marmon Silko's *Storyteller, SAIL,* vol. 6, no. 4 (Fall 1982), 19.

7. *Orality and Literacy: The Technologizing of the Word* (New York: Methuen, 1982), 148.

8. "The Man Made of Words" in *The Remembered Earth,* edited by Geary Hobson (Albuquerque: Red Earth Press, 1979), 167.

9. Let me emphasize that the section titles used here and elsewhere in this essay are of my own devise and meant solely to identify with facility the specific groups of narratives I have chosen to consider.

10. Per Seyersted, *Leslie Marmon Silko,* Boise State University Western Writer's Series 45 (Boise, Idaho: Boise State University Press, 1980), 38.

11. *The Remembered Earth,* p. 170.

12. *Ceremony* in fact had its genesis in a short story Silko began to write while she was in Alaska. Seyersted, *Leslie Marmon Silko,* 25–26.

13. Dexter Fisher, ed., *The Third Woman: Minority Women Writers of the United States.* (Boston: Houghton Mifflin, 1980), p. 22.

14. Evers and Carr, 29; Silko at first refers to "the gossip stories," but then quickly rejects this label: "No, I don't look upon them as gossip. The connotation is all wrong. These stories about goings-on, about what people are up to, give identity to a place."

15. Only in the *Storyteller* version of "Yellow Woman" is this short poem used as an epigram. A. LaVonne Ruoff provides a brief but useful summary, derived from Boas, of the nature and structure of the "Yellow Woman" stories. She also points out the enigmatic nature of Whirlwind Man, "who may be either an evil kachina or who may live among the good kachinas at Wenimatse. . . ." "Ritual and Renewal: Keres Traditions in the Short Fiction of Leslie Silko," *MELUS,* vol. 5, no. 4 (Winter, 1978), 10.

16. David V. Erdman, ed., *The Complete Poetry and Prose of William Blake* (Garden City, N.Y.: Anchor Press/Doubleday, 1982), 39.

17. Ruoff, 13.

18. "Story Telling: The Fiction of Leslie Silko," *The Journal of Ethnic Studies* 9 (Spring 1981), 53.

19. Ruoff, 14.

20. *The Way to Rainy Mountain* (Albuquerque: University of New Mexico Press, 1969), 12.

21. *The Way to Rainy Mountain*, 17.

22. Karl Kroeber, writing of Dennis Tedlock's "The Spoken Word and the Work of Interpretation in American Indian Religion," says that Tedlock "shows that a Zuni story *continues* precisely because each reciter is a reviser." "An Introduction to the Art of Traditional American Indian Narration," *Traditional American Literatures: Texts and Interpretations*, edited by Karl Kroeber (Lincoln: University of Nebraska Press, 1981), 21. The same may be said of the Laguna stories Silko "revises" in *Cottonwood* and elsewhere in *Storyteller*.

23. "'The Grace That Remains'—American Indian Women's Literature," *Book Forum*, vol. 5, no. 3 (1981), p. 381.

24. Franz Boas, ed., *Keresan Texts*, Volume VIII (New York: Publications of the American Ethnological Society, 1928), 122–127.

25. The changes Silko makes, of course, might well derive from a version of the story she herself had heard. In any case, Silko recalls, elsewhere in *Storyteller*, that "Aunt Susie and Aunt Alice would tell me stories they had told me before but with changes in details or descriptions. The story was the important thing and little changes here and there were really part of the story." In the oral tradition variants do not constitute a problem, as they often do where writing is concerned. Rather they are renewals which invigorate the tradition. Silko goes on to say, "I've heard tellers begin 'The way I heard it was . . .' and then proceed with another story purportedly a version of a story just told but the story they would tell was a . . . new story with an integrity of its own, an offspring, a part of the continuing which storytelling must be" (227).

26. It is as Momaday says of his grandmother and of his need to retrace the Kiowa migration: "Although my grandmother lived out her long life in the shadow of Rainy Mountain, the immense landscape of the continental interior lay like memory in her blood. . . . I wanted to see in reality what she had seen more perfectly in the mind's eye," *The Way to Rainy Mountain*, 7.

27. Evers and Carr, 29.

□ ARNOLD KRUPAT ■

# The Dialogic of
# Silko's *Storyteller*

Autobiography as commonly understood in western European and Euro-American culture did not exist as a traditional type of literary expression among the aboriginal peoples of North America. Indeed, none of the conditions of production for autobiography—here I would isolate post–Napoleonic historicism, egocentric individualism and writing as foremost—was typical of Native American cultures.[1] To the extent that the life stories, personal histories, memoirs or recollections of Indians did finally come into textual form (traditional Indian literatures were not written but oral), it was as a result of contact with and pressure from Euro-Americans. Until the twentieth century the most common form of Native American autobiography was the Indian autobiography, a genre of American writing constituted by the principle of original, bicultural, composite composition, in which there is a distinct if not always clear division of labor between the subject of the autobiography (the Indian to whom the first-person pronoun ostensibly makes reference) and the Euro-American editor responsible for fixing the text in writing, yet whose presence the first-person pronoun ostensibly masks. Indian autobiography may thus be distinguished from autobiography by Indians, the life stories of those christianized and/or "civilized" natives who, having internalized Western culture and scription, committed their lives to writing on their own without the mediation of the Euro-American. In autobiographies by Indians,

---

From *Narrative Chance: Postmodern Discourse on Native American Literatures,* ed. Gerald Vizenor (Albuquerque: University of New Mexico Press, 1989), 55–68.

although there is inevitably an element of biculturalism, there is not the element of compositeness that precisely marks Indian autobiographies.

The earliest examples of Native American autobiography are two by Indians dating from the decades surrounding the American Revolution. These did not attract much attention; indeed, the more extensive of the two by Hendrick Aupaumut was not even published until 1827 and then in a journal of rather limited circulation.[2] It was only six years later, however that the first Indian autobiography, J. B. Patterson's *Life of Black Hawk,* appeared. This book did gain widespread notice, coming as it did at a time of increased American interest in Indians (the book was occasioned by the last Indian war to be fought east of the Mississippi) and in the type of writing then only recently named autobiography (in 1809 by the poet Southey). Both of these interests are developed in this earliest type of Indian autobiography, which presents the acts of the world-historical chief or (of particular concern in the first half of the nineteenth century) the Indian hero. The historical orientation of Indian autobiography persisted in some form into the 1930s and 1940s after which none of the warriors was left alive to tell his tale. By that time there had already occurred a shift of interest on the part of Euro-American editors from history to science. In the twentieth century professional anthropologists rather than amateur historians would most commonly edit Indian autobiographies.

In our time Indian autobiographies continue to be co-produced by historians and social scientists working with traditional native people, but their labors have very nearly been overshadowed by the autobiographical writing of a new generation of Indians, educated in Western literate forms yet by no means acculturated to the point of abandoning respect for the old ways. These autobiographies are not only contributions to historical and scientific record, but also works of art (particularly the autobiographies of N. Scott Momaday and Leslie Marmon Silko, whose claim to national attention came not from their relation to American religion, history or anthropology, but from their relation to American literature as previously established in their fiction and poetry).

The history of Native American autobiography could be

186

charted thematically as a movement from history and science to art on a line parallel to the history of European and Euro-American autobiography.[3] To chart it thus would demonstrate that Native Americans have had to make a variety of accommodations to the dominant culture's forms, capitulating to them, assimilating them, sometimes dramatically transforming them, but never able to proceed independent of them. However, Native American autobiography differs materially from western European and Euro-American (though not strictly western American) autobiography through its existence in specifically individual and composite forms, or, both monologic and dialogic forms.[4]

To introduce the terms monologue and dialogue is to invoke an important recent development in literary theory: recent interest in the Russian theorist, Mikhail Bakhtin.

So much has been written on Bakhtin of late that any attempt to summarize his thought is bound to be incomplete.[5] In this country, at least, what is generally understood by reference to "Bakhtin," is very far from settled. To be sure "Freud" and "Marx" mean different things to different people as well; but there seems to be for Bakhtin, more than for these other major thinkers (and it is by no means generally agreed that comparison of Bakhtin to major thinkers is justified), a pronounced ambiguity. This openness may be functional, a practical illustration of what has been theoretically proposed. Perhaps it is not so much "openness," that Bakhtin's writing exhibits, but such inconsistency and ambiguity that it is difficult or pointless to specify the particulars of his thought. Hence, any attempt at an approximately neutral summary automatically becomes partial, a choice not between nuances but real differences. Nevertheless, the following briefly outlines what is at issue in Bakhtin and therefore at issue in any Bakhtinian reading of Native American autobiography.

Bakhtin calls human language "heteroglossic, polyvocal," the speech of each individual enabled and circumscribed not so much by language as a *system* as by the actual speech of other individuals. (In this he differs from Saussurian structural linguistics and its fascination with *langue*.) Speech is social and meaning is open and in flux, inevitably a dialogue among speakers, not the property or in the power of any single speaker. ". . . . [A]ll there is to know about the world is not exhausted by a particular discourse about it . . . ,"[6] Bakhtin notes in a typical statement. Still some forms of written discourse and social practice seek to impose a single authoritative voice as the norm, thus subordinating or entirely suppressing other voices. It is the genre Bakhtin calls the "epic" that provides models of this monologic tendency in literature, while the totalitarianism of Stalinism under which Bakhtin lived provides the socio-political model of monologism. In opposition to the totalizing thrust of the epic, the novel testifies to its own (inevitable) incompleteness, its ongoing indebtedness to the discourse of others. The novel is the prime literary instance of dialogized speech.

Bakhtin seems to be committed to dialogue on empirical grounds, inasmuch as the term claims to name human communication correctly, pointing to the way speech and social life "really" are. But Bakhtin seems also to be committed to dialogue on moral and esthetic grounds; he approves of and is pleased by that which he finds di-, hetero-, poly-, and so on. For him, truth and beauty are one, but what this equivalence is to mean ultimately in a dialogic theory of language and of social life remains to be determined.

Does Bakhtinian dialogic envision a strong form of pluralism in which all have legitimate voice: truth having its particular authority, beauty having its, and both having equal (cognitive) force over other voices, which, although worthy of being heard, can be judged decidably less forceful? Or does Bakhtinian dialogic envision a kind of postmodernist free play of voices with no normative means for deciding their relative worth or authority? We do not know whether Bakhtin's dislike of what he calls monologue permits some forms of relatively stable assertion, in particular truth and beauty. Such statements as "the last word is never said"—and there are innumerable such statements in Bakhtin's writing—may intend a radically ironic, a schizophrenic refusal (in Jameson's very particular sense)[7] of any form, however relativized, of grounded meaning. Or they may insist only that no single language act has the capacity to encompass the entire range of humanly possible meaning, as no single mode of political organization can give full latitude to human potential.

In this latter regard the issue is particularly complicated because, while we do know from Bakhtin that the novel is supposed to provide the fullest literary illustration of relativized, dialogic discourse, we do not know whether the nearest thing he gives us to a socio-political equivalent of the novel, Rabelaisian "carnival," represents an actual model for social organization or an escape from too rigid social organization. In either case, we do not know what Bakhtinian carnival might actually entail for current or future social formations. To examine Native American autobiography from a Bakhtinian perspective, then, is not only to consider it as a discursive type—a kind of literature, generically closer to the epic or the novel as Bakhtin understands these Western forms—but as a social model which allows for the projection of a particular image of human community.

Let me now offer a reading of Leslie Marmon Silko's *Storyteller* in relation to these issues.

Merely to consider *Storyteller* among Native American autobiographies might require some explanation, since the book is a collection of stories, poems and photographs as much as it is a narrative of its author's life. Of course a variety of claims have been made in the recent past for the fictionality of autobiographies in general, the autobiography being recognized as the West's most obviously dialogic genre in which a conversation between *historia* and *poesis,* documentation and creation, is always in progress. And some of these claims might easily be used to justify classifying *Storyteller* as an autobiography.

Indeed, to justify the book's classification as an autobiography in this way, would not be mistaken; it would, however, be to treat it exclusively from a Western perspective, failing to acknowledge that traditional Native American literary forms were not—and, in their contemporary manifestations usually are not—as concerned about keeping fiction and fact or poetry and prose distinct from one another. It is the distinction between truth and error rather than that between fact and fiction that seems more interesting to native expression; and indeed, this distinction was also central to Western thought prior to the seventeenth century. Thus the present "blurring of genres," in Clifford Geertz's phrase,[8] in both the social sciences and in the arts, is actually only a return to that time when the line between history and myth was not very clearly marked. But that is the way things have always been for Native American literatures.

From the Western point of view, Silko's book would seem to announce by its title, *Storyteller,* the familiar pattern of discovering who one is by discovering what one does, the pattern of identity in vocation. This is useful enough as a way to view Silko's text. In the West it has been a very long time since the vocational storyteller has had a clear and conventional social role. In Pueblo culture, however, to be known as a storyteller is to be known as one who participates, in a communally sanctioned manner, in sustaining the group; for a Native American writer to identify herself as a storyteller today is to express a desire to perform such a function. In the classic terms of Marcel Mauss, person, self and role are here joined.[9]

Silko dedicates her book "to the storytellers as far back as memory goes and to the telling which continues and through which they all live and we with them." Having called herself a storyteller, she thus places herself in a tradition of tellings, suggesting that her stories cannot strictly be her own nor will we find in them what one typically looks for in post–Rousseauan, Western autobiography or (as Bakhtin would add, in poetry) a uniquely personal voice. There is no single, distinctive or authoritative voice in Silko's book nor any striving for such a voice; to the contrary, Silko will take pains to indicate how even her own individual speech is the product of many voices. *Storyteller* is presented as a strongly polyphonic text in which the author defines herself—finds her voice, tells her life, illustrates the capacities of her vocation—in relation to the voices of other native and nonnative storytellers, tale tellers and book writers, and even to the voices of those who serve as the (by-no-means silent) audience for these stories.

It is Silko's biographical voice that commences the

book, but not by speaking of her birth or the earliest recollections of childhood as Western autobiography usually dictates. Rather, she begins by establishing the relation of "hundreds of photographs taken since the 1890s around Laguna" that she finds in "a tall Hopi basket" to "the stories as [she] remembers them."[10] Visual stories, speaking pictures, here as in the familiar Western understanding will also provide a voice; and Silko's developing relation to every kind of story becomes the story of her life.

Dennis Tedlock has made the important point that Zuni stories are fashioned in such a way as to include in their telling not just the story itself but a critique of or commentary on those stories, and Silko's autobiographical story will also permit a critical dimension, voices that comment on stories and storytellers—storytellers like her Aunt Susie, who, when she told stories had "certain phrases, certain distinctive words / she used in her telling" (7). Both Aunt Susie and Aunt Alice "would tell me stories they had told me before but with changes in details or descriptions. . . . There were even stories about the different versions of stories and how they imagined these differing versions came to be" (227). Silko's own versions of stories she has heard from Simon Ortiz, the Acoma writer whom Silko acknowledges as the source of her prose tale, "Uncle Tony's Goat," and her verse tale, "Skeleton Fixer," also introduce certain phrases and distinctive words that make them identifiably her own. Yet these and all the other stories are never presented as the final or definitive version; although they are intensely associated with their different tellers, they remain available for other tellings.[11] "What is realized in the novel," Bakhtin has written, "is the process of coming to know one's own language as it is perceived in someone else's language" (365) and so, too, to know one's own language as bound up with "someone else's language." Any story Silko herself tells, then, is always bound up with someone else's language; it is always a version and the story as version stands in relation to the story as officially sanctioned myth, as the novel stands to the national epic. Silko's stories are always consistent with—to return to Bakhtin—attempts to liberate "cultural-semantic and emotional intentions from the hegemony of a single and unitary language," consistent with a "loss of feeling for language as myth, that is, as an absolute form of thought" (367).

Stories are transmitted by other storytellers, as Silko wrote early in her book:

> by word of mouth
> an entire history
> an entire vision of the world
> which depended upon memory
> and retelling by subsequent generations.
> . . . . . . . . . . . . . . . . . . . . . . . . . . . . . . . . . .
> . . . the oral tradition depends upon each person
> listening and remembering a portion. . . .
>
> (6–7)

But the awareness of and respect for the oral tradition, here, is not a kind of sentimental privileging of the old ways. Indeed, this first reference to the importance of cultural transmission by oral means comes in a lovely memorial to Aunt Susie who, Silko writes:

> From the time that I can remember her
> . . . worked on her kitchen table
> with her books and papers spread over the oil cloth.
> She wrote beautiful long hand script
> but her eyesight was not good
> and so she wrote very slowly.
> . . . . . . . . . . . . . . . . . . . . . . .
> She had come to believe very much in books. . .
>
> (4)

It is Aunt Susie, the believer in books and in writing, who was of "the last generation here at Laguna, / that passed an entire culture by word of mouth." Silko's own writing is compared to oral telling by a neighbor, who, finding her "Laguna Coyote" poem in a library book, remarks:

> "We all enjoyed it so much,
> but I was telling the children

the way my grandpa used to tell it
is longer."

To this critical voice, Silko responds:

"Yes, that's the trouble with writing . . .
You can't go on and on the way we do
when we tell stories around here.
People who aren't used to it get tired."

(110)

This awareness of the audience is entirely typical for a native storyteller who cannot go forward with a tale without the audience's response. As Silko writes:

The Laguna people
always begin their stories
with "humma-hah":
that means "long ago."
And the ones who are listening
say "aaaa-eh."

(38)

These are the stories, of course, of the oral tradition. Silko invokes the feel of "long ago" both in the verse format she frequently uses and in the prose pieces, although perhaps only those sections of the book set in verse attempt to evoke something of the actual feel of an oral telling.

It is interesting to note that there are two pieces in the book that echo the title, one in prose and the other set in loose verse. The first, "Storyteller," is an intense and powerful short story which takes place in Alaska. The storyteller of the title is the protagonist's grandfather, a rather less benign figure than the old storytellers of Silko's biographical experience; nonetheless, the stories he tells are of the traditional, mythic type. The second, "Storytelling," is a kind of mini-anthology of several short tales of women and their (quite historical, if fictional!) sexual adventures. The "humma-hah" (in effect) of the first section goes:

You should understand
the way it was
back then,
because it is the same
even now.
     [aaaa-eh]
                    (94)

The final section has its unnamed speaker conclude:

My husband
left
after he heard the story
and moved back in with his mother.
It was my fault and
I don't blame him either.
I could have told
the story
better than I did.
                              (98)

In both these pieces ("Storyteller" and "Storytelling") we find
a very different sense of verbal art from that expressed in the
West in something like Auden's lines (in the poem on the
death of Yeats), where he writes that "poetry makes nothing
happen." In deadly serious prose and in witty verse, Silko
dramatizes her belief that stories—both the mythic-traditional
tales passed down among the people and the day-to-day nar-
rations of events—do make things happen. The two pieces refer to very different kinds of stories which, in their capacity to
produce material effects, are nonetheless the same.

     Among other identifiable voices in Silko's texts are her
own epistolary voice in letters she has written to Lawson F.
Inada and James A. Wright, the voices of Coyote and Buffalo,
and those of traditional figures like Kochininako, Whirlwind
Man, Arrowboy, Spider Woman and Yellow Woman—some of
whom appear in modern day incarnations. In stories or letters
or poems, in monologues or dialogues, the diction may vary—
now more colloquial and/or regional, now more formal—or the
tone—lyrical, humorous, meditative. Yet always, the effort is

to make us hear the various languages that constitute Silko's world and so herself. If we agree with Bakhtin that, "The primary stylistic project of the novel as a genre is to create images of languages" (366), *Storyteller* is a clear instance of novelized discourse, Native American autobiography of the dialogic type. It remains to say what the implications of this particular dialogic discourse may be.

I have tried to read *Storyteller* as an example of Native American autobiography in the dialogic mode, that is, against the backdrop of Bakhtin's meditations on language and society. By way of conclusion, it seems useful to see what Silko's book has to say about these important subjects, or more accurately, what projections about language and society might be made from the book. To interrogate the text in this way is not to treat it foremost as ethnic or hyphenated literature (although it cannot be understood in ignorance of its informing context), but as a candidate for inclusion in the canon of American literature conceived of as a selection of the most important work from among national texts (*American* literature) and texts (for all the blurring of genres) of a certain kind (American *literature*).

Let me review the possibilities. In regard to its understanding of language and the nature of communication, on one hand a commitment to dialogism may be seen as a recognition of the necessity of an infinite semantic openness. Here the inescapable possibility of yet some further voice is crucial inasmuch as that voice may decisively alter or ambiguate any relatively stable meaning one might claim to understand. On the other hand, a commitment to dialogism may be seen as a type of radical pluralism, a more relativized openness, concerned with stating meanings provisionally in recognition of the legitimate claims of otherness and difference. In regard to its implied model of the social, a commitment to dialogism may be seen as envisioning, "a carnivalesque arena of diversity," as James Clifford has described it, "a utopian . . . space,"[12] where the utopian exists as a category of pure abstraction, an image out of time and oblivious to the conditions of historical possibility: diversity as limitless freeplay. Or a commitment to dialogism may envision—but here one

195

encounters difficulties, for it is hard to name or describe the sort of democratic and egalitarian community that would be the political equivalent of a radical pluralism as distinct from an infinite openness. No doubt, traditional Native American models of communal organization need further study in this regard, although it is not at all clear how the present-day Pueblo or the nineteenth-century Plains camp circle might be incorporated into models of some harmonious world-community to come.

Let me, then, name the alternative to dialogism as carnival and polymorphous diversity, what Paul Rabinow has called *cosmopolitanism*. "Let us define cosmopolitanism," Rabinow writes, "as an ethos of macro-interdependencies, with an acute consciousness (often forced upon people) of the inescapabilities and particularities of places, characters, historical trajectories, and fates."[13] The trick is to avoid "reify[ing] local identities or construct[ing] universal ones," a trick, as Rabinow notes, that requires a rather delicate balancing act, one that the West has had a difficult time managing. For all the seeming irony of proposing that the highly place-oriented and more or less homogenous cultures of indigenous Americans might best teach us how to be cosmopolitans, that is exactly what I mean to say. But here let me return to *Storyteller*.

Storyteller is open to a plurality of voices. What keeps it from entering the poststructuralist, postmodernist or schizophrenic heteroglossic domain is its commitment to the equivalent of a normative voice. For all the polyvocal openness of Silko's work, there is always the unabashed commitment to Pueblo ways as a reference point. This may be modified, updated, playfully construed: but its authority is always to be reckoned with. Whatever one understands from any speaker is to be understood in reference to that. Here we find dialogic as dialectic (not, it seems, the case in Bakhtin!), meaning as the interaction of any voiced value whatever and the centered voice of the Pueblo.[14]

If this account of *Storyteller*'s semantics, or theory of meaning, is at all accurate, it would follow that its political unconscious is more easily conformable to Rabinow's cosmopolitanism than to a utopianized carnival. The social implications of *Storyteller*'s dialogism might be a vision of an American cosmopolitanism to come that permits racial and cultural voices at home (in both "residual" and "emerging" forms [15]) to speak fully and that opens its ears to other voices abroad. This is an image, to be sure, not a political program; and to imagine the "polyvocal polity" in this way is also utopian, but perhaps only in the sense that it is not yet imminent.

Silko's book says nothing of this, offering neither a theory of communication nor of politics. To take it seriously, however, is to see it as more than merely evocative, amusing, expressive or informative (to the mainstream reader curious about the exotic ways of marginalized communities). It is to see its art as a matter of values that are most certainly not only aesthetic.

## ☐ *Notes* ∎

1. For a fuller account see Arnold Krupat, *For Those Who Come After: A Study of Native American Autobiography* (Berkeley: University of California Press, 1985).

2. See Samson Occom, "A Short Narrative of My Life," *The Elders Wrote: An Anthology of Early Prose by North American Indians*, ed. Bernd Peyer (Berlin: Dietrich Reimer Verlag, 1982). Occom wrote in 1768; his manuscript reposed in the Dartmouth College Library until its publication by Peyer. Also see Hendrick Aupaumut, "Journal of a Mission to the Western Tribes of Indians," which was written in 1791 and published by B. H. Coates in 1827 in the *Pennsylvania Historical Society Memoirs,* II, part 1, 61–131.

3. This is William Spengemann's trajectory for Western autobiography which he sees as presenting "historical, philosophical, and poetic" forms, and a "movement of autobiography from the biographical to the fictive mode," in his *The Forms of Autobiography: Episodes in the History of a Literary Genre* (New Haven: Yale University Press, 1980) xiv.

4. An earlier and very different version of this paper was summarized as a presentation to the European Association on American Studies Convention (Budapest, March 1986).

5. I hesitate to offer even a selected bibliography of recent

work on Bakhtin, so voluminous are the possibilities. For what use it may be let me mention only two book-length studies. Katerina Clark and Michael Holquist's biography, *Mikhail Bakhtin* (Cambridge: Harvard University Press, 1984), is both indispensable and too-good-to-be-true in its shaping of Bakhtin's life and thought into a coherent, but largely anti-communist, whole. Tzvetan Todorov's *Mikhail Bakhtin: the Dialogical Principle,* trans. Wlad Godzich (Minneapolis: University of Minnesota Press, 1984) is a particularly subtle reading. Denis Donoghue's "Reading Bakhtin," *Raritan* 2 (Fall 1985): 107–19, offers a more sceptical account. The primary volumes in English of Bakhtin's work are *Rabelais and his World,* trans. Helene Iswolsky (Cambridge: MIT Press, 1968); *The Dialogic Imagination: Four Essays by M. M. Bakhtin,* ed. Michael Holquist, trans. Caryl Emerson and Michael Holquist (Austin: University of Texas Press, 1981); and *Problems of Dostoevsky's Poetics,* ed. and trans. Caryl Emerson (Minneapolis: University of Minnesota Press, 1984). The interested reader will find many special issues of journals devoted to Bakhtin, several with extensive bibliographies.

6. Bakhtin, *The Dialogic Imagination,* 45. All further quotations from Bakhtin are from this volume and page references will be documented in the text.

7. See Fredric Jameson, "Postmodernism, or The Cultural Logic of Late Capitalism," *New Left Review* 146 (1984): 53–82.

8. See Clifford Geertz, "Blurred Genres: The Refiguration of Social Thought," *Local Knowledge: Further Essays in Interpretive Anthropology* (New York: Basic Books, 1983), originally published 1980.

9. See Marcel Mauss, "A Category of the human mind: the notion of person; the notion of self." In M. Carrithers, S. Collins and S. Lukes, eds., *The Category of the Person: Anthropology, Philosophy, History* (Cambridge: Harvard University Press, 1985).

10. Leslie Marmon Silko, *Storyteller* (New York: Seaver Books, 1981) 1. All further page references will be given in the text.

11. In fact there *are* other tellings because many of the stories in *Storyteller* have appeared elsewhere, some of them in several places. (Pieces of Silko's novel, *Ceremony,* also appear elsewhere.) What to make of this? On the one hand it may be that Silko is just trying to get as much mileage as she can out of what she's done, a practice not unknown to both fiction and essay writers, native and

non-native. On the other hand, in the context of Native American storytelling, repetition of the "same" story on several different occasions is standard procedure, "originality" or noticeable innovation having no particular value. It should also be noted that the retellings of Silko's stories are not exact reprintings. For example, "The Man to Send Rain Clouds," as it appears in Kenneth Rosen's anthology of the same name (New York: Viking, 1974), and in *Storyteller*, have slight differences. In Rosen's anthology there are numbered sections of the story (one to four), while there are only space breaks in *Storyteller* (no numbers). In the first paragraph of the Rosen version, Levis are "light-blue" while in *Storyteller* they are "light blue"; "blue mountains were still deep in snow" (3) in Rosen while in *Storyteller* "blue mountains were still in snow" (182). If we turn to the story called "Uncle Tony's Goat" in both books, we find differences in the endings. In Rosen the story ends this way:

. . . Tony finished the cup of coffee. "He's probably in Quemado by now."

I thought his voice sounded strong and happy when he said this, and I looked at him again, standing there by the door, ready to go milk the nanny goats. He smiled at me.

"There wasn't ever a goat like that one," he said, "but if that's the way he's going to act, O.K. then. That damn goat got pissed off, too easy anyway."

(99–100)

The ending in *Storyteller* goes:

. . . "He's probably in Quemado by now."

I looked at him again, standing there by the door, ready to go milk the nanny goats.

"There wasn't ever a goat like that one," he said, "but if that's the way he's going to act, O.K. then. That damn goat got pissed off too easy anyway."

He smiled at me and his voice was strong and happy when he said this. (18)

The differences in the first example may not amount to much, while those in the second might suggest a slight change in emphasis; a systematic study of the differences in Silko's retellings (something I have not attempted to do) might tell us something about her development as a writer—or might not be all that substantial. My point here is that Silko's retellings in writing, whether she is aware of this or not (and it is always possible that different versions come into existence as a result of the demands of different editors rather than as a result of Silko's own determinations), tend to parallel what we know of the oral retellings of traditional narrators.

12. James Clifford, "On Ethnographic Authority," *Representations* 1 (Spring 1983): 137.

13. Paul Rabinow, "Representations are Social Facts: Modernity and Post-Modernity in Anthropology," *Writing Culture: The Poetics and Politics of Ethnography*, ed. James Clifford and George E. Marcus (Berkeley: University of California Press, 1986) 258.

14. This would not accord very well with what Silko said of herself in Rosen's 1974 volume, *Voices of the Rainbow* (New York: Viking Press, 1974) where she emphasized that "the way we live is like Marmons . . . somewhere on the fringes . . . our origin is unlike any other. My poetry, my storytelling rise out of this source." As glossed by Alan Velie, from whom I take this quotation, this means like "mixed-blood[s] from a ruling family" (in *Four American Indian Literary Masters: N. Scott Momaday, James Welch, Leslie Marmon Silko, and Gerald Vizenor* [Norman: University of Oklahoma Press, 1982] 107). It goes rather better with what Silko put in her contributor's note to Rosen's 1975 *The Man to Send Rain Clouds*. She wrote, "I am of mixed-breed ancestry, but what I know is Laguna. This place I am from is everything I am as a writer and human being."

15. These are values in relation to "dominant" values as defined by Raymond Williams in "Base and Superstructure in Marxist Cultural Theory," in his *Problems in Materialism and Culture* (London: Verso, 1980) 40ff.

# The Storytellers
# in *Storyteller*

In American Indian traditional cultures, good songs and stories are useful, fostering the survival of the people and their
culture. The verbal arts sustain cosmic relationships, testify to
sources of creative energy, teach young people, heal the sick,
bring lovers together, or reprimand the socially irresponsible.
Leslie Silko's *Storyteller* is an heir of such tradition and a tes-
timony to verbal art as a survival strategy. Moreover, the work
takes its spiderweb-like structure from the Keresan mytho-
logic traditions of female creative deities who think—or tell—
the world into existence (Thought Woman) and who offer dis-
ciplined protection to the living beings (Grandmother Spider).[1]
When we read *Storyteller* bearing in mind the significance of
both the spiderweb structure and the values underlying traditional verbal art, we realize that *Storyteller*, often dismissed as
an oddly assorted album, is a coherent work about how tribal
people survive. By making stories, people continue the tradition of Thought Woman and Grandmother Spider: they con-
tinuously create and protect themselves and their world.

Silko describes one of her own critical essays ["Language and Literature from a Pueblo Indian Perspective"] in a
way that could equally well apply to *Storyteller:*

> For those of you accustomed to a structure that moves from
> point A to point B to point C, this presentation may be some-
> what difficult to follow because the structure of Pueblo
> expression resembles something like a spider's web—with
> many little threads radiating from a center, criss-crossing

From *Studies in American Indian Literature* 1:2 (Fall 1989): 21–31.

each other. As with the web, the structure will emerge as it is made, and you must simply listen and trust, as the Pueblo people do, that meaning will be made.

In *Storyteller,* thematic clusters constitute the radiating strands of the web. While the radial strands provide the organizational pattern of the book, the web's lateral threads connect one thematic strand to another, suggesting a whole and woven fabric. Throughout the book, Silko spins such a lateral thread of attention to storytellers and the art of storytelling. These piece constantly guide the reader's attention back to the act of storytelling as creation, to the creative in all aspects of human interaction, to the female deities, and as well to the ordinary tribal women, Silko's most frequently selected narrators who carry on Thought Woman's function of speaking into being.

Grandmother Spider of course lives at the center of the web, giving *Storyteller* its authority. But Grandmother Spider, and thus the whole pantheon of protective, creative female deities, live also in the author and in all the aunts, grandmothers, and other people from whom she heard these stories. Silko specifically credits many of these others: Great-aunt Susie Marmon, Great-grandmother Maria Anaya Marmon, Grandma Lillie and Grandpa Hank Marmon, her father Lee Marmon, and her friend and fellow writer Simon Ortiz. For Silko certainly credits the creative power in men as well as women. At other times Silko credits the"they say" of oral tradition. "Everyone," Silko says, "from the youngest child to the oldest person, was expected to listen and to be able to recall or tell a portion, if only a small detail, from a narrative account or story. Thus the remembering and retelling were a communal process" ("Landscape, History, and the Pueblo Imagination").

Taking such a stance, Silko identifies herself and her community with the creative power of Thought Woman. Thus the creation of the world is something humans are responsible for, day after day. This sacred connection between Thought Woman and author, as ordinary human and as member of the community, is directly expressed in the prefatory poem to Silko's novel *Ceremony,* when Thought Woman "is sitting in her room / thinking of a story now / I'm telling you the story / she is thinking." If we read with a consciousness of structure and theme, we are reminded constantly of Grandmother Spider, and by extension of her other aspects as Thought Woman, the sisters Naut'ts'ity'i and I'tc'ts'ity'i, and Grandmother Spider. We are reminded of the nurture, creativity, and vitality of tribal people, especially the women; of how the people have survived by telling the stories of their lives and their collective past as well as by imagining their ongoing present; and of how the author's role contributes to this process. For it takes both memory and imagination to nurture and preserve life. "What we call memory and what we call imagination," Silko says, "are not so easily distinguished" (*Storyteller* 227). We see the interplay of both functions in all of Silko's storytellers. The proportions may vary, but both functions are always present.

At the beginning of the first filament of the spiderweb are the literal and literary grandmothers, the living embodiments of Grandmother Spider, the first sources instead of the last consulted, as in so much work by (primarily male) anthropologists. By placing them first, Silko suggests that these stories and these women's voices have mattered to her and to the survival of the culture. In "Aunt Susie had certain phrases," Silko emphasizes the personal, performance, and interactional elements, and so tells a story about telling stories. She begins the story of the little girl, Waithea, with, "This is the way Aunt Susie told the story." As Silko recreates the narrative Aunt Susie told, we are aware of the audience of little girls, possibly Leslie and her sisters; this story contains lessons about attentiveness and the right way to live. Aunt Susie's text is from tribal memory, but her recreation of it involves acts of imagination, as when her asides indicate that she recognizes these modern grandchildren's need for information: "There used to be a trail there, you know, it is gone now but it was accessible in those days." At the end of the narrative Silko, completing the contextual frame she has introduced, focuses on the qualities of Aunt Susie's voice, the way she sounded telling a story, and the way the sound of her voice affected the hearers. For Silko, the fact of storytelling is as important as the content of the story. Aunt Susie shapes the event in her hearers' minds, just as Thought Woman shapes the universe. The same creative energy may shape cosmic events or nurture the tribal and personal self-perception of a small girl.

The book's title story is set in Alaska, far from Laguna country; nonetheless here again the grandparent generation is a source of power, and storytelling is a way of being, of creating oneself and the world. From the old man, the central character learns the manner and need for telling the stories, which ensure the survival of a way of life and a world view. Just as her sexual relationship with the old man symbolizes her absorption of cultural traditions, similarly a putting on of old ways is suggested when she wears the wolfskin parka she has inherited from her grandmother. It is from her grandmother, too, that she learns the subject of her own story, beginning with the death of her parents.

Then she must live out and tell her story in the face of an invasive colonizing culture that would deny her the right to both her way of life and her own story. Her synthesizing imagination joins the old man's manner and valuation of storytelling with the content of the family story, to create both action and a new narrative. She comes to understand what the old man means when he says, "It will take a long time, but the stories must be told. There must not be any lies." But she insists on the integrity of her own story: in revenge for her parents' death years before when an opportunistic storekeeper had apparently sold them canned heat as drinking alcohol, she has lured the present storekeeper onto the weak river ice, where he has chased her and fallen through to his death. In her jail cell her liberal white attorney makes excuses for her: She couldn't possibly have planned it; her mind was confused. But she insists, "I intended that he die. The story must be told as it is." Her stance is both heroic and pathetic as she directs her story to those who have no ears to hear it.

The white characters—whether oil field workers, priests, educators, or functionaries of the Law—are all unable to accept who the protagonist is or what she says. Her curious, active sexuality causes them to try either to use her or reform her. The lawyer cannot accept that she may with justification have planned the death of the storekeeper. Kate Shanley Vangen suggests that if some legal functionary finally does believe her, the system will want to punish her for murder or hospitalize her. But the teller's spirit survives with her story in the face of colonialism.

Like the young Inuit woman in "Storyteller," the old Navajo woman, Ayah, in "Lullaby," tells the story of encounters with a hostile culture, though she recreates the story for herself, in her mind, rather than for an audience of foreigners. Though "Lullaby" lacks the apocalyptic tone of "Storyteller," nonetheless, Ayah's review of her pitifully ordinary life story and her identification with Grandmother Spider both lead her to reclaim her power to deal with her own situation. Ayah is no mere victim. The structural context of the spiderweb, combined with the story's imagery, associates Ayah with Grandmother Spider. And in her capacity to use her own story to govern her life and offer mercy where it is needed, she is also Thought Woman. Thus the story goes far beyond the pathetic cliche we might be tempted to see without the awareness of tribal traditions and the power of stories to shape reality.

The next radiating filament of *Storyteller's* web structure involves stories of Kochininako, or Yellow Woman, which explore the creative power and survival value of this Everywoman figure among the Keresan holy people.[2] Kochininako's power, Paula Gunn Allen observes, is that of an agent or catalyst. She enables the seasons to follow their appointed rounds, for example. Not only does she catalyze the seasonal progression, but, as A. LaVonne Ruoff points out, she renews tribal vitality through "liaison with outside forces."

Her fictional character in "Yellow Woman," Silko tells us, joins "adolescent longings and the old stories, that plus the stories around Laguna at the time about people who did, in fact, just in recent times, use the river as a meeting place" (*Sun Tracks* interview 29). Besides addressing an audience she assumes is sympathetic, this narrator is also telling herself the story she wants to hear, justifying herself, but with enough self-awareness and humor to recognize the doubtful elements in her story. She does bring renewal to her sense of mythic reality through her adventure with Silva, the "outside force," as she almost convinces herself that she really is Yellow Woman. The proposition is not utterly unlikely. Yellow Woman exhibits the desires and weaknesses of ordinary women; why should the protagonist not be Yellow Woman? Through her adventure, at any rate, she livens up an apparently dull existence. She identifies with the freedom of Yellow Woman in her grandfather's stories, reminding us that modern women embody the potential of Yellow Woman, bring the vitality of imagination to everyday life. After all, the power to make a convincing excuse or to fool oneself is yet one more version of the power to create the universe.

Silko's story of a young woman going off with an attractive stranger whom she meets on a riverbank closely follows the beginning of a Laguna story published by Franz Boas under the title "Cliff Dweller." The stranger, Silva, smilingly goes along with her suggestion that they may really be Yellow Woman and a ka'tsina spirit. Eventually, the narrator makes her way back to the pueblo, reorienting herself to ordinary reality as she goes, speculating about what the family is doing in her absence.

In the course of the adventure she has renewed the power of the myth by imagining what Yellow Woman's life and state of mind would have been like:

> I was wondering if Yellow Woman had known who she was—
> if she knew that she would become part of the stories. Maybe
> she'd had another name that her husband and relatives called
> her so that only the ka'tsina from the north and the storytell-
> ers would know her as Yellow Woman.

Finally she sees her story as an artifact that only her grandfather could properly appreciate because the Yellow Woman stories were what he liked best. But it is not by chance that out of her grandfather's repertory the narrator recollects a Yellow Woman story involving a sexual encounter with Coyote. Silva, of course, is more opportunistic than evil, and thus more Coyote than Cliff Dweller. And the narrator shares the same appetite-driven opportunism. As there is a bit of Grandmother Spider and Yellow Woman in all women, so there is a bit of Coyote in all people. For storytellers are tricksters like Coyote as well as agents like Yellow Woman, or creator-deities, and this character certainly contains all three possibilities.

This is the first point in the book where we see strongly

and explicitly the suggestion that Coyote is part of storytelling and creative life, as much as the mother gods, whose creation he is, after all. We should have guessed, for memory and imagination are virtually inextricable, and while Coyote is short on memory, he is long on the experimental and playful part of the imagination. Coyote may not always be admirable. But a Navajo informant once remarked to J. Barre Toelken, "If [Coyote] did not do all those things, then those things would not be possible in the world." Out of chaos, exaggeration, and impropriety comes the possibility of a new synthesis. This pool of possibility is the source of strength and growth, of creative response to the yet unimagined future.

This story looks toward the end of the book with its cluster of Coyote stories. It also prefigures the poem "Storytelling," which perfects the fine art of gossip, tale bearing, and excuse-making in daily life. "Storytelling" begins with a reprise of the Buffalo Man and Yellow Woman story from "Cottonwoods Part Two"; this leads to someone's modern-day Yellow Woman escapade, and concludes with several romance, kidnapping, and seduction vignettes from local gossip, including one in which four aggressive Laguna women and three evidently bemused Navajo men lead the FBI and the state police on a trail

> of wine bottles
> and size 42 panties
> hanging in bushes and trees
> all the way along the road.

In "Storytelling," Silko loops back in a recursive spiral, spinning together several themes found thus far in the book. Besides varying the Yellow Woman theme, the comic poem's title reminds us of the title story and counterpoints its serious view of storytelling as a kind of cultural holding action: the gossip in "Storytelling" reassures people of their place in the community, all the while laughing at and controlling their excesses. With its lusty appetites and proliferation of self-serving tales, this poem, like "Yellow Woman," anticipates the Coyote stories in the final section. Furthermore, its position just at the end of a sequence of hunting stories emphasizes that sexual encounters involve cooperation between the hunter and the hunted. Silko had presented the serious mythic version of this same clustering of sexual encounter, hunting, and cooperation in "Cottonwoods Part Two: Buffalo Man." Just as Silko had reminded us in the poem's title of the range of serious-to-comic narrative purposes and ritualistic-to-casual modes of telling, these thematic echoes simply suggest once more that the world is all one. Gossip and comedy, too, take on sacred and creative power.

In the next two filaments, Silko's focus shifts away from the interactions of people in communities and social settings, toward the use of power to create harmony or conflict in the universe. Among the several major narratives that portray destruction of natural harmony as a result of someone's ill-intention manipulation—witchery—one is specifically a story about a storyteller. "Long Time Ago" portrays a witch speaking into being the white people and their obsession with technology and power. Prophecy about the coming of white people is part of Keresan and many other tribal traditions.[3] But the details of "Long Time Ago" seem to be Silko's invention. During a contest among witches to see whose magic is most spectacular or repellant, an unknown witch offers simply a story of white people discovering uranium and producing nuclear cataclysm, promising, "as I tell the story / it will begin to happen" (133). When the other witches ask the storyteller to call the prophecy back, of course it cannot be done. The frightened, individualistic white race, remote from nature and other people, has already been called into existence.

In "Long Time Ago," the power of a story is simple, literal, and monolithic, as when Thought Woman thinks something into existence. But the same kind of power that could create a harmonious universe instead creates a destructive force that would seem utterly fantastic did it not sound so familiar. Likewise, experimental try-anything-once Coyote power can create both comedy and stark disaster. Power itself is neutral. Any being, Silko suggests, might use the power for good or ill on different occasions, and in fact, "the balance could come undone and any character could change" in its relation to good or ill use of power (interview in *Persona* 34).

The spokes of *Storyteller's* spider web structure circle

back through a cluster of pieces in which family members reappear as the sequence moves from the cosmic back into the community of animals and humans, co-existing through love and ceremonial interchange. But by now we realize that memory is not the only way to resist the ill-speaking of witchery, Silko's term for negativity, manipulation, and destructiveness. Whatever there is of foolishness or selfishness in Coyote, his saving grace is spontaneity and imagination. Like Grandmother Spider, Coyote is a maker figure, albeit a spirit of disorder, appetite, play, and potential. In the last part of *Storyteller*, this disorder, instead of the orderly creation of the mother gods, becomes the focal point. But then, the Coyote spirit of play and uncontrol always was part of the larger scheme. According to the emergence story told by W. G. Marmon's widow,

> *Iyetik* said to her sisters, "I wish we had something to make us laugh. We sit around here so quiet without anything to make us laugh." *Iyetik* rubbed her skin. Rubbing both hands she got a ball like dough. She put it aside and covered it with cloth. Out of the rubbings came the *kashare* [sic].
> (Parsons, *Notes on Ceremonialism at Laguna* 144).

Coyote, like the koshare, both subverts and transcends the rules and the ceremonies. From Coyote's readiness to fulfill his appetites comes the power to adapt and experiment. Coyote power fuels the continuance of life as much as Grandmother Spider protects life.

The woman protagonist of the narrative poem "Storyteller's Escape" exhibits this adaptive power as she speaks into existence the story of her own escape from an enemy tribe. Not explicitly a Coyote story, it is positioned significantly in the midst of Coyote stories. The storyteller understands the value of stories for adaptation and survival:

> she says, "With these stories of ours
> we can escape almost anything
> with these stories we will survive."
> (*Storyteller* 247)

She also understands the importance of memory to the survival of both individuals and the tribe:

> "In this way
> we hold them
> and keep them with us forever
> and in this way
> we continue."

This storyteller combines the creator gods' memory, love for the lost members of the tribe, and sense of responsibility with Coyote's sense of possibility, ability to seize the main chance and to enjoy a trick. Like Yellow Woman, even in a tight spot, she delights in her artifact:

> This one's the best one yet—
> Too bad nobody may ever hear it
> (252)

For the first time, in Silko's sequence of women storytellers, this one seems to have a publicly acknowledged role. She is in some sense in charge of the stories. We might even suspect Silko of a subtle reference to the phrasing of the Thought Woman poem at the beginning of *Ceremony*:

> This is the story she told,
>> the child who looked back
>> the old teller's escape—
>> the story she was thinking of . . .

The action of "Storyteller's Escape" once again echoes and this time inverts that of the book's title story. Like the earlier story, this one involves a pursuit, but with a happier ending than posited for the central character in "Storyteller." This time the storyteller is not forced to an inevitable ending. Rather, grasping luck and chance, she makes a Coyote-style escape. Having fallen behind her tribe as they flee from the enemy, she mourns, for how will the people now remember the lost ones, and who will remember her? Deciding that she will make up a story while she is waiting to die either of the heat or at the hands of the enemy, she suddenly sees things from a new angle, gets up, walks home, and is there waiting when the tribe returns.

One can hardly avoid the parallel with all those tales in which Coyote wins a race by hiding along the race course and resting while others run. The storyteller intends to cheat only the enemy tribe—which hardly seems like cheating. But she rescues herself through a fresh, direct, self-interested perception of the situation, like Coyote. Thus she protects and preserves history, of which she is the tribal guardian. But despite her regard for history and tradition, she is not stuck in old assumptions and ceremonies. She recognizes a need for a new approach.

Throughout the Coyote section we hear echoes and inversions of subjects and themes developed earlier. Police officers at a feast echo "Tony's Story," but this time the police resemble Coyote, not witches. Politicians, gas company officials, Marmon ancestors, Mrs. Sekakaku's opportunistic admirer, and Mrs. Sekakaku herself are all cast as Coyotes. In these parallels we are reminded of the need for open possibility, comedy, flexibility. This complex of threads connecting elsewhere in *Storyteller* reminds the reader that this is Grandmother Spider's web, and Thought Woman, Nau'ts'ity'i, I'tc'ts'ity'i, and Grandmother Spider are the ground of nurturance and continuance in the world. The children of Thought Woman continue to preserve and to speak the world into being. But the modern-day Coyotes renew and refresh its possibilities—the survivors, the foolers and the fooled, those who, like Coyote in so many traditional stories, are just "going along."

### ☐ *Notes* ∎

1. For a full analysis of the spider web structure in *Storyteller,* see Danielson, "*Storyteller:* Grandmother Spider's Web," where "Aunt Susie had certain phrases," "Storyteller," and "Lullaby" are discussed in greater depth.

2. Boas comments that "girl heroes" are generally called Yel-

low Woman (*Keresan Texts* I, 218). The plural *Yellow Women* is found in Boas's text entitled "Sunrise" (89).

   3. John M. Gunn, for example, gives a Laguna version of a widespread southwestern traditional prophecy that light-skinned, bearded warriors in metal shirts would come from the east. (*Schat-Chen* 101)

Works cited are:

Boas, Franz, ed. *Keresan Texts*, Volume VIII, Pts. I and II. New York: Publications of the American Ethnological Society, 1928.

Danielson, Linda L. "Storyteller: Grandmother Spider's Web." *Journal of the Southwest* 30 (Autumn 1988): 325–355.

Evers, Larry and Denny Carr. "A Conversation with Leslie Marmon Silko." *Sun Tracks* 3, no. 1 (Fall 1976): 30.

Gunn, John M. *Schat-Chen: History, Traditions and Naratives (sic) of the Queres Indians of Laguna and Acoma.* Albuquerque: Albright and Anderson, 1917.

Parsons, Elsie Clews. *Notes on Ceremonialism at Laguna,* Anthropological Papers of the American Museum of Natural History XIX, Pt. 1. New York: Trustees of the AMNH.

Silko, Leslie Marmon. "Landscape, History, and the Pueblo Imagination." *Antaeus* 57 (Autumn 1986): 83–94.

———. "Language and Literature from a Pueblo Indian Perspective." In *English Literature: Opening Up the Canon*, edited by Leslie Fiedler and Houston A. Baker, Jr., 54–72. Baltimore: The Johns Hopkins University Press, 1981.

# The Web of Meaning: Naming the Absent Mother in *Storyteller*

> They think
> I am stronger than I am.
>> I would tell this like a story
>> but where a story should begin
>> I am left standing in the beat
>> of my silences.
> There has to be someone to name you.
>>>> —WENDY ROSE, "Naming Power"

*Storyteller* by Leslie Silko begins with the image of "a tall Hopi basket . . . inside the basket are hundreds of photographs." The form and structure of the text reflect this image; it is a collage of stories, poems, myths, folktales, autobiographical notes, letters and pictures. And, like the photographs in the basket, the subjects are frequently the same—only the details change. Silko tells us that the photographs, many of which were taken by Grandpa Hank, "have always had special significance with the people of my family . . . [They] have a special relationship to the stories/ . . . because many of the stories can be traced in the photographs." The book itself is shaped like a picture album or a scrapbook, creating a certain intimacy and familiarity between text and reader. Silko seems to invite the reader to share with her a personal as well as a mythological, historical and fictional set of memories.

---

This is the first publication of this essay.

The book is, in fact, autobiographical in the sense that it places the emphasis on the shaping of the author's developing self through the influence of her family and friends, the myths and stories she was told, and the place where she was raised. In an interview with Per Seyersted, Leslie Silko says that she sees *Storyteller* "as a statement about storytelling and the relationship of the people, my family and my background to the storytelling—a personal statement done in the style of the storytelling tradition, i.e., using stories themselves to explain the dimensions of the process." By "naming" the people, places and stories that were important to her, she defines herself through her relationship to the family, the community and the land. Storytelling for Silko is more than "just . . . sitting down and telling a once-upon-a-time kind of story" (Barnes 86). It is rather "a whole way of seeing yourself, the people around you, your life, the place of your life in the bigger context, not just in terms of nature and location but in terms of what has gone on before, what has happened to other people . . . a whole way of being" (Barnes 86). This is a characteristic Native American point of view according to Simon Ortiz, who regards storytelling as "a way of life . . . a trail which I follow in order to be aware as much as possible of what is around me and what part I am in that life" (quoted in Lincoln 223). The reader, as he or she turns the pages of this "album," is privileged to participate in the journey.

We are introduced to Silko's family through the pictures and the stories. We see and hear about her father, her sister, Aunt Susie, Grandpa Hank, Uncle Walter, Great Grandmother Anaya, Great Grandfather Marmon, Grandma A'mooh, Aunt Bessie, Great Grandpa Stagner and his brother Bill, Grandma Helen and even old Juana, who raised Grandma Helen. Each photograph tells a story and the story is "written" in the images present, the juxtaposition between photographs and text, and in the pictures omitted. We "read" the pictures as we read the myths and stories, looking for broader connections between them and Silko's life as she presents it in the text. Terry Eagleton, in *Literary Theory: An Introduction,* suggests that "the process of reading . . . is always a dynamic one, a complex movement . . . unfolding through time" (77). The oral storytelling tradition which forms the basic structure of Silko's text involves the reader in such a dynamic process. The reader, in effect, becomes participant in the text, connecting stories, finishing them, rewriting them, and constructing his or her own stories in the "gaps." These gaps exist in every text according to Wolfgang Iser in "The Reading Process" because

> no tale can ever be told in its entirety. . . . [It] is only through inevitable omissions that a story gains its dynamism . . . [T]hus whenever the flow is interrupted . . . the opportunity is given to us to bring into play our own faculty for establishing connections-for filling in the gaps left by the text itself.
>
> (55)

The gaps in Silko's *Storyteller,* however, form a greater and more significant part of the story than those found in traditional texts. Like many Native American and modern texts, it is so fragmentary in form that "one's attention is almost exclusively occupied with the search for connections between fragments" (Iser 55). As we are seduced into the storytelling session, distinctions blur between the teller and the told, and where one story ends, a new one begins.

The most notable gaps and silences in *Storyteller* revolve around the absence of Silko's mother. In a book that appears to be substantially autobiographical and largely about the significance of female myths and forebearers, Silko's mother is mentioned only once in the entire text and then only in connection with Grandma A'mooh:

> It was a long time before
> I learned that my Grandma A'mooh's
> real name was Marie Anaya Marmon.
> I thought her name really was "A'mooh."
> I realize now it had happened when I was a baby
> and she cared for me while my mother worked.
>
> (33)

Stories about fictional, mythological and surrogate mothers, however, abound in the text. Not only does the book begin with Aunt Susie who functioned as surrogate mother to Silko, listening to her, answering her questions, and passing "down an entire culture / by word of mouth / an entire history / an entire vision of the world" (5–6), but it is dominated by the myths and stories of Yellow Woman. The Yellow Woman myths originate in traditional Cochiti and Laguna Pueblo stories. There are many versions of the story of Yellow Woman, but in each telling of the story Yellow Woman is abducted or seduced by the sexually exciting, potentially dangerous ka'tsina spirit. When she is drawn to him, her "physical sensations and desire . . . blot out thoughts of home, family and responsibility" (Ruoff 12). She leaves her husband and children to follow him. Sometimes she returns to the family; other times she does not. This union, however, almost always results in positive benefits for the tribe. According to Paula Gunn Allen in *Spider Woman's Granddaughters,* Yellow Woman may be "a Spirit, a Mother, a blessed ear of corn, an archetype, a person, a daughter . . . an agent of change and of obscure events, a wanton, an outcast, a girl who runs off with Navajos, or Zunis, or even Mexicans" (211). Whichever role she assumes, Yellow Woman functions as a powerful image of freedom, sexuality, power and creativity. She is simultaneously the "good" mother who fulfills the traditional role of wife and nurturer and the "bad" mother whose sexuality is a powerful force, capable of both creation and destruction. As a daughter and as a woman, Silko must come to terms with the female power and sexuality she recognizes in her mother and in herself; she must negotiate the dangerous territory between mother and daughter, self and other, freedom and responsibility, saint and wanton. To name her mother is to name herself; to acknowledge her mother is to acknowledge her own divided self. Silko must, therefore, silence the literal mother whose power, whose potential for wildness and wantonness, frighten her. Only by putting her into a story, weaving both the mother's and daughter's stories into myths and stories of Yellow Woman, can Silko find her own voice, unite the dual aspects of her own psyche, and take her rightful place in the line of strong women who preceded her.

Like Wendy Rose in "Naming Power," Silko "tells this like a story" but where we expect her own personal story to begin, with her own birth, with her own mother, we are "left standing in the beat / of [her] silences." The mother becomes simultaneously and paradoxically both absent from the text, and through her palpable absence, the very center of the text. This is a crucial "gap" in the text and one which leads the reader to struggle for connections. The mother is traditionally the central figure in a child's life and perhaps even more significantly so in a female child's life. It is generally through the mother that a daughter defines herself, her sexuality and her place in the world. As Susan Gubar suggests in "The Blank Page' and Female Creativity," the gaps and silences in the text, the blank pages "contain all stories in no story, just as silence contains all potential sound and white contains all colors" (305). The absence of the mother implies her importance to Silko's sense of self. Furthermore, Silko's repeated retelling of stories of other mothers and wives, particularly in the form of the Yellow Woman stories, seems to reinforce this significance.

The centrality of the mother figure in Laguna life is discussed by Paula Gunn Allen in "Who is Your Mother? Red Roots of White Feminism." She writes that "at Laguna Pueblo in New Mexico, 'Who is your mother?' is an important question . . . [Y]our mother's identity is the key to your own identity" (209). Clearly Silko, who is of mixed Laguna, Hispanic and Anglo ancestry and who spent much of her childhood in and around the Laguna Pueblo, is aware of the importance of the mother figure on a mythical and metaphorical as well as literal level. The exclusion of the mother, then, from a text that focuses so strongly on the mythological aspects of motherhood, acquires increased significance. Certainly, as readers, we cannot overlook the silence; we must assume that this omission is both intentional and telling. Arnold Krupat suggests in "Post-Structuralism and Oral Tradition" that in reading Native American texts, we must "acknowledge that any meanings which appear to be present are never fully present" and conversely, "meaning (according to Terry Eagleton) . . . is a matter of what the sign is *not* as well as of what the sign seems to be" (128, italics added). The literal absence of the mother, therefore, invites us, as readers, to look for her in Silko's subtexts.

The mother, so conspicuously absent from Silko's personal memories, appears repeatedly in fictional and mythological forms. The opening story is one told by Aunt Susie about "the little girl who ran away" and drowned herself in the lake because her mother "didn't want [her] to have any *yashtoah*" (13). Yet after the child's death, the mother grieves and is "very sad" (14). In her grief, she scatters "the little clothing— / the little *manta* dresses and shawls / the moccasins and the *yashtoah*— / they all turned into butterflies— / all colors of butterflies / *And today they say that acoma has more beautiful butterflies—*" (15). The mother fails, at least in Western terms, to meet the child's needs and desires; yet, ultimately, good results for the community out of the individual tragedy. Aunt Susie's voice, relating the story, reflects this as she "spoke the words of the mother to her daughter / with great tenderness, with great feeling / as if Aunt Susie herself were the mother / . . . But when Aunt Susie came to the place / where the little girl's clothes turned into butterflies / then her voice would change and I could hear the excitement and wonder / and the story wasn't sad any longer" (15). Significantly, it is Aunt Susie, the surrogate mother, who tells this conflicted story of motherhood and establishes the sense of ambivalence and duality that is reflected in the many versions of the Yellow Woman stories that follow in the text.

Motherhood in Silko's stories has a duality that is based in history, tradition and myth and creates conflict for the Native American woman today; motherhood for the Lagunas is greater than a personal and familial state but has implications for the community and for the earth as well. This scope and the conflicts inherent in it are explored in the various tellings of the Yellow Woman stories. In their context Silko opens up the possibility for exploring the many dimensions of motherhood for herself and indirectly for the reader as well. The silences and the gaps in the text allow the reader the freedom to write and rewrite his or her own versions of Silko's stories just as Silko writes and rewrites them herself. The construction of Silko's text integrates the oral tradition into the reader's own experience. Just as Aunt Susie and Aunt Alice told Silko's stories "they had told . . . before but with changes in details," the text is open for our own storytelling. Silko remembers that

> The story was the important thing and little changes here and
> there were really part of the story. There were even stories
> about the different versions of stories and how they imagined
> these differing versions came to be. . . . I've heard tellers begin
> "The way I heard it was . . . . " and then proceed with another
> story purportedly a version of a story just told but the story
> they would tell was a wholly separate story, a new story with
> an integrity of its own, an offspring, a part of the continuing
> which storytelling must be.
>
> (227)

In the spirit of such a storytelling tradition, I will tell the stories "the way I heard it was . . . and then proceed with another
story," my own version of the story just told and yet a "wholly
separate story" as well.

In my first version of the story, I imagine that I am
telling the story of Leslie Silko's childhood—the story of a
little girl who grew up "around Laguna life without begin immersed in it . . . [living] somewhere on the fringes" (Smith,
Allen 188). Silko knew that she was not full Laguna and that

> the white men who came to the Laguna Pueblo Reservation
> and married Laguna women were the beginning of the half-
> breed Laguna people like my family, the Marmon family. . . .
> I suppose at the core of my writing is the attempt to identify
> what it is to be a half-breed or mixed blooded person; what it
> is to grow up neither white nor fully traditional Indian.
>
> (Lincoln 233)

Like Yellow Woman, the women in Silko's family had been
seduced into marriages that separated them from their culture, leaving Silko "somewhere on the fringes" of Laguna life.
If, as Paula Gunn Allen suggests, two of the roles that Yellow
Woman may take are that of an outcast and an agent of
change, then the responsibility for the isolation and dissonance that Silko feels as a result of her mixed blood lies with
the mother. By merging her mother's story and her own with
the myth of Yellow Woman, Silko attempts to bring the disparate pieces together, to identify "what it is to be a half-breed."
The process of the telling, revising and retelling of the old

stories, the conversion of the traditional into the contemporary, binds Silko to her heritage, allowing her, like Yellow Woman, to return home with a new story to tell.

Since Laguna heritage is strongly matrilineal, the mother's story is particularly crucial in identifying the daughter and establishing her place in Laguna society. Women control the houses, the property, the lineage of the children, and many of the decisions about marriages (Fisher 23). The women in Silko's family provided strong role models for her. With her mother away at work, she was raised by "her grandmother Lillie, who had been a Model A mechanic, and her great-grandmother Marie or 'A'mooh,' a full blood from Paguate who . . . had gone to Indian School at Carlisle as soon as her many children were grown" (Seyersted 13). Aunt Susie attended Dickinson College and "when she returned to Laguna / she continued her studies / . . . even as she raised her family / and helped Uncle Walter run their small cattle ranch" (*Storyteller* 3). These women were not only remarkable in their accomplishments but in their ability to mesh the modern, westernized world of formal education and jobs with their traditional values and heritage. Grandma A'mooh "washed her hair in yucca roots and told the child about the old days" (Seyersted 13). Aunt Susie kept the oral tradition of storytelling alive and passed it down to Silko. Silko thinks of these women with affection and pride, saying "I grew up with women who were really strong, women with a good deal of power," but she adds a line which shows how difficult it is for her to reconcile this power with her mother's power, which she sees as negative: "And I think about that, and I try to think about my mother: is there something about the way she and I have gotten along, or how we related to each other? . . . If someone was going to thwart you or frighten you, it would tend to be a woman; you see it coming from your mother, sent by your mother" (Barnes 96–97). She can only "try" to think about her mother.

Silko's mother was a "mixed blood Plains Indian" and she kept Silko on the "customary cradle board until she was a year old" (Seyersted 13). Yet she also went out to work when Silko was a young child leaving Grandma A'mooh and her aunts to mother her. Thus, the mother is both present and absent in Silko's life; she weds the traditional Native American customs of mothering with the Western need to leave the home to work. Since much of Leslie Silko's sense of her place in the community is vested the identity of her mother and her mother's family, this dissonance sets up an inevitable conflict.

> Among the Keres, every individual has a place within the universe—and that place is defined by clan membership. In turn, clan membership is dependent on matrilineal descent . . . . [N]aming your own mother . . . enables people to place you precisely within the universal web of your life, in each of its dimensions: cultural, spiritual, personal, and historical.
>
> (Allen, "Who Is Your Mother?" 209)

Because of her mixed blood, Silko's position in the community was on the periphery. Her house was "situated below the village, close to the river . . . on the fringe of things" (Silko, "A Conversation," 29). She was included in clan activities, but not to the same extent as the full bloods; she helped out at ceremonial dances but did not dance herself (Seyersted 13). Silko seemed to belong nowhere and everywhere. Her place in the community is largely determined by her mother and, if her relationship with her mother is distanced or problematic, the consequences, according to Paula Gunn Allen, are the "same as being lost, isolated, abandoned, self-estranged, and alienated from your own life . . . Failure to know your mother, that is, your position and its attendant traditions, history, and place in the scheme of things, is failure to remember your significance, your reality, your right relationship to earth and society" ("Who is Your Mother?" 209–210). The issues of motherhood in the literal, the figurative, and the metaphorical sense become central, therefore, to Silko's sense of self—her identity both as an individual and as a part of the whole.

Silko, then, must write about her mother in order to understand herself and her place in the community. Yet as Adrienne Rich points out in *Of Woman Born*, "the cathexis between mother and daughter—essential, distorted, misused—

is the great unwritten story" (225). The daughter must both identify with and separate from the mother. It is difficult to see our own mothers in any way other than through their relationship to us, and if that relationship is conflicted, as it often is, we must look for our mother's stories and our own story in the stories of other women. It is both difficult and threatening to imagine our mothers with sexual and emotional needs similar to, yet separate from, our own. It is hard, in fact, to acknowledge those same feelings in ourselves. We, too, are daughters, and perhaps mothers, and in these roles, we bury the stories of our own sexuality as deeply as we do those of our mothers. Our sexuality makes us vulnerable and leaves us open to seduction. We are seduced by men, by words, by stories, by the experiences of others, and by our own needs and desires. The repeated storytelling of the Yellow Woman stories in *Storyteller* is an attempt on Silko's part to place her life in a larger context—to grapple with the sexuality and seduction of her mother, her grandmothers, herself and her people, to create a new story, a new myth, out of the old stories and the fabric of her life.

In *Storyteller,* the story of Yellow Woman is told at least six different times and each telling is both the same and different from the preceding telling. The effect of this succession of stories, merged with the content of each story, suggests that, like Silko, we all are caught in a web of storytelling in which the mythical stories that we have known since "time immemorial" inform the patterns that our lives take, the stories that we will live. Kenneth Lincoln in *Native American Renaissance* says that

> Words are believed to carry the power to make things happen, ritualized in song, sacred story, and prayer. This natural force is at once common as daily speech and people's names. The empowering primacy of language weds people with their native environment: an experience or object or person exists interpenetrant with all other creation, inseparable from its name. And names allow people to see themselves and the things around them, as words image the spirits in the world.
> (143)

The act of telling and of naming is an act of creation. Naming makes it so. In the Yellow Woman stories, Silko tries out a variety of stories and myths, telling each from a different stance. She tells traditional stories, mythological stories, modern versions, versions in which Yellow Woman goes home to her family and versions in which Yellow Woman is killed. Some stories are funny and others are sad; some stories are cynical and brittle, others are lyrical and touching. It is as though Silko tries on a new persona for each story, envisioning both herself and her mother as the Yellow Woman of the story, exploring the choices available to women and the compelling needs and desires that drive women to make those choices.

In "Yellow Woman," it is the act of telling and naming that transverses the distance between myth and reality, between story and life, and merges the two into one. The stranger by the river calls the woman "Yellow Woman," and she is seduced into the story, drawn inextricably into its pattern. She follows Silva: she "did not decide to go . . . [She] just went. Moonflowers blossom in the sand hills before dawn, just as . . . [she] followed him." Like the pattern in a spider web, the replication is inevitable. She wonders if

> Yellow Woman had known who she was—if she knew that she would become part of the stories. Maybe she'd had another name that her husband and relatives called her so that only the ka'tsina from the north and the storytellers would know her as Yellow Woman.

The story becomes her story. When Silko tells the story, it becomes her story as well; both Silko and Yellow Woman are "drawn inextricably into [the] . . . pattern" of the stories they create. Yellow Woman thinks that she "will see someone . . . and then I will be certain that he is only a man . . . and I will be sure that I am not Yellow Woman. Because she is from out of time past and I live now and I've been to school and there are highways and pickup trucks that Yellow Woman never saw." But all she can know is the moment. All she can feel is "the way he felt, warm, damp, his body beside me. This is the way it happens in the stories, I was thinking, with no thought beyond the moment." Perhaps we all live only in the moment and the moment is beyond our control, our stories written and determined by the stories that have gone before, that have already been told; we live out the stories unaware that we are recreating new versions of old stories and it is only in the telling that the patterns become real. In an interview in *Sun Tracks,* Silko suggests that "you know you belong if the stories incorporate you into them. There have to be stories . . . People tell . . . stories about you and your family . . . and they begin to create your identity. In a sense you are told who you are or you know who you are by the stories that are told about you" (29–30). Our very lives are an act of creation—making new versions of old stories for future storytellers.

Silva tells Yellow Woman that "someday they will talk about us and they will say, 'Those two lived long ago when things like that happened.'" And Yellow Woman knows that "if old Grandpa weren't dead he would tell them what happened—he would laugh and say 'Stolen by a ka'tsina, a mountain spirit. She'll come home—they usually do.'" In the end Yellow Woman decides to tell them "that some Navajo had kidnapped me, but I was sorry that old Grandpa wasn't alive to hear my story because it was the Yellow Woman stories he liked to tell best." In the telling, the story will become a new legend, a new myth, reinforcing the pattern that will inform the next story. As Elaine Jahner suggests, "transmission of the knowledge of 'stories,' . . . involves not only the sharing of knowledge but the sharing of how knowledge has been shaped through one's living with it" (41–42). It is through such stories that Silko is able to integrate past and present, to resolve the conflicts and to restore balance in her life.

In each telling of the Yellow Woman story, Yellow Woman abandons her family and goes off with the ka'tsina spirit, drawn to "his skin slippery against [hers]." Each time her actions are understandable, forgivable, inevitable. This story leads me back to the gaps, the silences, in the text about Silko's own mother. I imagine that this contemporary version of the myth is Silko rewriting her mother's story, justifying her mother's actions. In the story we are told that the "mother and grandmother will raise the baby like they raised me. Al will find someone else, and they will go on like before, except that there will be a story about the way I disappeared while I was walking along the river." Whether Silko actually felt abandoned by her mother physically, emotionally or spiritually is not relevant for, as Silko reminds the reader, "sometimes what we call 'memory' and what we call 'imagination' are not so easily distinguished." The telling of the story makes it real, turns pain into celebration.

Yet, in writing the Yellow Woman story, I imagine that Silko not only rewrites her mother's story, but writes her own story as well. This is a story conceived in both memory and imagination and its genesis is in both the myth and the modern world. In the *Sun Tracks* interview, Silko tells us that girls meet boyfriends and lovers at the river and that she used to

> wander around down there herself and try to imagine walking around the bend and just happening to stumble upon some beautiful man. Later on I realized that these kinds of things that I was doing when I was fifteen are exactly the kinds of things out of which stories like the Yellow Woman story [came]. I finally put the two together: the adolescent longings and the old stories, that plus the stories around Laguna at that time about people who did, in fact, just in recent times, use the river as a meeting place.
>
> (29)

Silko weaves together both her own stories and her mother's stories and in the process explores the power and dimensions of female sexuality. In the Yellow Woman stories, women are overcome time and again by their own overpowering passion. They are almost unhesitatingly willing to abandon one life for another. These women must negotiate between two worlds— the world of the family and that of self. The Native American version of this conflict, however, differs significantly from the Western version. In the Western tradition the mother who leaves her family is punished; in the Native American tradition she is celebrated. The Yellow Woman stories validate female sexuality, viewing the wildness and passion that leads to such improper, non-conformist behavior as an ultimately creative act. This sense of self as a sensual and sexual being may at certain times even work for the greater good of the community. Simon Ortiz suggests that "pueblo societies see the survival of the group as more important than the existence of the individual . . . [and] man as a minute part of an immense natural cycle" (Seyersted 17). The perpetuation of that cycle serves to "bring new blood into the pueblo [and] Yellow Woman becomes a symbol of renewal through liaisons with outside forces" (Ruoff 10). The sexual act, then, "channels the awesome power and energy of our human sexuality—the preserve of wilderness in human beings—into socially useful channels" (Smith, Allen 178). Accordingly, women who step outside the bonds of propriety often bring not disgrace but great good to the tribe. This pattern is reflected repeatedly in the various versions of the Yellow Woman stories.

In "Cottonwood Part One: Story of Sun House," Yellow Woman leaves "precise stone rooms / that hold the heart silently" and "her home / her clan / and the people / (three small children / the youngest just weaned / her husband away cutting firewood)" (*Storyteller* 64). She is seduced by the "colors of the sun," in the form of a spirit who is the sun himself. She is inextricably drawn to him despite the fact that "the people may not understand." She does it "for the world / to continue / Out of love for this earth / cottonwood / sandstone / and sky." Because of her actions the sun comes again and again "out of the Sun House," and the earth will not freeze over and die.

This pattern is repeated in "Cottonwood Part Two: Buffalo Story," in which Yellow Woman's actions result in bringing food to her people in a time of drought and starvation. Yellow Woman, who goes out searching for "water to carry back to her family," is seduced by "water . . . churning . . . [where] something very large had muddied the water." Frightened by her own sexuality, she turns "to hurry away / because she didn't want to find out," but it is too late. She is seduced by a spirit who is "very good to look at / . . . she had never seen anyone like him / It was Buffalo Man who was very beautiful," and when he says "Come with me," she follows. She is killed by her husband when he discovers she is unwilling to leave the Buffalo people whom she "loves." Yet, her death results in plentiful meat for her tribe. The community benefits from her actions:

It was all because
one time long ago
our daughter, our sister Kochininako
went away with them.

(76)

Seduction stories follow one after the other and whether "Yellow Woman" (or her contemporary counterpart) is abducted by "that Mexican / at Seama feast," or "three Navajo men / headed north along / the Rio Puerco river / in a red '56 Ford" or is seduced "Outside the dance hall door / late Friday night / in the summertime," the result is always the same. When she is asked "Have you seen the way stars shine / up there in the sand hills?" she usually says "No. Will you show me?" The result of this acknowledgement and acting out of human sexuality generally climaxes in a positive outcome for the community or tribe in the form of the birth of magical children, the acquisition of food or water in time of need, or the gift of a new ceremony. Female sexuality is seen as a positive and creative force in the world, even outside the bonds of marriage.

I imagine that there is another story embedded in this story, however, and it is the story of the land. In "Lullaby," Silko writes "The earth is your mother / she holds you / . . . There never was a time / when this / was not so" (51). The earth, as mother, is connected to the human, animal and spiritual world as mother/woman is to a lover. In an interview with Kim Barnes, Silko suggests that

> What's operating in those stories of Kochininako is this attraction, this passion, this connection between the human world and the animal and spirit worlds. Buffalo Man is a buffalo, and he can be in the form of a buffalo, but there is this link, and the link is sealed with sexual intimacy, which is emblematic of that joining of two worlds. . . . there's a real overpowering sexual attraction that's felt. The attraction is symbolized by or typified by the kind of sexual power that draws her to the buffalo man, but the power which draws her to Buffalo Man is actually the human, the link, the animal and human world, those two being drawn together. It's that power that's really

operating, and the sexual nature of it is just a metaphor for that power.

(95–96)

So Silko weaves a new story out of the old one—a story about power, sex, love and the earth. Intercourse occurs between mother earth and the spirit and animal world. And, like the other seductions in the Yellow Woman stories, this union results in good for the earth and the community. The mother, as sexual and sensual being as well as mother figure, is of central importance. For Silko to acknowledge and understand her own sexuality as well as her mother's, she must see it in the greater context of mother as earth as well as mother as individual. She must see sexuality as ultimately creative and productive; she must once again tell the story so that the mother's choice between self and child is not only an acceptable but a necessary act. Smith and Allen write:

> In such comings-together of persons and spirits, the land and the people engage in a ritual dialogue. . . . The ultimate purpose of such ritual abductions and seductions is to transfer knowledge from the spirit world to the human sphere. . . . the human woman makes little attempt either to resist or to tame the spirit-man who abducts her. Nor do men . . . attempt to control or dominate [the women]. . . . the human protagonists usually engage willingly in literal sexual intercourse with the spirits. . . . This act brings the land's power, spirit, and fecundity in touch with their own, and so ultimately yields benefit for their people.
>
> (178)

The mother who acknowledges her own sexuality and who acts on that acknowledgment offers men and women a paradigm for healthy and whole relationships with each other; a woman's role as wife, mother, earth is no longer viewed as constricting but as liberating.

This connection to the land must be particularly important to Silko. Today the Jackpile Mine is located in Laguna land, near Pagute. It is the largest open pit uranium mine in existence. The deepest uranium mine shaft is sunk into

Mt. Taylor, the sacred Laguna mountain, which is the traditional home of the ka'tsina spirit. These mines have brought economic prosperity to Laguna but at the same time cancer is spreading at an alarming rate; the number of children born with birth defects at Laguna is growing significantly; the ecosystem is contaminated and drinking water has radiation levels two hundred times greater than those considered safe (Seyersted 12). If the mother is to survive, if the earth is to survive, Silko suggests that the relationship between the spiritual, the physical and the human must be one of passion, intercourse and love: We must sleep "with the river" and find "he is warmer than any man." We must listen to voices and stories that inform us:

> Aging with the rock
> of this ancient land
> I give myself to the earth,
> merge
> > my red feet on the mesa like rust, root
> > in this place with my mothers before me,
> > balance end by end like a rainbow
> > between the two points of my birth, dance
> > into shapes that search the sky for clouds
> > filled with fertile water.
> >
> > Across asphalt canyons, bridging river
> > after river, a thirty year old woman
> is waiting for her name.

Like this speaker from Wendy Rose's "Naming Power," through accepting and embracing our own passion and sexuality we can "give [ourselves] to the earth," connect with and come to understand "[our] mothers before [us]," and in so doing, achieve a "balance . . . like a rainbow."

The stories merge and converge. The absent mother at the center of the text is the figure around which all the other figures revolve. Each story is her story, Silko's story, and, in a sense, our story also. Just as the stories can be traced in the photographs in the Hopi basket, the stories are told through the blank pages, the silences, and the gaps in the text. When we look through Silko's album of pictures, the absence of a picture of her mother tells a story just as loudly as the presence of the pictures of others. Iser says in "The Reading Process" that

> although we rarely notice it, we are all the time engaged in constructing hypotheses about the meaning of the text. The reader makes implicit connections, fills in the gaps, draws inferences and tests our hunches. . . . [T]he text itself is really no more than a series of "cues" to the reader, invitations to construct a piece of language into meaning.
>
> (76)

The series of stories about Yellow Woman, like the pictures, each serve as a different pose, a different landscape, but the subject remains the same—the identity of woman as mother and wife and the tensions between those roles and her sexuality, creativity and productivity. In leafing through the album, telling the stories of the pictures, we see ourselves as well as others. Similarly, in reading the "gaps" in the text, we come to know a series of stories—some of them our own.

In Silko's *Storyteller,* we must listen to the silence as well as the words, and out of that silence construct our own stories to propel us into the future and connect us to the past. Leslie Silko is the storyteller and

> The storyteller keeps the stories
>    all the escape stories
>       she says "With these stories of ours
>       we can escape almost anything
>       with these stories we will survive."
>          "The Storyteller's Escape"(247)

 *Notes* ∎

My interest in the absent mother in *Storyteller* originated in a seminar class in American Indian literature taught by Melody Graulich at the University of New Hampshire in the spring of 1989. I am indebted to Melody Graulich for first raising the question of the absent mother and for her insights and encouragement on this paper.

Works cited are:

Allen, Paula Gunn. "Cochiti and Laguna Pueblo Traditional Yellow Woman Stories." *Spider Woman's Granddaughters: Traditional Tales and Contemporary Writing by Native American Women*. Edited by Paula Gunn Allen. New York: Fawcett Columbine, 1989. 210–218.

———. "Who is Your Mother?: Red Roots of White Feminism." *The Sacred Hoop: Recovering the Feminine in American Indians Traditions*. Boston: Beacon Press, 1986. 209–221.

Barnes, Kim. "A Leslie Marmon Silko Interview." *The Journal of Ethnic Studies* 134 (1986): 83–105.

Eagleton, Terry. *Literary Theory: An Introduction*. Minneapolis: University of Minnesota Press, 1983.

Fisher, Dexter. "Stories and Their Tellers—A Conversation with Leslie Marmon Silko." *The Third Woman: Minority Women Writers of the United States*. Edited by Dexter Fisher. Boston: Houghton Mifflin, 1980. 18–23.

Gubar, Susan. "'The Blank Page' and Female Creativity." *The New Feminist Criticism*. Edited by Elaine Showalter. New York: Pantheon Books, 1985. 292–313.

Iser, Wolfgang. "The Reading Process: A Phenomenological Approach." The Johns Hopkins University Press, 1980. 50–69.

Jahner, Elaine. "An Act of Attention: Event Structure in *Ceremony*." *American Indian Quarterly* 5.1 (1979): 34–47.

Krupat, Arnold. "Post-Structuralism and Oral Tradition." *Recovering the Word: Essays on Native American Literature*. Edited by Brian Swann and Arnold Krupat. Berkeley: University of California Press, 1987. 113–128.

Lincoln, Kenneth. "Grandmother Storyteller: Leslie Silko." *Native American Renaissance*. Los Angeles: University of California Press, 1983. 222–250.

Rich, Adrienne. *Of Woman Born*. New York: W. W. Norton & Company, 1986.

Rose, Wendy. "Naming Power." *That's What She Said: Contemporary Poetry and Fiction by Native American Women*. Edited by Rayna Green. Bloomington: Indiana University Press, 1984. 218–220.

Ruoff, A. LaVonne. "Ritual and Renewal: Keres Traditions in the Short Fiction of Leslie Silko." *MELUS* 5.4 (1978): 2–17.

Seyersted, Per. *Leslie Marmon Silko*. Western Writers Series 45. Boise: State University, 1980.

Silko, Leslie. "A Conversation with Leslie Marmon Silko." *Sun Tracks* 3.1 (1977): 29–32.

——. *Storyteller*. New York: Seaver Books, 1981.

Smith, Patricia Clark and Paula Gunn Allen. "Earthly Relations, Carnal Knowledge: Southwestern American Indian Women Writers and Landscape." *The Desert is No Lady*. Edited by Vera Norwood and Janice Monk. New Haven: Yale University Press, 1987. 174–196.

# ❑ Selected Bibliography ■

## Works by Leslie Marmon Silko

Silko, Leslie Marmon. *The Almanac of the Dead: A Novel*. New York: Simon and Schuster, 1991.

———. "An Old-Time Indian Attack Conducted in Two Parts." In *The Remembered Earth: An Anthology of Native American Literature,* edited by Gerry Hobson, 211–216. Albuquerque: University of New Mexico Press, 1981. (First published in *Shantih* 4 (Summer/Fall 1979): 3–5.)

———. *Ceremony* New York: Viking, 1977.

———. "Language and Literature from a Pueblo Indian Perspective." In *English Literature: Opening Up the Canon,* edited by Leslie Fiedler and Houston A. Baker, Jr., 54–72. Baltimore: The Johns Hopkins University Press, 1981.

———. *Laguna Woman: Poems By Leslie Silko*. Greenfield Center, N.Y.: Greenfield Review Press, 1974.

———. "Landscape, History, and the Pueblo Imagination." *Antaeus* 57 (Autumn 1986): 83–94.

———. *Storyteller*. New York: Seaver Books, 1981.

Wright, Anne, ed. *The Delicacy and Strength of Lace: Letters Between Leslie Marmon Silko and James Wright*. St. Paul, Minnesota: Graywolf Press, 1986.

## Suggested Further Reading

Allen, Paula Gunn. *Spider Woman's Granddaughters*. Boston: Beacon Press, 1989.

———. *The Sacred Hoop: Recovering the Feminine in American Indian Traditions*. Boston: Beacon Press, 1986.

Anderson, Laurie. "Colorful Revenge in Silko's Storyteller." *Notes on Contemporary Literature* XV (September 1985): 11–12.

Antell, Judith. "Momaday, Welch, and Silko: Expressing the Feminine Principle Through Male Alienation. *American Indian Quarterly* XII (Summer 1988): 213–220.

Coltelli, Laura. "Leslie Marmon Silko." *Winged Words: American Indian Writers Speak*. Lincoln: University of Nebraska Press, 1990.

Danielson, Linda L. *"Storyteller*: Grandmother Spider's Web." *Journal of the Southwest* 30 (Autumn 1988): 325–355.

Evers, Larry and Denny Carr. "A Conversation with Leslie Marmon Silko." *Sun Tracks* 3:1 (Fall 1976): 28–33.

Fisher, Dexter. "Stories and Their Tellers: A Conversation with Leslie Marmon Silko." *The Third Woman: Minority Women Writers of the United States*. Boston: Houghton Mifflin, 1980.

Jahner, Elaine. "The Novel and Oral Tradition: An Interview with Leslie Marmon Silko." *Book Forum: An International Transdisciplinary Quarterly* 5:3 (1981): 383–388.

Lincoln, Kenneth. *Native American Renaissance*. Berkeley: University of California Press, 1983.

Lucero, Ambrose. "For the People: Leslie Silko's *Storyteller*." *Minority Voices: An Interdisciplinary Journal* 5 (Spring/Fall, 1981): 1–10.

Parry, Donna. [check with Leslie Mitchner about whether she would like this book cited and for title, etc.]

Ruppert, Jim. "Story Telling: The Fiction of Leslie Silko." *Journal of Ethnic Studies* 9 (Spring 1981): 53–58.

Seyersted, Per. *Leslie Marmon Silko*. Boise: Boise State University Western Writers Series, No. 45, 1980.

———. "Two Interviews with Leslie Marmon Silko." *American Studies in Scandinavia* 13 (1981): 17–33.

Thompson, Joan. "Yellow Woman, Old and New: Oral Tradition and Leslie Marmon Silko's *Storyteller*." *Wikazo Sa Review: A Journal of Indian Studies* 5:2 (Fall 1989): 22–25.

234

# ❏ Permissions ■

235

CPSIA information can be obtained
at www.ICGtesting.com
Printed in the USA
LVHW04s2003181018
594071LV00001B/10/P